CHI...

Came...

CHINA'S DANCER
Cameos of Life in China

Belinda Mackay

alpha

Alpha is an imprint of Paternoster Publishing,
PO Box 300, Carlisle, Cumbria, CA3 0QS, UK
http:www.paternoster-publishing.com

British Library Cataloguing in Publication Data
A catalogue record for this book is available from the British Library

ISBN 1-89893-876-8

Cover Design by Mainstream, Lancaster
Typeset by WestKey Ltd, Falmouth, Cornwall
Printed in Great Britain by
Caledonian International Book Manufacturing Ltd, Glasgow

Dedication

This book is dedicated to my late mother who put aside her natural tendency to protect her girls, and instead gave her blessing for my work in China, no matter where it might lead me.

Biblical Reference

The Holy Bible New King James Version, Thomas
Nelson Publishers Inc, Nashville, USA 1984

Contents

Author's Note

The events of the book take place during my academic year spent teaching English in a college in southern China. In order to protect the identity of friends in China, their names and some details, such as the name of my city, have been changed or omitted. I hope the reader can forgive me and understand the necessity for this caution. Beyond this, all other events and circumstances have been recalled as accurately as possible. Since prior to my residency in the Middle Kingdom, I visited China often over an eleven-year span, I have included many anecdotes from other provinces, to give a wider view of the country. A history section on conflicts with the West partially explains Chinese attitudes towards Westerners. The names of cities and other Chinese words are generally written using the common Pinyin transliteration.

We read a lot about what is happening in China on the national, macro level particularly on politics and economics. My aim is to show something of the life in China on the everyday, grassroots level, from the viewpoint of an Australian resident. My hope is that some readers will be moved enough to pray for

China's people and some will want to visit or work there. For the latter group, I have included practical tips in the Chapters, and an Appendix to assist with preparations before departure and in adjustment to the new culture after arrival. I pray that for them, as it was for me, living in the Middle Kingdom will be 'an experience of a lifetime'.

Thanks

The author would like to thank her family and friends who have kept up their enthusiasm for this project all the way through. I greatly appreciated the assistance given by my teachers of my professional writing course. Special thanks also to the staff at Paternoster Publishing and the various helpers in the various computer crises along the way. But most of all, I give thanks to our Heavenly Father who thought a term in China would be a great way to prove to me that he 'is able to do exceedingly abundantly above all that we ask or think, according to the power that works in us'. (Ephesians 3: 20)

TEARS IN YOUR EYES

It's coming again, time and again
Things to do and places to go.
Only for a while, you say with a smile.
Reassurance that don't change the feelings.
It's not just the time or the measure of miles
I just hate being apart.
But that's the purpose of love
When it comes from above
You've got to give it away.
Living every day, by a heart and a mind
With reasons better than feelings.
I just want to give you the best
And leave you with a love that never dies.

With tears in your eyes
You might say goodbye
Holding hands that don't want to let go.
But the love in your heart, it will never die
So you're lonely, but not ever alone.
It's only for a while.

So it all begins, without an end
You're out there walking the road.
You start with a smile, then after a while
You're talking deep with the feelings
You're looking at eyes and you share in a life
You're here with more than a friend
But that's the purpose of love
When it comes from above.
You've got to give it away.
Living every day, by a heart and a mind.
With reasons better than feelings.
I just want to give you the best
And leave you with a love that never dies.

And time is your friend when you know its never ending.
We'll be together again in love
We'll be together again.

With tears in your eyes
But the love in your heart it will never die
Oh I don't want to let go
With tears in my eyes
I don't want to say goodbye.

Gary Houston

Introduction

'Are you coming with us to Beijing or not?'

I opened an eye groggily.

'I need to know now because I'm putting a deposit down with the travel agent today.'

'Um, yes I'll come', I said slowly.

Six thirty in the morning is not the best time to make important decisions about going overseas. My friend was anxious to finalize who was going on the holiday in January 1987 to Beijing. I had been dithering about whether to go or not.

On the eve of departure, one of the eight who had signed up was wondering how he could justify before the Lord the cost of this holiday, when there were so many pressing financial needs on the mission field to which he could have given the money.

'God can use a holiday overseas to show a person the needs of a country and inspire them to go and work there.' As I said these words, a feeling came over me. Is this the sensation the prophets experienced when they spoke God's word to the people?

'Belinda, you're getting too dramatic,' my sensible self corrected me. 'Anyway, if it is a prophecy, it's probably for him. Yes, that's it. It's not for me, I'm only the messenger.' That was a comforting thought.

Wearing alpine-like gear, borrowed or bought, we played tourist around all the historical sites in Beijing – the Forbidden City, Summer Palace, Beihai Park and elsewhere. The section of the Great Wall of China near Beijing is spectacular, even through a gale blowing snowflakes in your eyes. Standing on a parapet, hanging onto the wall, to stop myself from falling on the slippery snow, I was pleased I had not been on sentry duty in the middle of winter 2,000 years ago. During the whole trip of seventeen days the temperature did not rise above 5 degrees C, and it must have been as low as minus 10 degrees the day at the Wall, up in the mountains. At such temperatures, feeling 'cold' is a whole new experience compared with what is experienced in an everyday 'cold' Australian winter.

It was easy to see from the effects of the climate alone, why so many workers tragically perished in the building of the Wall. (Summer temperatures reach 37 degrees C and winter temperatures can drop as low as minus 28 degrees C in Beijing.) How do people grow crops, bring up families and carry out all the everyday activities of life in such a harsh climate? I admired the Chinese tenacity which enabled them to live and thrive for thousands of years despite such adversities. God showed me though, how fragile their hold on life can be.

We went to Tiananmen Square on our first day. Driving in heated taxis, we passed people manoeuvring and balancing bicycles on the treacherous, icy roads. Weaving in between trucks, cars and horse-drawn drays, were carts pulled by bicycles.

On one sideless cart was a person lying motionless with only a mop of black hair visible above a thick quilt. Was the person sick? Was the man pedalling so laboriously a relative? I wondered how far they had to go before they reached a hospital.

A few days later, the images from that first day repeated themselves in my memory, like a video-tape on a continuous loop. One night, the others congregated in one of the rooms for a game of cards. I didn't want to play, so stayed in my room. There the Lord unexpectedly spoke to me about praying regularly for China. Easy to do, but dangerous: this could lead in future to all sorts of destinations.

Surprisingly, within half an hour, I was vomiting violently from food poisoning. Now, when I am sick, nothing in the world penetrates my consciousness. All I can think about is that I'm sick and sorry for myself! This time was different. During the six hours of my illness, my mind was filled with the vivid sights I had seen in Beijing. The Lord also showed me, through mental pictures, what he sees in the *hutongs* – the back streets and the faceless tenement blocks where the majority of people dwell. He showed me people living in poverty and despair; the difficult conditions exacerbated by extreme temperatures.

I saw the contrast between what happened when I became ill and when the average citizen became ill. I was attended by the hotel doctor and nurse in the comfort of my own warm room. (More serious cases would be treated at the hospital for foreign patients only.) An ailing Chinese person has to rely on a relative to negotiate the traffic in a risky journey to a general hospital.

As these images were burned into my mind, God imparted his heart towards the Chinese people into my spirit. God's heart was yearning to remove their suffering and give them 'life abundant'. Next morning I was weakened from the effects of the bug, but a precious share of God's concern was lodged permanently inside me. This impartation of God's heart for China changed my heart and propelled me through all the exciting and rough patches of succeeding years of China involvement.

A month later a friend, tossing me a pamphlet said: 'Hey Belinda, do you want to go back to China?' Silly girl doesn't she know what my bank balance is?

Nine months later I was on a plane heading back to China as the dance leader on my first cultural exchange concert tour. This was the most adventurous experience of my life to date. Fortunately I was blissfully naïve enough *not* to conjecture where the tour might lead in the coming years. I had forgotten the prophecy, given years earlier, in Perth, that the Lord would open the door for me to dance in many, many places in the world, places I couldn't possibly imagine at the time.

1

'And teach English too?'
— Getting There —

'Well actually, Belinda would like to teach dance in a college in China,' said our Music Director matter-of-factly. All eyes turned on me.

'Oh, er, yes I would like to.' I wanted to appear confident, but I was stunned by this admission.

'And teach English too?' The English teacher asked.

'Oh yes, I can do that.'

I felt a strange mixture of emotions evoked by my seemingly casual reply to this important question. But at a deeper level, I suspected that my life was going to take a sharp turn – northward – in the future. This city was going to be 'home' for a time. How long for? Heaven was yet to tell me.

At the time of this conversation, we had been part of a cultural exchange concert tour to China. For years, ever since my world had been turned around by that eventful holiday in Beijing, I had been part of these almost yearly pilgrimages; to perform and make friends with the Chinese people. Included in the team was a performing troupe comprising a rock band and dance group. I was the mother hen over the latter and was greatly enjoying my comfortable place in the scheme of things.

The team included many old 'China hands' who had been on two or three tours in preceding years and were well and truly bitten by the 'China bug'. In richer theological language this meant that God had individually shown us his heart and concern for the people of China, which had left an indelible mark on our own hearts. So, like homing pigeons, we kept coming back to China ...

> *'It's coming again, time and again,*
> *Things to do and places to go.'*

With expectant ears we were constantly listening to the whisper of the Lord's call to us for each tour and our individual part in it. Visiting designated key universities, one of which had students from influential families of China, forced me to the awesome realization that the Lord can set me in *any* circumstance when he wants certain people exposed to the gospel through me.

In some cities it was wonderful to have some of the same students in the audience as the year before and to meet up with old friends. Receiving surprise telephone calls from friends at our hotels, made us feel part of the local community, though the ones who called at six in the morning, following a performance the night before, received a less-than-intelligent response from me. The students lapped up all our western songs and the presentation of their own cultural forms in traditional dance, folksongs and the latest chart hits by popular Chinese singers. These performance items struck a chord, earning an immediate response from students and staff wherever we went. We produced an entertaining, largely secular musical programme; respectful of Communist policy on religion.

However, it was liberating to know that as a dancer, I could make statements of faith without having to worry about censorship. (After all, I was only dancing!) It was exciting to know that the Holy Spirit would be working through the dances to touch members of the audience. Often enough at home I have seen people weep during my dances, as the Spirit touched them, to know that he could do the same in China. (No, they didn't cry because my dancing was woeful!) For each tour the Lord encouraged me to produce one dance on the programme which looked to the audience like an ordinary item, but which he wanted to be an intercession for China. Each year the dance form changed, but not the purpose.

To fulfil our brief to provide 'cultural exchanges' I blended East and West in one of the items by choreographing an Aussie-style bush-dance set to a toe-tapping Chinese folk-tune. The finale was a surprise acrobatic stunt by our team gymnast. We wondered some nights if he would land on the key-board! This appealed to the Chinese taste for a wide variety of performing arts combining together, as expressed in their own musical/dramatic productions.

Working this piece out during rehearsals gave me the opportunity to consider the meaning of 'culture'. The reproduction of my own cultural forms and the adoption of Chinese styles, such as Chinese dancing, raised nagging questions. How precious was my western culture to me? Also, how much of it was I willing to forsake to adopt Chinese cultural styles instead? Indeed, it seemed, on the emotional level at least, that by adopting the latter I had to let go of some of the former. That was the painful part. The heart of the matter was really not outward behaviour but, as I perceived it, a change in identity. It was a pertinent issue that the Lord put to me ever so gently. He wanted my future to be in China, on a teaching contract. I came to realize over the next few years that this would mean a shift in my Australian identity in order to serve the people of another culture. As Paul said: 'To the Jews I became as a Jew, that I might win Jews' (1 Cor. 9:20). I need not have worried, because I didn't lose any of my 'Australianness' during my time in China; rather, I became what is called 'a bi-cultural person'. I kept all of my Australian identity and gained layers of Chinese culture. My life became enormously richer for the blend.

So here we were, part-way through our concert tour, sitting with the Dean, Vice-Dean and other teachers of the English Department of the Normal College, eating frogs' legs and other delicacies for dinner, after our concert. The talk at the table revolved around the need to find more foreign teachers to teach English at the College. Then the remark about teaching Dance broke into the conversation, re-directing my life's course. A year before I had mentioned to our Music Director my desire to teach Dance in a college; how had he remembered it after all this time? Teach Dance and English in this hot and steamy place for a year? I would have to think and pray ardently about this one! I knew it might not be difficult getting the position, because I had a Bachelor of Arts degree and wondered if I had already had the interview! I wonder if they serve up frogs' legs in ordinary meals at the College? Taste a bit like chicken . . . quite nice really . . .

I returned home, my mind churning over what had happened that evening. Praying all the time for guidance was mixed with a desire not to know the answer anyway, in case it was '*Go!*' Deep down I knew what God wanted; fear didn't want me to admit it.

A few weeks later I contacted the College again and yes, they were interested in receiving an application. But it was several months with long gaps in between, when I did not know if I was coming or going, before they definitely gave me the job. At one point the delays in faxes were so long, I gave up hope altogether that I would get the job. In one fax they asked if I would buy some English teaching videos for them. I checked out prices and asked if they wanted to reimburse me if I bought some. I didn't get a reply to that, nor to several other important questions included in the same fax. I learnt early on that Chinese authorities give only the information that they consider absolutely necessary, that is, what you need to know, for their goals to be accomplished. Even with the best intentions in the world, they probably can't appreciate what a culture shock it is for a Westerner to go to China, because few have ever lived overseas themselves. The Vice-Dean was eventually forthcoming with a brief letter answering my questions about accommodation, salaries and other necessities. That was a relief, but there were still a million other questions left unanswered, hanging in the air somewhere above the South China Sea.

I asked if one of the foreign teachers I was to replace, would correspond with me. His hilarious volumes of loquacity filled in gaps in my understanding. He knew how I felt wanting to prepare psychologically and practically for what I was to meet in China. The letters were full of hints about the flat, 'Nothing quite works the way it is supposed to.' sounded somewhat unpromising. He talked a lot about teaching and the students and his estimation of the Dean was encouraging: 'Overall it's a nice team to work with (the English Department). Mr Chen, the Dean is a kind of fatherly figure.' I drew strength from, 'In case I haven't got the feeling across, coming here is the experience of a lifetime.' Well if he can be happy, I suppose I can be too?

I told the Lord that I wasn't prepared to live in China by myself. He said that he would provide a friend. I jokingly asked two friends of mine who had strong teaching backgrounds to apply for the other positions vacant at the College. To my amazement they both did, but months of negotiations ended with our dream of a threesome fizzling out. The College gave one position to a Chinese girl from Sydney. Was God unfaithful in his promise to send me a friend or did I just hear it wrong? Either way, this issue was a crisis in faith – faith in God and faith in myself.

Eventually Mr Chen wrote: 'Our department will certainly invite you to come to our College to teach advanced English for grade three students and some other conversational courses. All of us are very happy that we are going to have a foreign teacher from Australia. We'll meet all the terms you mentioned.'

Well that's it. I'm *going*!

But I wished I had been more excited about going: a full dose of adventurous enthusiasm would have served me well in the preparation time. Deep down, I have the spirit of adventure – if it wasn't there, I would not have gone to China on that life-changing holiday in Beijing. But now, with only months to go before I became a foreign resident of the Middle Kingdom, my spirit of adventure had decided to pull the covers up and hibernate when I needed it most. Going to China on cultural exchange concert tours was easy; I had been on so many and knew the ropes backwards. This was an academic year away in unknown waters; I had no precedent in my experience to fall back on and instead of being with a team, I was going alone.

What propelled me into daring to pray, daring to say 'yes' and daring to go at all, was the irrefutable knowledge that God wanted me there. It was a decision made out of cerebral obedience rather than emotion. That would have sounded strange to people around me, who saw my stint as a resident as just a natural progression, after years of short 'hops' over to China. Their logic was, 'Belinda *loves* China, so Belinda will *love* to live there.' My pastor said that it was 'a dream come true'. They didn't know how far from the truth these ideas were. The trouble was, although I was deeply committed to the Chinese people, I knew something of what China was like, albeit inevitably from a western viewpoint. I simply didn't know if I could cope if circumstances at the College were really bad.

The Lord filled out my education about China and its people, both good and bad, during my time away, to an extent far greater than I could have imagined before I left Australia. To shape my education was one of the multitude of reasons why he wanted me there.

Obtaining a three-month visa, (later extended after arrival in China) required medical tests. Difficulties in this gave me a taste of how bureaucracy can make a simple process unnecessarily lengthy. By contrast, I appreciated the professional service from airlines and other organizations who went out of their way to help me wind up my affairs in Australia and to facilitate my passage northward.

Also my family were very patient and helpful when I needed them most and assisted in a myriad of ways, especially in communications. Many fax machines in China are manual. The person telephones first to say that they want to send a fax. My brother-in-law would go blue in the face trying to make the Chinese person understand they then had to 'Press the button!' (Meanwhile his family was falling around laughing silently at their dad's predicament.) This scenario repeated itself, fax after fax, for reasons we couldn't fathom. Another long-suffering brother-in-law contacted the world at large searching for the best airline ticket price and connections and gained a sizeable discount into the bargain.

One of the unsung heroes behind an ex-pat's life is the person(s) living with her before she takes off to the adventure in her country of calling. Friends, family and church people lend vital support with kind words, prayers, finance and practical assistance but they, unlike the house-mate, are in a fortunate position: they don't have to *live* with the person. I'm sure there is a quiet corner in heaven reserved just for house-mates; an eternity away from the ravings, tears, fears, hopes, and mayhem generated by the calling.

My friend Kaye, who shared my turbulent eighteen months prior to going to China, backed up my efforts and put on a brave face. Day and night, to soothe away anxieties, she would recite: 'Eye has not seen, nor ear heard, nor have entered into the heart of man, the things which God has prepared for those who love him' (1 Cor. 2:9).

The Lord branded this scripture firmly on my soul by relaying it to me via countless friends and acquaintances. I played a new tape by a singer from church: '*No eye has seen . . .*' Knowing beyond a doubt that the Lord had great plans and experiencing his sovereignty was wonderfully comforting. He wanted me primarily to concentrate on pumping as much English as possible into the students.

The excellent *Perspectives on the World Christian Movement* course set a firm understanding about God's plans for mankind in my mind. The *Perspectives* literature states:

'This course carries with it a certain danger. Quite possibly, the experience of taking this course will, in itself, set you apart in certain ways from even your closest friends. There is something terrifyingly lonely about the cross of Jesus Christ. The full implications of our obedience to our Lord may not make us feel at home in all human circumstances and diversions. A whole new pattern of relationships may develop if you *"hang in"* with great determination concerning a Commission which pertains urgently and crucially to people who are outside the range of normal conversation, beyond the awareness of normal church life, thinly and almost meaninglessly, if at all, in the prayers of the average Christian . . . It is the element of loneliness with which the Great Commission itself attempts to deal . . . This is why Jesus said: "*I will be with you.*" ,[1]

Going to China was an expensive business: money disappeared into a bottomless black abyss labelled 'Pay this, buy that.' Friends, family and even anonymous donors lightened the burden, earning my undying gratitude. I circulated a list of do's and don'ts about letter-writing, predicting that my letters and faxes might be opened.

'I've got the easy part. I'm just pleased that I'm not called to go!' said Jane as she jabbed me with the syringe. She happened to be practising as a doctor, at a travellers' medical centre and generously donated my injections to 'the cause', free of charge. My list of inoculations was quite impressive by the end of the jabbing sessions.

The foreign teacher wrote that shampoo and other toiletries were expensive and not readily available. Buying a year's supply of everything, including a first-aid kit would be prohibitive. So I asked my church to donate items to a small basket I placed at church one Sunday. The circulated list included shampoo and Band-Aids (for a joke I mentioned 'Glow in the Dark' ones.) One day the church office girl rang asking me to collect my basket of goods. When I arrived, she gave a knowing giggle and ushered me to a room where sat in grand state an enormous basket, the size of a trunk,

---

[1] Hawthorne, S.C., *Perspectives on the World Christian Movement Part I: Study Guide* (Christchurch: Centre for Mission Direction, NZ, 1994, 2nd Edition) p. 3.

filled to overflowing with goods both on and off the list and all manner of weird and wonderful hospital supplies, including the gadget with the unpronounceable name used for taking blood-pressure. It was hard to believe such generosity. The concept of a 'year's supply of everything' seemed to capture the imagination of donors and some lines were inflated into two or three years' supply. A year after my return, I was still using some of the shampoo and two years later, the conditioner. The Band-Aids caught on: there were fluorescent ones, 'Wow, Awesome, Cool' and 'Mickey and Pals'. They looked great on the toes of this highly sophisticated teacher in the classroom in summer. I wonder whatever happened to my little basket?

'You're looking at eyes and you share in a life'

Strangely, the prospect of teaching was the least of my fears. Years of knocking dance teams into shape and dancing on stage had tested my ability to teach and put performances together. Sitting in the comfort of home, I was relatively confident of being able to construct worthwhile lessons. I looked forward to the challenge of teaching and I had confidence in the knowledge that knew the Lord would help me greatly.

For three months I scoured the bookshelves of friends and family searching for old magazines, newspapers, junk mail, calendars, pictorials and examples of 'authentic English' to ship off in advance. Chinese colleges are poorly resourced and teachers must rely on their own initiative and materials.

'The first thing to understand about teaching or studying in China is that however you prepare . . . reality will probably turn out quite different from expectation. Conditions in China change rapidly. Then too, few people before they arrive can pin down Chinese institutions on just what they'll study or teach. Those that do often find everything changed on arrival. History lectures become economics seminars, and composition classes conversation classes, often without apparent reason or consideration.[2]

So to have all bases covered on every conceivable possible type of class or topic, I begged, borrowed and bought all sorts of resources. No literature, sitting quietly gathering dust, was safe. Everyday items – telephone book pages, train timetables, leaflets, calendars etc. were commandeered for a 'higher purpose'. Friends couldn't understand why I fell on junk mail in utter delight; they papered the bird-cage with theirs. I saw afresh how tawdry are most popular magazines sold in Australia. So I ripped out squeaky-clean articles and stapled them between thick card, and discarded the rest.

The day came when the two boxes of literature, were lined with plastic, packed, taped and roped, ready for the post-office. The post-office staff had never heard of the little-used 'printed matter only $2 kg rate'. After numerous annoyed mutterings interspersed with phone calls to more knowledgeable post offices, we finally established that yes, the rate did exist beyond my imagination and I bade farewell to

---

[2] Weiner, R., Murphy, M. & Li, A., *Living in China* (San Francisco: China Books & Periodicals, Inc., USA, 1991) p. 7.

my boxes with a prayer for travelling mercies. They arrived before me, the medical supplies soon after and though slashed by Customs, nothing was amiss.

I thought I had better get some training in TESL (Teaching English as a Second Language). Several colleges in Australia offered the Cambridge Royal Society of Arts intensive TESL course. The procedure for getting into a course was quite lengthy, requiring tests of English proficiency and a long interview. I gained an inkling about TESL methodology from this rigmarole. The vast amount of preparation expected in addition to nine to five classes all week was daunting, but I was overjoyed to be accepted. It was a crushing blow not to be able to get funding for the course; the Lord had something better in mind. I learnt the hard lesson that I must put my faith in God's ability to provide, not man's.

Someone suggested I do an intensive 'Language and Culture' course offered by a Christian organization. I looked forward to learning the nitty-gritty of my own language, methods of learning another language, phonetics and anthropology. I gained an exemption from the latter because it had been a major subject at university. My adopted language was Pidgin English. The course gave me confidence and resources for teaching. Stammering through phonetics tutorials proved worthwhile because my students, I subsequently found, were also trained in phonetics. During the course, I could feel the Lord changing me into the person I needed to be in my new role. The warmth, patience and good humour of the teachers and other staff was appreciated by all the class. The Holy Spirit poured into my life abundant rivers of blessing in a hundred different ways. The staff and students in the Language and Culture course were channels for encouragement, teaching, and rich friendship and ministry.

I went to church services twice every Sunday and the Holy Spirit ministered his peace, healing, strengthening and heaven knows what else. He knew how much spiritual input I needed in order to face future challenges. It seemed as though the Lord crammed several years of ministry into a few short weeks. My spirit was willing for all that God had for me but my flesh heard frequent 'calls' to idyllic beaches in Queensland.

I finished the course a week early because the start of the semester in September was fast approaching. My parents flew from their home to spend the last week with me. This was the last time I saw my mother in good health.

'Only for a while, you say with a smile.'

My family and a friend came to the airport to see me off on my adventure. Normally saying goodbye at the airport amidst laughter and 'butterflies' had been an exciting time, because I was going for only two weeks. But this time the thought of leaving family and friends I love, put a huge leaden lump in my heart that wouldn't go away. Mum was upset and cried but I had to keep the tears back. It was up to me to face the future with more strength than I felt I had at that moment. Since God had started the adventure, he wouldn't let me down even though my knees threatened to.

The flight to Kuala Lumpur was uneventful. A taxi took me to the extremely comfortable Pan Pacific

Glen-Marie Hotel. The excellent service was a sooth-
ing balm. The receptionist quaintly called me 'Miss
Belinda'. How many times would I hear people call me
that during the coming months? In the comfortable
hotel room I felt terribly alone.

Next day at KL airport crowds of people, possessions and trolleys enveloped me. In the waiting
lounge, I sat near a friendly Chinese woman. Mandarin for 'What is your name?' had fled from my mind,
but crystal clear came the Pidgin English: 'Nam bilong
mi Belinda, nam bilong yu?' Great help. So I did learn
something on the course!

It was a good thing I changed my connecting flight
from Guangzhou for a later one because we sat on the
Kuala Lumpur tarmac for over an hour. A Chinese
friend was waiting for me at Guangzhou airport. We
enjoyed a long chat about past tours, future plans and
general gossip about people we know. After a couple
of hours, it was time to say goodbye. Now I really was
alone.

I headed for the upstairs lounge. Having to wait
for an hour or more, continuously looking at the
departure monitor screen to tell me which gate to go
to, was testing my faith in human efficiency and
modern technology. My flight number still failed to
appear though the time was getting dangerously close
to take-off. Then a girl appeared out of nowhere, saw
my T-shirt from the College I was going to, and came
over to talk to me. I would come to know over the
next few months that walking up to strangers was a
very Chinese thing to do. In this case I was greatly
relieved she did, because we were catching the same
plane. She guided me through the crowds to wherever

we were supposed to go. Can angels be Communist Party members like her? While we were tossing about in the airport bus on the bumpy trip out to the plane, she was excitedly showing me photos of her trip to Sydney.

At the airport I was greeted by a full welcome committee: the Dean of the English Department, the Chief Foreign Affairs Officer (FAO), his Assistant and Ramona, an English teacher whom I had met the previous year. Having collected my bag, I headed for the door, but was confronted by one of the staff yelling at me in rapid Chinese. I couldn't understand a word he was saying nor the shouts of the rest of the throng who joined in, and looked around totally bewildered. The teacher thought she would help matters by shouting the loudest of all, this time in English. After what seemed like several minutes, everyone's frustration, I realized, what they should have quietly told me in the first place, that I had to show my plane ticket to this ranting stickler-for-the-rules before I could be set free into the crowd. I was wondering at this point if I wanted to be freed at all, since their 'welcome' comprised so much yelling. Perhaps getting back on the plane was a quieter alternative, especially if it was heading south.

We drove through the dark streets of my new adopted city, past shapes and intermittent lights and fleeting appearances of bicycles and motor-bikes. The car paused at the imposing College gates, while a uniformed guard clanked their metallic bulkiness out of the way to let us pass. The dim streetlights revealed little of what I had seen of the buildings in the campus grounds the previous year. Students faded in and out of the headlights as we slowly meandered along the narrow lanes. Before leaving Australia's comfortable shores, I had told myself that I would just have to grin and bear whatever was given – stiff upper lip – that's what is needed.

Even though we arrived at night, I could tell that my alley was dirty and old. Baggage in hand, we picked our way carefully through piles of rubbish, building rubble and other refuse to get to the entrance. We climbed four flights of very dirty stairs. The walls of the stairwell were losing their whitewash and were stained extensively by years of traffic. At the top we encountered a padlocked gate, a few feet away from the front door. 'Great fire trap,' I thought. *Bleak House.*

The only adornments to the bare walls of the lounge were a giant world map stuck on crookedly, next to a large calendar depicting mythical characters. The latter gave me the spiritual horrors. The map and calendar leaned towards each other at crazy angles. There was a calendar in each of the three bedrooms leaving the rest of the walls bare, though raw would be a better word. Whitewash was flaking off every wall, exposing the first coat of grey paint. Here and there chunks had fallen out of the walls, presumably when workmen had been trying to drill into the soft sand-stone-like cement. All the electrical wiring ran along the outside of the walls like veins. 'Oh well, I can always put up pictures,' I mused. I was horrified by the state of the flat, but I put on my pleasant and amiable front to the English Department.

There was a tiny kitchen outside the front door near the stairwell. They showed me how to turn the gas on from the bottle for the two gas rings, and hot water service in the bathroom. Bone weary and depressed, I was beyond being able to take in all the instructions and just nodded absently. Someone was dispatched to buy food. He returned with a bottle of mineral water and some dry biscuits.

Everyone found a seat in the lounge and I perched gingerly on the edge of a very dusty chair. The conversation that night passed me in a blur, but I gathered that the assembly was trying to make me feel welcome. I recollect hoping they would leave so that I could sleep.

'Oh a mouse!' I said as the biggest, meanest-looking rat ran across a doorway and disappeared behind a cupboard. The visitors were surprised, but noone challenged its right to occupancy. I thanked God that he had given me the grace to say 'mouse' instead of 'rat'.

After telling me that breakfast would be at eight and someone would come for me, they finally left me alone. Well, not exactly alone, there was still Ratty for company. How many more companions had he invited for the evening entertainment?

Someone had been in the flat before my arrival, evidenced by a green and yellow striped bath towel lying on the bed. The mystery person had obviously left immediately – his job complete – without glancing at the thick dust that shrouded concrete floors, furniture, window-sills – everywhere. The dust had impregnated the only sheet on the bed in the main bedroom. My predecessor had advised that I bring a pillowslip and a pair of sheets with me. On the first night I could use only one of my sheets because the second had lain on the side of my suitcase which had somehow become saturated with water during the journey. I wished I had lined my case with plastic. I reckon the dust of Methuselah came out of the College sheet on the bed.

I tentatively inspected the furniture in my bedroom. Apart from a number of startled lizards who were indignant that someone bigger had taken up residence, I couldn't see any rats. Thank God. I closed the bedroom door, hoping to keep vermin out – and not in. Despairing about the miserable predicament I had landed myself in, I went to bed while the rats had a party in the next bedroom.

Mr. Chen had mentioned that the other mystery foreign teacher from Sydney had left two days previously. 'Do you think Jeanette would reconsider coming to China?' he asked wistfully. Oh, I hope she does!

I always said it was strange that I was the only one going to China.

2

'Will you stay two years?'
— The First Two Months —

'We are going to have a welcome party for the new students. You will sing a song,' announced Mr Chen next morning on the way to breakfast.

'You don't know if I can sing!' I teased.

'I am sure you can.' The instruction sounded dictatorial but the twinkle in his eye suggested the party was going to be more fun than ordeal. For the next three weeks, with the event written up in the calendar, there was constant discussion, clandestine rehearsals and speculation about what all the main players would perform. What strange sounds would come from the Australian? I irritated the neighbours for hours singing 'Tears in your eyes' – a song written with Chinese students in mind. (I later learned there were singing teachers downstairs. What did they think?)

'Could you dance for us as well?' a fourth year asked eagerly.

'I've been told I am going to sing a song.'

'Well, perhaps you could sing a song at the same time as dance?' she enquired wistfully. And leap tall buildings in a single bound? No problem!

The night was a great success and we all enjoyed the song and dance items immensely. The students were eager from then on to learn western songs; a hilarious task in a noisy classroom with forty voices all chortling at different speeds. Every College concert I attended during the stay in China was a good night out. The Art Department turned out spectacular traditional and 'western' dances in full, colourful costumes, which put all my efforts at dressing up our teams to shame. Still, they usually had a cast of twenty to forty dancers on stage at the same time, compared to our handful trying to fill the stage.

In a letter a missionary writes about new recruits: 'They have just joined the work and the first steep cliffs of entering a foreign language and culture where the skin of self may be rubbed raw and weak muscles stretched.'

My student Ruth's commiseration was a welcome gem of empathy: 'I get homesick because my hometown is a long way away. I can't go home much. But you must get a lot more homesick than me because your family is a *lot* further away than mine.' Another girl announced that 'It's childish to get homesick.' How far was she from her family home, I wondered.

The combination of feeling homesick for everything that is familiar and having to adapt to everything that is strange, creates a new perception of how you view yourself; a new 'you' emerges. Fortunately I am not the only person on planet earth who has undergone this strange metamorphosis. Gillian Bouras is a Melbourne woman who lived for years in a village in Greece with her Greek husband and children.

'The great temptation of extended travel or migration is the chance to reinvent yourself. You begin in the spirit of high endeavour and resolution: no more ... worry about what other people think. But this spirit lasts about a day, because paradoxically, you discover that you do not really want to start again. You begin to worry about your old self, feel it threatened and want it back just as it was. And further irony: that's exactly what you cannot have, because migration strips away all the cocoon layers, all the supports, takes away the boltholes of Mummy's arms and best friend's packet of Kleenex, until there is just you, reduced to a minimum, unprotected and exposed as never before.'[1]

This work of the Lord ushered in a new transformation in my understanding of myself; I often didn't feel that I knew myself at all. As I spoke the correct responses in any given situation, I was viewing myself from the stance of an outside observer. The new emotions which welled up on the inside belonged to someone else, surely. I thought I knew myself so well; now I was walking around in the body of a total stranger. It was comforting to read later that the experience is shared by others who live in a foreign country.

At miserable times, when I felt the Lord was a long way off (though I never fell for an instance for the enemy's lie that he had deserted me), I was reminded that this sense of disconnectedness with a higher power, was the way people without the Lord felt when

[1] Bouras, G, *A Foreign Wife*, (Melbourne: McPhee Gribble/Penguin, 1988 3rd edition) pp. 8–9.

adversity struck them. But how much more terrifying for them than for me? How rich in the Lord I really was, despite the circumstances. I 'felt' so clearly the need for the gospel in others' lives, that they too could know they are never abandoned. How could I have felt this way expect through a taste of this disconnectedness?

The friendliness of the students was the best medicine for all these negative reactions. Within my first week I had an official visit from the class monitors of one of my classes. They came bearing a delicate carving of a shrimp and fish swimming through seaweed, made out of deer antler and a card. This was 'National Teacher's Day'. All over China students honour their teachers. Even on TV there were musical programmes showing squads of young ones out in their Sunday best, singing songs to their teachers. It was a nice idea. I was really touched by the thought, especially since I had not even started teaching them yet. They had no doubts about my abilities. The occasion cemented the relationships between the monitors and myself, which were important because everything I did in and out of class would be relayed back to the English Department hierarchy in the future, most probably through this pair. All the monitors in all my classes were certainly the best for the job and I maintained good friendships with them throughout my time.

One of the most threatening things I found about living in China especially in the first two months, was the intrusion of others into my flat and private life. Some of the intrusion was necessary because the flat was in such a poor state of disrepair that tradesmen had to make endless visits to mend or replace appliances and fixtures. The process was a major exercise entailing seemingly a cast of thousands. Girls were sent to sit with me while the men were there and also to help clean up the accumulated dust and grime.

Further, my arrival was apparently such a history-changing event that the local press blurted it to the city. Strangers came in droves to my door to see what I looked like. Once satisfied, I wouldn't see them again. Mr Chen warned in the first week this would happen and advised me to keep people out. I am not talking here about students or people who had a desire to be sincere friends.

The trouble was that I didn't know who was friend, merely curious, mischief-maker or someone sent from the Lord. I didn't know, but I didn't get a prompting either from the Holy Spirit. An Australian acquaintance who had worked in China for several years, warned that many visitors would just waste my time. I thought it was a harsh comment at the time, but had to trust her more extensive experience. It didn't take me long to experience the reality of what she said.

I interviewed visitors through the padlocked gate and let only girls or male students beyond it. Most of the time the students arrived in groups. Disappointed young men from outside the College who landed on the doorstep alone, would look bewildered when I refused entry after they had asked if they could come in. After all, they had given me an introduction to themselves – all thirty seconds in length.

I could see the newspaper headlines: 'Foreign Teacher Entertains Strange Men in her Flat – in the

First Week of Arrival.' Visitors who did get beyond the gate, would immediately wander right through the flat – bedroom and all without asking permission, all the while busily asking a million questions, some quite personal. I knew that whatever I said would be taken down and used in a thousand conversations with who knows who. The main stream of curious people had slowed down by the time Jeanette arrived. But I wondered if her appearance might herald a fresh wave of visitors. Fortunately the second wave was smaller than the first.

Students were always welcome in the flat and they brought a greater degree of respect and courtesy than outsiders. By comparison, it was so good to relax into everyday conversation with them. They were always a lot of fun to be around and cheered me up just by their effervescence. By the next summer I realized how much I had changed regarding my privacy. Once I had got to know the students and a more casual and realistic understanding of each other had been formed, I didn't mind them looking around the flat and they were always genuinely interested in what we were up to. By then we had shifted into another set of flats, and on the hottest days I'd invite girls to enjoy the air-conditioner located in my bedroom. It seemed mean not to, considering the stifling, spartan conditions they endured in the cramped dormitories.

Students invited me to the English Corners organized by individual classes, as well as the general one on the plaza outside the English Department. (English Corner was an hour or so a week spent under the fig-trees speaking English with students.) This was a good chance to get to know the young people, especially the fourth years whom I didn't teach during the day. Everyone was keen to talk and especially to proudly talk about their hometowns; it was quite an education.

Jasmin, an eloquent fourth year, invited me to talk with her primary school students she tutored in English every Saturday in a school across the city. By the time we arrived there, the children had finished chalking a welcome message for me on the board and decorated it with beautiful, complicated pictures. I was really touched. They were very polite and shyly showed off their English skills. Jasmine told them to sing me a few songs. Instantly everyone burst into song without any hesitation or fumbling over half-remembered words. I was very impressed. After talking with them for a while, I asked for a piece of paper. Again instantly, the children all clambered excitely for paper, and someone was dispatched to find a person who could get some. A minute later an old man arrived carrying paper for everyone. They all launched into making paper-folded masterpieces; the room was filled with boats, cranes and birds of several varieties and sizes, hats and all sorts of shapes which made my humble Sydney Opera House look rather ordinary. The children's creations filled my flat and cheered it up no end.

I was beginning to learn one of the treasures in Chinese culture, namely the attitude that art in all its forms is part of everyday life. The children so naturally took to 'performing' without any self-consciousness at all. What a contrast to Australian culture which prizes the highly skilled professionals to the extent that art is not so much a part of everyday life, but most of the time a spectator sport for the masses. Chinese society encourages the ordinary person to take part in spontaneous entertainment, even if they have mediocre skill in the area. This was a recurring theme which I noted throughout my stay.

Ramona took me to the home of Charlotte, the College Dance teacher, for dinner. The family could not understand English, nor could I understand Chinese, but we had a brilliant night together nonetheless. The evening was alive with musical and dance items. The father was a music teacher and most proficient on a small stringed instrument. His son was a remarkable pianist for his age and played Chinese and western classical pieces. Ramona's nine-year daughter danced a traditional piece, then somehow I found myself dancing western style, accompanied by the piano.

They insisted I try on a gorgeous red and cream Mongolian dancing dress, and a headdress with a heavy fringe of glass beads to hang across the forehead. The dancing teacher conjured romantic images while she talked about her days in a dancing troupe in Xinjiang, one of the remote north-west provinces of China. The troupe travelled around the country on horse-back! It was such a feast of fun that I felt at the end of the night that I had been to a concert in a theatre. Oh if only Australians could loosen up enough to perform spontaneously without fear of ridicule.

'You must pray now. This isn't just another storm. Satan wants to wreak enormous destruction against the city and people.'

This urgent message from the Lord spurred my heart into action as the rain and wind thundered outside. From my eyrie on the top floor, I saw palm branches thrashing about in the gale, lashing other trees and buildings around them. With so many windows in the bedroom and elsewhere, and rain pouring across the concrete floors, I felt as if the flat was in a fragile glass globe poised upon a slender pedestal, a plaything, buffeted by savage elements. The rotting casement windows couldn't hold the water back. I feared they would explode, scattering glass and water across my bed. I was relieved to realize that being so high up, I was above the level of flying missiles from broken up homes. The full force of the gale fortunately hit the building almost directly side on. The only window there was in the bathroom: so only a slice of the wind's trajectory threatened the panes. I prayed earnestly that the typhoon wouldn't change direction and hit straight on.

Vivid memories came back of windows exploding one after the other, unable to stand against the pressure of the blast of Cyclone Tracy in Darwin on Christmas Day 1974. A giant can-opener ripped our roof into oblivion in one screaming movement. Darwin city was razed to the ground. Our house was one of the few still possessing walls at the end of that terrifying night. I remembered the lengths of roofing timber which had ricocheted around my bedroom and landed in the hall. One of them was over ten feet long. My sister's home was reduced to nothing but bare floor boards in the morning. (The family was unhurt after spending the night in their caravan under the house.)

Remembering the nearby power-pole which instead of standing tall, next morning ran parallel to the ground and the weighty steel girder whipped into a circular 'art form', later moved to a prominent spot at my high school, reinforced the reality of the power of nature's violence. I was sickened to think of what was happening outside my concrete eyrie. What protection did the people have, who lived in the makeshift huts and ancient dwellings? Flying rubble crashed unhindered into man, beast and home with chilling velocity. I thought of the popular blue and pink tarpaulins stretched as awnings outside shops taking flight.

I later learnt that typhoon Sibyl caused the most devastation in the Philippines, sending a hundred and eight people to their deaths with another hundred listed missing. The bill for damage was $US38 million. This was not surprising since the wind force peaked at 95 knots. After venting its anger there, it visited Hong Kong, then mainland China, losing some of its force as it crossed the coast. Tracy was one of Australia's worst natural disasters and extremely intense by world standards. Its wind velocity was greater than Sibyl's.

The *China Daily* reported:

'At least eight people were killed and more than 30 injured when typhoon Sibyl battered South China's Guangdong Province on Tuesday . . . Some of the streets in Guangzhou and Shenzhen were flooded, causing heavy traffic jams in the two cities. Shenzhen Reservoir reached its warning line on Tuesday. Electricity and water supplies in some of the towns and villages were cut off. Fields and crops including sugar cane and rice were flooded.'

I was amazed that no one mentioned the typhoon to me before or after the event, since every detail of every other occasion at College was eagerly relayed in triplicate. Possibly, however people might not have received the warning and what could we have done anyway?

'We get typhoons every year. We always have about ten days or two weeks of typhoons,' reported one of my students who had grown up in the area. Her local knowledge gave her a veneer of calmness since she had lived through these ordeals for years, but underneath I sensed she was agitated just like the rest of us. It was Friday afternoon, a week or two after Sibyl, at a grade two Practical English class. We were four flights up; the tropical storm raged outside. There were forty students not wanting to work but wanting a distraction from their fears. I felt a responsibility to keep them calm, but felt just as powerless.

The brunt of the wind force was taken by the windowless side walls of the structure. The remaining front and back walls were louvered glass from desk height to the high ceilings. Thick, wide and cumbersome, the louvers were wedged into corrupted metal clips defying closure against the weather. There was really no need to close them because most of the year the breeze was welcome. As I tried to keep my voice even and loud over the gale – and my beating heart – I wondered if the wind would change direction and strike the classroom broad-side. Would the glass shatter? We would be all drenched in seconds. There was nowhere to run to, no safe room. It was best to keep the lesson going. We didn't achieve much.

By the end of the class, the wind had abated sufficiently to allow us to walk carefully along slippery paths littered with branches, rubbish and other debris, and running with streams of water. Drenched, I reached home, and grateful that I would be in Australia before the annual frightening fortnight struck again.

'Employers still insist on employees going to work during a typhoon. They aren't allowed to stay home,' Elly said knowledgeably. How fierce does the hurricane have to be before this rule is relaxed? Not for the first time I marvelled at the Chinese capacity to keep business-as-usual in the face of enormous adversity.

At times the Lord impressed upon me the sight of the thick, oppressive cloud cover which shrouds much of China for months on end, as a symbolic reminder of the work of the enemy keeping the country bound. This gave me much to pray about.

'How long are you going to stay in China?' From day one at the College, this was the question on everyone's lips, as if they were in a tacit conspiracy to encourage me to reconsider.

'One year.'

'Please will you stay two years?' they insisted.

'You don't know me. I may not be a good teacher!' I teased.

'Yes, I am sure you will be,' was the emphatic and trusting response. What faith!

It was overwhelming to find so many people, so recently met, wanting me to be a semi-permanent fixture in College life, or were they just desperate and would take anyone? The signing of the contract made my intentions known and sealed my fate for the next

year. The event wasn't half as bad as I thought it
would be.

> 'Teachers contracts . . . vary across the map, both
> between and within institutions. It is necessary to
> negotiate vigorously. Too many foreigners, starry-eyed
> about Asia, inexperienced at negotiation, and perhaps
> succumbing to an unscrupulous waiban (College Foreign
> Affairs Officer) pressured to sign a contract while still
> gripped by jet lag, neglect the contract's importance, or
> sign without careful scrutiny. When they later discover
> their colleagues teach half the courses for twice the wage,
> they howl and scream, but to no avail.'[2]

I didn't know how the penny would fall in my case
concerning the timing of signing the contract.

> 'Pre-arrival contracts allow more time for reflection and
> consultation with friends, but tend to be abstract, as you
> sign them without knowing details of local conditions.
> Post-arrival contracts allow inclusion of nitty-gritty
> details like which building you'll sleep in and whom
> you'll teach, but can be subject to time pressure; much
> paperwork can't be completed till you sign, and your
> waiban may push for speedy negotiations.'[3]

The contract, when at last it appeared three or four
weeks into the semester, was fairly written overall,
though the rosy picture of the flat described in the

---

[2] Weiner, Murphy & Li, *Living in China*, p. 61.
[3] Ibid., p. 60.

accommodation paragraph, would have elicited
indignant coughing from the seriously-minded. No
mention was made of the state of the flat at the
signing. Since by this time things were moving satisfactorily in that direction, with a great deal of help
from long-suffering Mr Chen, I thought it politic to let
matters drop. There was no point mentioning all my
arguments with the Foreign Affairs Officer (FAO)
about getting my flat fixed. Mr Chen was casual and
chatty about the contract and the only clause he mentioned was, predictably, the one on religion: 'Party B
shall respect China's religious policy and shall not
conduct activities incompatible with the status of an
expert.'

The Lord gave me the wisdom to wave it aside
politely and change the subject by asking a question.

'Are we going to have, er, "meetings" every day?'
Jeanette asked during her first week. If one of us was
fussing around doing something other than coming to
order at the meeting, the other would complain
loudly: 'It's hard to get a quorum when half the
committee is absent!'

Our nightly prayer meetings revolved around the
worries of the students and staff, the city, more generally of the nation, and our daily needs. It would have
been nice to write that we experienced mighty mani-
festations of the Holy Spirit, so that we returned
home spiritual heroes. We were not led to engage primarily in deep intercessory prayer ministry for hours
on end, but to use our teaching skills to raise the standard of language fluency as much as possible. God
has plans for using such proficiency which are far
wider than we mere mortals could ever imagine.

Simply to love the students and show we believed in
them as much as we could, was a crying need. Certainly the Lord was present and ever working to
change us and people around us.

Belinda is going to the banquet

October 1st is National Day in China. The solemnity
of the occasion is signified by a three-day holiday each
year. On October 1st 1949, Mao Zedong rode
through Beijing in an American jeep to the dais at
Tiananmen Square and proclaimed the founding of
the People's Republic of China. Victory for the
Communist Party was sweet but they faced gigantic
responsibilities to feed and govern such a vast population. A new foreign policy had to be quickly drafted
because they were confronted with international hos-
tilities from countries supportive of the ousted
Kuomintang or Nationalist Party (especially the USA,
though it remained officially neutral). In the cities,
much of the food and consumer goods were imported
and many Chinese cities had more commercial links
with other countries than with regions inland.

I wrote home: 'On September 30th I am going to a
banquet with the College President at the most prestigious hotel in town to celebrate National Day. None
of the other English Department teachers have been
invited, so I'm it! There will be other foreigners there,
so it will be good to chat in English, French, Japanese
. . . perhaps I'd better brush up on my Chinese.'

Mr Chen said in a fatherly fashion, 'There will be
many foreigners at the banquet you can meet so you

won't be lonely any more!' The annual banquet for foreigners was hosted by the Municipal Foreign Affairs Department.

My students were agog with the news that the year before I had actually *stayed* at the hotel where the banquet was to be held. I hastened to add that in my bleary-eyed state on that particular night, I remembered little of the room because we arrived very late after performing at the College and then left at 4 a.m. next morning. To my mind, two hours' sleep barely fitted the description of 'stayed there' – a term which conjures visions of lazing beside the pool or casually eating exotic food in the hotel restaurant. The townspeople are very proud of their hotel because President Jiang Zemin himself stayed there a few years earlier, while attending municipal meetings. (I hope he had more sleep.)

All the English Department buzzed with the news that I was going to the banquet. By their excitement, anyone would have thought they were going too. I certainly wished one of them was, because I suspected the President couldn't speak English. Who would translate? I was accustomed to people constantly milling around me, helping with communication and practical details, so this evening was going to be a new experience in more ways than one. Every day of the preceding week, the vicarious enjoyment of my grand night out bubbled from the teachers and FAO people in a multitude of well-intentioned instructions – which changed every day. The most important of them all was: *Don't be late for the President!* (a crime I take it that was up there with the big ones like murder and treason).

I was excited and a little inattentive to my class on the fateful Friday afternoon. Everyone was hoping that I could dash home after the class ended at 4.30 p.m., have a shower, get changed and be ready to meet the President, cool and poised by 5.15 p.m. at the designated location (which had been changed a couple of times during the day). Would I get lost on the way? In the middle of my shower, George arrived and asked if I was ready. 'I would be if I was allowed to get on with it,' I muttered under my breath. Having held me up for a few minutes, his job complete, he retreated downstairs.

In the alley a knot of teachers and FAO staff were waiting for me in nervous anticipation. Relieved that I had appeared on time, they hurried me up a side alley to the College car. They had dispensed with the plan to find the car (behind the basketball courts near the garage, wherever that was) and thought a safer plan was to ask the driver to find me instead. Compliments about my dress and wishes for a pleasant evening abounded before the majority of teachers went home. I sat in the car and waited. Keeping a foreign teacher waiting wasn't a crime up there with the big ones. I didn't mind, I was practising my phrase of greeting to a superior and better. When the gentleman did arrive, my greeting had the desired effect and he broke into a surprised grin. We were off to a good start.

Living a cloistered existence for the past few weeks meant little opportunity to see the rest of the city outside the immediate shopping district. The suburbia beyond the car's tinted windows was a fascinating world and I had to keep telling myself that I was still in the same city. A disconnected sense of belonging, but not belonging, to the city was heightened when we reached this modern section. The spacious streets with wide, clean footpaths and new, impressive buildings were foreign intrusions into the familiar cityscape of old crowded alleys and dingy tumble-down dwellings. The structures here seemed as impervious to the ravages of tropical heat and typhoons as the older areas seemed vulnerable.

The car purred through the hotel gate, past lush gardens, tennis courts and villas dotted between, and came to rest outside the main building. There was a sense of the Cinderella story as I alighted from the car and was welcomed by the staff. The dining-room was decorated for the occasion and buzzing with the arrival of foreign guests, each accompanied by one or two Chinese officials from their establishment. I searched the crowd for some hint of an Australian identity, all the time telling myself that there was probably an assortment of nationalities here, not necessarily Australian. Friendly smiles made me yearn to mingle but a smartly-dressed waiter with table manners to match, curtly directed us to our table.

The seating was arranged with consideration. Beside me was the President from the Education College, (a similar establishment to my College) a sociable man with flawless English. Beside him was our College President with several Chinese men whom I didn't know. To the left of me were two western English teachers – a man and woman from two other colleges.

My companions and I had a great time. The two ex-patriates understood what it felt like to be the new kid in town. Laughing and talking rapidly (for the first time in weeks) and eating course after course of sumptuous Chinese food was wonderful. The College President enjoyed the night too with his friends. The culinary delights (topped by 'Chinese Pizza') brought the chit-chat inevitably around to 'what I miss from home'. Mention of cheese produced a swift response: 'I buy cheese twice a year. Go to a shop in a side street behind such and such hotel, tell the man there you want some cheese. He'll hop on his bike and peddle to a friend and buy a block for you. Cost you a bit though.' My cravings wanted to try it out, but what a roundabout way of getting the cheese!

The official speeches by the mayor and senior government men revealed that there were representatives from nineteen nations in the room, including Denmark. 'This is it, the entire ex-pat community?' I queried. There wouldn't have been more than 150 of us. I realized gloomily that they would all live in this part of town or thereabouts and the majority work in business enterprises anyway. A wave of 'feeling lonely in a crowd' passed over me. Still, there was no use fretting. I might as well enjoy the night. Following the speeches, a group of dignitaries shook hands from table to table. Buoyant with good food, wine and company, they chatted informally and sincerely welcomed each of us in turn.

Abruptly all the Chinese people stood up as though a silent command had been given. We looked at each other bewildered, quickly gathered our handbags and followed the cue of our escorts. Ushered into line to shake hands with the officials at the door, I said the formal thanks and a moment later found myself outside the door.

It was 9 p.m.

A heaviness of heart descended, all the enjoyment had ended so early. The night had been the closest thing since my arrival, to the kind of interaction I was used to with people at home, and it had restored my equilibrium greatly.

The front car door was opened for me. I met the grins and embarrassed smirks of two unknown Chinese men and the President, all crammed into the back seat. We meandered through the grounds, then suddenly stopped outside a bar. Everyone emerged from the crowd and we entered a karaoke bar. The volume of the music made up for the dim lighting. A woman descended on us chatting in English. Lip-reading rather than hearing, I learnt that she taught at our College, and would I like to sing a song? My protestations fell on already half-deaf ears and before I knew it, I was singing 'Country Road' to the delight of the audience. Well, I'm not sure if delight was the word, politeness may have been nearer the mark. What I heard of my voice in fold-back sounded way off-key, though I knew I was singing in key. There was also a time-lag between the music and vocals. As I crossed the empty dance-floor back to my seat, I thought perhaps the darkness in the bar was a good idea after all.

The evening had been so refreshing, my cameo performance of Cinderella's story in a distant country. But looking around my shabby College quarters thinking about the arguments with the FAO, made me question the meaning of the phrase 'We welcome you to China'.

Hobbies

During the first two months, the only hobbies I had were cross-stitch, letter-writing and cards. Playing patience with a cheap pack of cards under an unshaded light bulb transported me to the austere set of a 1950's black and white film. I put out of mind the familiar image of the solitary performer down on her luck, waiting for the big break that might come any day now. Patience filled the night hours but left the empty cup of loneliness.

I rationed the chapters of a book I had bought at the airport before departure, resisting the temptation to devour it in a week. I yearned to take books out of the College library but alas, no library card, no book. It was weeks before I received my very own card. When the plastic treasure arrived, I raced to the library and lost myself amongst the floors, corridors, mezzanines and alleys created by crammed rows of volumes in the confusing building. Seeing me entering the labyrinth, the staff, unseen by me, dispatched an attendant who spoke a little English to find and direct me to the English section.

Here I found two stacks of dusty ESL books, English literature analyses, classic novels and a few sets of donated text-books on the USA. There wasn't a book on Australia and very few on other countries. I came home clutching some classics, wondering how much of the language of the last-century novels my students would understand if they read them. How incongruous to be an Australian living in the 1990s reading in a flat in China *The Great Gatsby* by the American F. Scott Fitzgerald? If I had been in Shanghai, a city harking back to those hedonistic days of grand hotels – Peace, Astor, Cathay, Burlington – it would have felt less strange.

' "There were parties at hotels every night, and you could go from one to the other and still be dancing at four o'clock in the morning", recalls the breezy voice of an old Shanghailander (as foreign settlers in Shanghai were known) . . . in Hong Kong half a century later.'[4]

The library held knitting pattern books. The tight College schedule and tight living quarters left little room in the students' week for hobbies beyond sport. But amongst the girls, knitting was a popular pastime at weekends.

'Many girls knit for the boys they like,' giggled several girls looking deliberately at a red-faced room-mate busily knitting away. I was just as intrigued to see the inside of a Chinese wool-shop, as I was in the intricate designs created on four needles by deft fingers. One Saturday morning, Sally, Elly and I set off with great expectations for the wool-shop. Inside was yarn and wool in every colour from muted tones to dazzling pink and orange, echoing the oriental taste for bright colours in bath towels and bed linen. The girls negotiated a reasonable price on some blue wool and a set of needles – pointed at both ends. Surprisingly there was the abbreviated 'Australia' character on the wrapper. What a pleasant change to see our exports going overseas, instead of hearing bad news in the media about our trade imbalance.

---

[4] Findlay, Ian, *Shanghai*, (London: Harrap Ltd/Hong Kong: The Guidebook Co. Ltd., 1988) p. 18.

I wrote triumphantly to Jeanette about the wool-shop discovery, suggesting she bring any favourite knitting needles (with ends). It wouldn't be long before she arrived.

I wrote home: 'Well, I've hit the big smoke! (the Provincial capital). Tomorrow we're going to meet Jeanette at the airport. She faxed us to say that she couldn't book an internal flight. So in a show of masculine bravado, Mr Chen decided to save her the rigours of the Chinese railway system, by sending George (FAO assistant) to the airport to pick her up. I pointed out that he doesn't know what she looks like; Mr Chen asked if I wanted to go, so here we are! It feels peculiar and lonely to be in a hotel suite. But I wanted to make sure that Jeanette actually got back "home" safely. With a punctured tyre (later fixed along the highway), traffic jams, rain, mud and stretches of bad road, it took us 12 hours to arrive. Coming here is a big deal for the students – they were all goggle-eyed at the news that we were going. Most have lived such sheltered lives in their hometowns, that going to the Big Smoke sounds to them a very great distance away. One of my students rang last night to *complain* that I was cancelling Friday's class (in order to come here).'

True to her reputation for creative projects, Jeanette flew in bearing luggage dangerously bristling with knitting needles and a book of the world's top forty most difficult fairisle designs. She announced that I was to knit the one at the top of the list – a cardigan with Welsh pansies frolicking all over it.

'I can't make that, it's too hard.'

'Yes you can, it's easy.'

Her faith in my ability as number one knitter faded like a pansy in summer within a week.

'Jeanette I've made another mistake. What do I do now?' Sigh.

Searching for the next stitch, swimming elusively on the graph, reminded me this was a long-term project for a long-term stay in China. Slowly I got the gist of bringing pansy blossoms to bloom before my eyes. Oh bliss, Oh rapture! Meanwhile the second number one knitter jumped ahead, creating large colourful squares, worked into a cheerful patchwork cardigan and in no time was sewing it up. The knitters amongst the girls checked regularly on the progress of both garments and made approving noises. (The students took to Jeanette like ducks to water, following weeks of endless indoctrination: 'My friend is coming from Australia! You'll like her!')

'You are very clever,' one remarked to her, 'you can make lots of things.' Jeanette also brought from home a delicate cross-stitch pattern to work on fine linen.

The students were fascinated as flowers and birds fluttered onto the fabric.

The same girl enthused to her: 'You are so clever, *you can do everything*!'

Well, that was that for the training in humility. For the rest of our stay, every little incident even vaguely involving some sort of minor achievement by Jeanette, elicited from her the unchanging remark: 'Don't you know I can do everything?' The Chinese are by nature very complimentary and she scooped up compliments wherever she went and tacked them onto the phrase. Hereafter my ears rang with the familiar refrain: 'Not only do I have a beautiful nose, beautiful hair and eyes, can sing and dance, but *I can do everything* as well!'

The 'singing' stretched credulity a bit because the only song we could both sing together in any semblance of harmony was 'Waltzing Matilda'. There was a difference in keys in other songs or was it that our powerfully agile voices wanted to soar between a whole range of keys? Anyway, we sounded dreadful singing any other ditty together. So 'Matilda' became our standard party item. We had to make our own fun and entertainment at home because of the absence of night-life, and enjoyed trying to remember songs – taking turns to fill in the gaps in the less familiar verses.

It was so good to have someone to fill in all the gaps in my existence in this foreign land.

Travelling insights

'Where are you going?' the conductor yelled out of the bus window, holding a grimy card with (Route) '1' on it.

'Route Two' we answered. In a flash he reversed the card to show '2' and the man yelled for us to quickly get on board. What a bus service; it changes route just to please its passengers! Such is aggressive private enterprise in modern China. These men were going to get customers no matter how. Bumping along the city roads, the conductor loudly accosted every foot-sore pedestrian wandering along the road and many took advantage of this user-friendly bus service. Yes, there are bus stops, but the bus could screech to a halt at any point along the road as well. I looked around the interior of the crowded bus and felt the hardness of the seat under its tattered bamboo matting; clearly not much money was ploughed back into 'interior decoration' for the passengers', comfort. I checked my own expectations of any bus service and concluded that I would much rather have buses run frequently (and change route to suit me) than wait half an hour for padded seats to come along.

From the stares, chattering and discussions with my companions, I had obviously made the other passengers' day. While I gazed outside, they gazed inside at the strange girl with the blue eyes and brown hair. In the Chinese cities where foreigners are a common sight, the 'staring and chattering' treatment is not so intense, but here, where there is only a tiny ex-patriate population, the game of 'spot the *guilo*' is a popular pastime for the locals, conferring instant stardom on the unsuspecting.

Taxis are common and range in size from motorbikes and scooters to minibuses and sedans. For those liking a gentler pace, there's the two-seater with a canopy on top, but no sides, pulled by a bicycle. The latter always reminded me of the bicycle version of the 'surrey with a fringe on top' from *Oklahoma*. I loved going for sedate rides in them.

You have to admire drivers of tourist coaches in China. These intrepid, unsung heroes worm their way through seething, honking rivers of vehicles flowing like treacle along the streets, fly-overs and highways in cities, and then flood out into the countryside.

Fortunately, because of traffic density, the pace of travel is fairly slow. I would stare in amazement, as the driver negotiated past trucks, cars, motorcycles, carts pulled by buffaloes, bullocks or donkeys, pedal-powered 'tray-tops' and a wide selection of vehicles defying categorization by western minds. Of course there are bicycles, bicycles, bicycles . . . In the midst of all this, are the most courageous of all, the pedestrians who need to cross the road . . .

One year on a past tour, while travelling on a coach in the Pudong docks area of Shanghai, our driver had to cross over a vast bridge, served by confusing spa-ghetti junctions at both exits. Coming from Nanjing, the area was unfamiliar to him, so he became lost in the maze of roads and sign-posts. He crossed the bridge but somehow turned around and drove back to the start. Arriving for the second pay-in at the toll-booth, my companion quipped: 'I wonder if they give a discount for the second time around.'

One imagines endless traffic jams and accidents in every Chinese city every second of the day. On a street in wintry Beijing, I arrived soon after a minor car crash had caused the line-up of sixteen trolley buses in the vicinity, and a second line-up of similar proportions around the corner. 'No-one was going nowhere' until the policeman arrived.

The worst possible scenario which one predicts will happen at any moment, does not necessarily occur because of the attitude of road-users. They realize the obvious fact that the only way everyone is going to get from A to B, is for everyone to extend an incredible degree of space-grace to other users. One vehicle is 'allowed' to cut off another – what a contrast to

Australian drivers! The Chinese have learnt through thousands of years of hard times and crowded conditions, that a huge degree of give and take in all aspects of life is required, in order to avoid accidents and disharmony in society generally. Once the initial shock that everyone is driving on the 'other' side of the road had dissipated, I was rarely nervous while travelling in China.

Civil engineers in Guangzhou have found an ingenious solution to traffic congestion and the differing speeds of road-users. If you have a road on the ground, why not build a road above, parallel to it? As I ascend the approach to one of these roads, past experience tells me that I am going to go along a flyover and soon descend to the ground again. Instead, the road goes on and on . . . Looking right and left, I notice just how close I am to the adjacent buildings. I suddenly feel uncomfortably like a peeping-tom, because I can clearly see the picture on a TV screen in someone's living-room. The elevated sensation in my stomach reminds me that the family lives not on street-level, but on the third floor of the building. Flying through the city like this gives a fascinating perspective of the cityscape, otherwise invisible from the ground. Seeing space used so efficiently and the variety of vehicles, I am impressed by the inventiveness of the Chinese to turn their resources into solutions for their problems, commensurate with their circumstances and income. We have much to learn from them.

3

'Table-top dancing ducklings'
— Food —

What we ate, how we ate it, and when we ate it, were burning questions uppermost in the minds of seemingly each and every person whenever we met them. Nervous students at English Corner, unprepared with any other questions, would blurt out one of these standard lines – often several students would rattle them off within the hour. My own students and regulars to English Corner knew that I expected more substantial topics of conversation. I had to remind myself that these young people had just recently left the nest where Mum would have been chief cook and organizer of meals, so they would not have had the experience of fending for themselves. Most are expected to put in many hours of homework after school during their secondary years.

'What do you eat?'

What do they mean by that question? The ingredients for our food was available for them too in the markets and shops. I suppose they think that strange people eat strange food. One day I was in the kitchen mashing potato, when a student wandered in to see what I was doing. 'Oh my . . . what's that?' reverberated around the tiny room.

'It's potato,' I said lamely. She was unconvinced. Perhaps she wondered why anyone would go to the trouble of beating an unsuspecting potato to a pulp.

'Do you cook by yourself?'

This question used to amuse me because of its ambiguity. What did they mean?

Am I capable of cooking by myself?

Do I have a hired cook? On a teachers' salary?!

Does the College expect us to eat College food or do our own cooking?

The list of questions engendered by this question goes on and on. I never did satisfactorily answer this one. To reply, 'Yes I do, because College food often makes me sick,' was tempting and had a ring of truth about it, because Jeanette and I often had stomach problems after eating canteen food, but it's hardly diplomatic. I refrained.

'Have you had your supper?'

To the newly-arrived western resident, this question posed as a greeting, sounds rather odd, especially when asked frequently and at an hour in between meal-breaks (both western and Chinese). Why would

I have had my supper at two o'clock in the afternoon?
The Chinese have meals at times of the day different
from us. They are up with the birds, already exercised,
breakfasted and ready to start classes at 7.30 a.m. So,
they must have lunch early; 11.30 a.m.–2.30 p.m. was
the official 'lunch-three-hours'. Then there is another
burst of academic endeavour until 4.30 p.m. when
everyone has their 'supper'. I surmise that the Chinese
adopted the word 'supper' from British customs.

I ceased my questioning and irritation when I learnt
the sobering history of the greeting. Students told me
that years ago, when people were very poor and frequently went without food, it became the custom to
inquire into the welfare of another person by asking if
they had eaten that day. If the person had, then they
were doing relatively well – at least for that day. A
three-year drought in North China in 1876–79
resulted in the deaths of between 9 and 13 million people. Another in 1920–21 affected 20 million and killed
500,000. In 1928–29 a famine comparable in extent
and severity to the famine of the previous century,
affected Shensi, Honan and Kansu Provinces. In
Shensi Province alone 3 million people died. The students of this better-fed generation, said laughingly
that it was a silly saying. I was reminded, though, of
the precarious life of a third of the Chinese population
still living in poverty today.

While I was getting my flat fixed up and settling in,
the week before classes started, I was given three days
of free VIP meals at a nearby college canteen. Every
meal was one of strange experiences; I didn't know
which emotion to retain out of a whole collection
which the occasion elicited. The canteen floor was

habitually dirty, so I would sit on a small stool at a table, with my skirts tucked up out of the water that the staff sloshed about every day. The tables were usually covered with the remains of the meals of the previous patrons – heaps of rice, bones and other left-overs were scattered everywhere by students to be later cleared away by the staff. The food was delicious.

Once upon a time the concrete walls had been painted but most of the paint had crumbled away and been replaced by stains, dirt and mould. The kitchen next door was a centre of activity and blackness. The high walls were black from cooked-on oil, the smell of which wafted from below. The food was laid out on a wide bench in the middle of the kitchen and in one corner was a huge, raging fire which heated what must have been the biggest wok known to man. It must have been a metre in diameter. Bellows of probably similar dimensions fed draughts of air to the fire and though unseen, made their presence felt: conversation was almost incomprehensible above the din. Mr Chen told me that the canteen staff came from inland country areas and were employed on a casual basis, so that the College didn't have to pay pensions; and, no doubt, compensation for the loss of hearing in the young workers. Despite the environment from which it came, the food they gave me during the first week was tasty and there was enough for a family of four. They must have thought I needed feeding up. (A few months of living in China made me lose a lot of weight and I became as waif-like as those around me.)

After the false start at organizing meals at the canteen, we developed a routine of cooking in the flat with weekly forays to the local market accompanied by one

or two students. The students insisted we did not go to
the market alone because 'They will cheat you.' Every
Wednesday afternoon in the first semester, Anita
would appear as regular as clock-work to escort me. In
the second semester, Pauline and Kelly took their turn
at being my 'vegie girls'. I enjoyed their company and
they enjoyed asking me innumerable questions about
the west and about the English language.

I wrote home: 'There's a mini-market in a side alley
off the main road near the College . . . It is such a sad
sight – the people are what the students call "peasants", so they must travel from outside the city to
bring in their produce. The food is put out on sacking
on the ground in the mud, and I can't see how they
would make enough money to feed their families. No
purchase I make is more than 5–6 jiao (just a few
cents) . . . I tell Anita to bargain only once – to let them
know that they can't put the price up just because I am
a foreigner. But honestly, I don't mind paying much
more because my salary can certainly cover the cost.
The sellers smile at me, but from their dirty clothes and
weather-beaten faces, I can see great hopelessness. The
women carry their babies in slings on their backs. The
contrast between rich and poor is starkly seen
here. Flash, air-conditioned cars go down the same
roads as bikes and bullocks.'

We would arrive home, with our bags bulging with
fruit, vegetables, beans, eggs, sometimes a freshly-
killed fish and any other unnamed something-or-other,
convinced that 'Jeanette would know how to cook it!'
Sometimes she'd say: 'You know that something-or-
other you bought last week? Well, don't get it this
week!'

Once the season for a particular vegetable was over, that was it, until the next season. The up-side of this meant gorging ourselves on delicious bananas, lychees, mangoes, green-skinned mandarins and watermelons before they ran out. We could buy most of the ground and green-leaf vegetables we knew back home, but often different varieties of each and flavours varied as well. Watercress, water-chestnuts, egg-plant and snow peas, which were not staple foods for me at home, regularly appeared on the table in China – that is, when they were in season. They vanished at the end of the season just as quickly as they had appeared. Our shopping lists were made tentatively, because the available produce changed markedly from week to week. Often I came home very disappointed at having missed out on a particular item, knowing that it might not re-appear for another twelve months. This unpredictability was a serious concern to us. We existed on fruit and vegetables and often I would wonder if the day would come when there would be lean pickings indeed for several months. As I write this, I am reminded of this problem in a letter from a friend working in another province. She writes: 'I am finding enough fruit and vegetables to keep me going, but please keep praying that it continues as it is very seasonal and things can disappear at the drop of a hat.'

Chinese cooks plan a dinner after going to the market to see what there is available to buy. Variety in vegetables was important because Jeanette is a vegetarian and one visit to the meat market turned me into one too. Meat of all descriptions, including dog, hung in hunks, open to flies and for people to see. It wasn't that we feared one day nothing would be available in the markets, but we feared that all the foods we knew, and knew how to cook, would disappear and all that would be left would be unfamiliar Chinese vegetables which we could not stomach and didn't know how to cook anyway. Fortunately that did not happen. Eggs, peanuts, cashews, rice, pasta, and tinned fish were important supplements. Jeanette used to make very tasty fritters out of navy, haricot, kidney and other types of beans. Although Queensland is the land of the Big Pineapple, I must say that the Chinese pineapples were sweeter than ours.

Just as the produce was seasonal, so was the distribution of processed groceries erratic. After regularly buying products for a while, we discovered that supplies quickly dried up. I was overjoyed to see Horlicks on the shelves and just as disappointed to see it disappear again suddenly from every shop, a few months later. It seemed strange to see Chinese Horlicks in shops when I returned home. Is that where they disappeared to? Presumably, once the shipment ran out, that was that until the next one, whenever that would be. Like squirrels hoarding nuts, we bought up large amounts when supplies were plentiful and staggered up the hill towards home with our treasures.

Feeling slightly hungry much of the time became a common feeling. (My family would say at this point that I am always hungry anyway. My mother didn't call me 'Hollow Legs' for nothing.) I learnt the hard way just how important a varied, tasty diet is to one's happiness in a foreign land. There is the cry from one's physiological make-up, which is used to being fed certain foods and tastes since birth. I think what cries out, just as loudly, is the psychological yearning for something familiar when all around is strange and at times hostile. You can put up with a difficult day if you know that there's a delectable dinner at the end of it. If there isn't, then life becomes depressingly miserable. I can now sympathize with people who have to go on restricted diets. Living so close to people in poverty, I frequently thought about what life must be like for people living daily on the edge of starvation. But I wouldn't be so arrogant as to say that I understood their situation, even in a small way.

Most dishes tasted like an imitation of the same dish at home because of differences in some ingredients or the lack of them. The highest accolade we gave to one another's cooking was: 'That almost tasted like . . . from home.'

Meal-times, particularly in the first two months, were very dismal because of the lack of variety. So I spent many hours exploring shops and markets ferreting out suitable groceries. I'd almost shout 'Eureka!' when I found something that I recognized and was worth buying. By the time Jeanette arrived, I had a mental map of all the local shops selling particular goods and were named accordingly. The 'flour shop' was just near my flat. The helpful shop-keeper got to know that we always bought the same amount of flour each time. There were red-letter days when I discovered peanut paste, cereal (wheat, rice and cornflakes), honey, powdered and condensed milk, coffee, and other simple treats.

People back home could not understand my absolute delight at finding such mundane commodities. In letters they would add insult to injury by going into long descriptions about special dinners they had had, eating foods unattainable here. They live in a society that has an endless supply of whatever they want to eat at any time of the night or day. In our city, western staple foods like cheese, bread or baking powder were unattainable in the shops. This must have gnawed away at my subconscious because once I dreamt about a cheese grill. As it came out of the griller, the bread, cheese and meat suddenly flew away and all that was left was tomato – the only ingredient that I could buy.

The previous teacher bemoaned: 'Same goes for seasoning . . . This part of the country is known for having the blandest/most natural cuisine . . . in the country.' Before going to China, I took scant notice of his advice to bring condiments and other additives to supplement the local produce. In hindsight I wished I had taken over more herbs, spices, packet sauces and blocks of cheese. In the flurry of packing and finalizing all the numerous details of flying out, food was not a big concern. I thought I'd just eat what the locals did. Little did I know that eating would be such an issue once I got there, especially in the first two months.

Jeanette arrived in China bearing yeast, baking powder, bread improver and other ingredients and worked hard making bread, scones, buns and all sorts of dishes. Though not always exactly the same as those at home, they had a great psychological effect on us, brightening our spirits. Much of our daily speech revolved around food. Jeanette sniffed out all sorts of aromatic additives from hessian sacks at the market. Some of these little treasures were complete mysteries to us. One container in the kitchen we labelled 'things wot go in curries'. Who knows what they were, but they certainly gave the food zest. Other things were recognizable, such as a piece of cobwebby cinnamon bark and a star anise for flavouring peanut brittle. I was ecstatic to discover a little nutmeg and cinnamon left by our predecessors. Then I could flavour fritters, pumpkin . . . anything. O joy! But not everything turned out as planned. We assumed shrivelled mushrooms would swell and soften after soaking and cooking. No, they were still just as chewy as Grandpa's old boots.

Friends and family sent us food parcels with all sorts of delights. One damaged parcel arrived containing amongst other things, cinnamon and candy canes – yes, both together. The escaped cinnamon gave a most interesting flavour to the sweets. I must introduce this unusual taste sensation to an Australian confectionery company. When I came home unexpectedly during the semester break in January, I filled a long shopping list we had compiled, and returned with my suitcase stuffed with more food than clothes. Fortunately I didn't have to explain myself to customs.

The students would bring us food when they came to visit, or when they thought our stay in China would be incomplete without the cultural excitement of a new taste experience. Many such experiences made us increasingly wary, as people approached us with mysterious goodies, though we were touched by the kind thoughts behind the gifts. One such gift was a sticky dark grey concoction bound with grey leaves. It looked a most unappetising morsel. We thanked the girl for her thoughtfulness, but put it in the refrigerator – at the back. A few days later, we noticed liquid oozing through the leaves, so decided to chuck it out. Inevitably, the giver asked us later what we thought of it. I never was good at lying. Since we enjoyed the last one so much, would we like another?

'O . . . yes.' There was no choice, we had to eat it. Tentatively we pulled the leaves apart and ate . . . it was really tasty. Inside the grey sticky mass were peanuts, sesame seeds and other recognizable ingredients. This only goes to prove the old adage that you can't tell a food by its colour. Taste is the only true test.

My culinary dilemmas were helped by a visit with a student to an expensive supermarket-cum-department store in the modern section of the city. When we arrived, uniformed security guards were milling around the entrance and carpark. Inside, the place was bristling with store workers in bright orange outfits in every aisle, making sure that no-one pocketed the imported goods. Many of the customers were only looking because the prices were beyond the average wage. It was a sad 'look but don't touch' situation which made me feel exceedingly uncomfortable. As well as the Chinese, the place must also cater to the small ex-patriate community, but, sadly, I did not see anyone on my shopping trip.

My appearance at the store suddenly thrust me into the limelight, as I tentatively walked around with the invisible tag around my neck 'wealthy foreigner going to spend a lot of money'. All eyes followed my every move. Here I could buy such treasures as tinned *(Australian)* margarine, meat, sardines, sauces, English jam and other basic items, which would barely rate a mention on one's shopping list at Safeways. It was hard to contain my excitement at seeing these precious additions to my bland diet. I lived up to the expectations of those around, by buying as much as we could carry. I could almost hear the people say 'She must earn a lot of money!' as I left. Subsequent visits proved that supplies quickly evaporated here too.

It is a mammoth task to feed over 4,000 students three times a day. The Chinese do not have a well-developed fast food mentality. Lunch and tea ('supper') are sit-down affairs, bought from the half-dozen canteens around the campus. Each student has a round enamel bowl with a lid and spoon which is carried around during class or deposited on every available window-sill inside or outside the buildings. The bowls are all the same shape and size and have the same decoration. They are distinguished by three or four colours and areas of chipped enamel resulting from accidents. I was surprised that the students could pick their own out of the dozens around. I suppose they gain a good eye for spotting belongings, after years of spotting their own bicycles from crowded bike-parks. They can either eat their dinner at the dining-room tables or go to the dormitories. The cuisine is quite extensive and covers several dishes of fish, duck, chicken, beef, seafood and vegetables of all kinds with noodles and rice.

A few students went to the dining-rooms for a cooked breakfast. But most bought breakfast at dinner-time, ready for eating the next day. The catering staff arrange racks and cabinets on tables near the dining-rooms and sell buns, cakes and other goodies. Since the government or the parents/extended families pay for the meals, and for many money is scarce, the

buns are the cheapest source of breakfast, taken home
in plastic bags. Given the rodent population roaming
the campus at night, including the dormitories, I pondered the wisdom of this arrangement. I concluded
that given the enormous cost and scale involved for
4,000 students, it would be difficult to find a better
solution. Rat-proof containers in each dorm would
require too much money. Cooking in the dorms was
banned, possibly because of fear of fire and one,
would hope, fear of rats.

During the first few months at the College, the students used a token system to pay for food and some
other items from campus shops. They would buy small
pieces of yellow, blue, white and green plastic denot-
ing various monetary values from campus shops and
then cash them as needed. The reasoning behind the
system was never explained to me. Perhaps it was
introduced to alleviate some of the hustle and bustle of
everyone descending en masse on the canteen staff.
Being a novice at handling this system, I was chroni-
cally clumsy with the tokens trying to pay for cakes. I
could never remember what each colour meant,
except green was for one yuan, or was it for two? Jostled from every side by eager, hungry buyers, I would
just smile weakly at the girl serving and hand over a
random collection of colours, hoping that I would not
be cheated. There were no prices displayed.

Through the yelling and gesticulating back and
forth across the tables, everyone learnt the prices
and names of everything. Well, almost everyone. As in
all our major and minor crises in China, help was
always close at hand – there was always someone who
wanted to practise their English and be helpful at the

same time. The serving girls did not cheat us and became most co-operative whenever they saw us.

Our days of bun-buying were numbered though. Eating the same food the students ate, at times resulted in minor stomach ailments for us. The worst was my bout of food poisoning resulting from eating a bun. The timing could not have been more ironic. It was the night before we were to go to Hainan Island for a few days' holiday with some of the teachers. I was too weak after six hours of vomiting, to move beyond the bedroom, so Jeanette and the others went without me.

The token system for buying food was replaced later by an electronic card system. Cards were purchased for 50 or 100 yuan. The students were quietly impressed by the very attractive cards which, being the latest technology, were a status symbol.

Confined by restricted diets and our cloistered existence, it was good to go out to dinner occasionally with our western friends and eat Chinese or quasi-western cuisine. One restaurant was keen to offer their patrons an intimate, candle-lit atmosphere. We stumbled our way up narrow steps in near-darkness and found ourselves in a room made like the Ames room I remembered from my studies in Perceptual Psychology. Or was it that we had instantaneously grown like Alice? We just did not fit the dimensions of the place at all. We could easily touch the ceiling without stretching. The small tables were so low that squeezing around them to sit down was difficult. The only light came from small candles on each table, placed on top of torn orange tablecloths. Instead of being romantic, I found the room mysterious and gloomy. Could we fit into the dimensions of the downstairs room instead?

Thankfully downstairs was designed for people without romantic inclinations. Our bodies resumed their normal size as we entered the room. The food was delicious. The dishes on the menu had weird and wonderful 'western' names. They were written perhaps directly from the Chinese meaning without consideration of English expressions. The Chinese language is pictorial, unlike the English alphabetic form, so it does not lend itself to straight translation of names with colloquialisms. I wonder how you would translate 'Bubble and Squeak', 'Toad in the Hole' or 'Yorkshire pudding'? The result is what my students call 'Chinglish'. Lateral thinking helped us work out what we were ordering. Absolutely delicious! I ate and ate and ate and . . . grew like Alice.

Our friends ran a classy ice cream shop. Needless to say we went there often. It was a pleasure to enjoy the atmosphere of fastidiously clean premises and of course, to eat their ice-cream made from rich ingredients. They always knew what to bring when they visited our place.

Whenever we were invited to the homes of people in the college or neighbourhood, they were always wanting to spoil us by serving the best that money could buy. Crabs, sea-worms, prawns, shell-fish of all sorts and a wide collection of sea-going creepy-crawlies I could not describe, would be served. My system does not agree with a lot of seafood, so I would tend to take as much as I could of the humble fish and only sample the rest. It was embarrassing not to take full advantage of the hospitality offered, especially since the meal cost so much.

I must confess that the plucky yellow ducklings in the ordinary restaurant in the Provincial capital were gorgeous and the only spot of colour and entertainment in the place. Jeanette and I were having a meal in the restaurant following an invitation to attend a big official function in the city. The purpose? To receive the official medal, certificate and hand-shake from the Vice-Governor for services rendered to the country. At least the venue for the presentation was impressive – the finest five star hotel the city could offer. The prospect though of spending twelve hours on the train to get there lessened our enthusiasm for being so honoured. Then it was extinguished completely when we learnt that a lad who could barely speak a word of English, was going to escort us. We suggested to our College, that perhaps their money would be better spent buying English books for the library. This piece of logic floated mid-air in the negotiations, then drifted away to the far-off place where all untried ideas forever live in limbo. The Higher Education authorities *ordered* us to attend. *We were going to be publicly honoured*, even if dragged kicking and screaming.

A few days later the College found a compromise, since we were not happy about going by train. On the weekend before our arrival, the lad was despatched by train to secure the hotel booking in person. Return air-flights for the weekend were arranged for Mr Lu, Jeanette and myself. We were informed that our time away would be reduced as a consequence of the change in arrangements.

Having arrived safely in the 'Big Smoke', here we
were sitting in the hotel restaurant where we were to
stay overnight. Perhaps not the Beijing Hotel nor the
classy venue of the presentations, but you can't have
everything. To our annoyance, we were the prize topic
of conversation amongst the other patrons. People
asked our companions everything there was to know
about us – 'Exhibits A and B' as we ate our dinner. At
the next table was a family comprising Mum and Dad
and two little girls. To entertain the children, the staff
put two yellow ducklings on the table. They enjoyed
the unaccustomed freedom and tap-danced about,
pecking at discarded bones and vegetables. The
children were enthralled.

'Belinda, take a shot of the tap-dancing ducklings.'
The sight of my camera had a transforming effect on
tiny tot and duckling alike. While the older child
beamed radiantly, the duckling turned on profile,
stretched its neck and fluttered its insubstantial wings,
as if to say, 'You must get my best side!'

Jeanette and I were silently horrified at the lack of
consideration for hygiene, but the ducklings had no
such squeamishness about eating food that had been
picked over by humans. The incident reminded me of a
woman I saw on TV who kept a pet giraffe. During
meals, the giraffe would lean through the French windows and be hand-fed from the table. Friends asked
her if she was concerned about the hygiene of this
habit. In mock horror she replied: 'Of course I am, you
never know what the giraffe might pick up!'

This ordinary restaurant contrasted greatly with
the big affair at the posh hotel. As the taxi doors were
opened by the hotel bell-boys, all irksomeness about

ducklings and the restaurant's blandness vanished. *This* hotel is truly impressive. A large waterfall dominates the grand foyer. The water-course, home to the fattest goldfish I have ever seen, meanders amongst tropical plants. Wooden bridges and steps here and there provide vantage points for trigger-happy photographers. Everything is immaculately clean and the architecture and furnishings tastefully co-ordinated.

The ceremony took place in a vast room, the size of a theatre, packed with hundreds of foreign teachers and experts of all nationalities working in the province. The speeches were by the Vice-Governor, other government people and 'foreign friends'. A woman from a West Australian university gave a most perceptive speech. She included a diplomatic request that we be called 'Australian friends', not 'foreign friends'. Quite a number of long-term teachers and experts were given special awards out of recognition of their commitment to China.

The food was glorious! Gone was the memory of the ducklings tap-dancing on the table-top. Their plumper cousins were prepared in a most fastidious manner, as were all the Chinese dishes. Elegant waitresses in traditional garb expertly served the guests. I headed for the tables where western food was laid out. Dishes as homely as potato salad, pasta, roast meat and trifle were haute cuisine to me and so, above all, was the cheese.

It was refreshing to be able to chat, at a normal speed, to the other teachers and laugh and commiserate over similar experiences. Everyone was keen to meet new people because, like us, they probably felt isolated. I could not believe I could eat so much and talk so much to people I had never met before and pack so much enjoyment into a few short hours. The combination of good company and delicious food, similar to what we eat at home, had a wonderfully restorative effect on everyone we spoke to. Conversations were condensed into what was important, because we had only a short time together. The dinner suddenly ended at about 9 p.m. Every mouthful of food was savoured because, for most of us, there were still a few weeks to go, if not longer, before we could again experience 'good old-fashioned food, like Mum used to make'. Like Cinderella on the stroke of midnight, we returned reluctantly to our homely hotel. The next night we flew home.

4

'Why did you not come sooner?'
— Witness —

Students, like everyone else on the planet, have a great need to be loved by others and are seeking security for their lives. They are drawn therefore to the notion of a sovereign God in whom they can find such security when circumstances become unpredictable.

Living in the world's most populous nation is not conducive to each individual's feeling special and unique. The Chinese culture emphasizes the corporate good over the desires of the individual. Even many place names are not specific. A Chinese atlas revealed that there are no less than 21 cities called Taiping – owning the same characters and pinyin spelling. Six of these cities are located in Guangxi Autonomous Region. There are 24 cities spelled Gucheng with the same Pinyin spelling, 19 of which share the same characters. Baisha, Banqiao, Daqiao and scores of others have multiple counterparts.

Young people are looking for role models to follow, in order to know how to manage their lives. They live in a world of conflicting ideologies, pulling them onto divergent pathways. In the lives of followers of Christ, they want to see integrity, trustworthiness and long-term caring, commitment both to themselves and to China's future, regardless of whether they themselves are able to reciprocate.

Chinese people have seen through the superficiality of some Christian people on 'quick visits' to the extent that 'don't preach Jesus to me' has now become a catch phrase in southern provinces. What perhaps is at the heart of such cynicism is again the desire to see established integrity, whole-hearted and long-term commitment to friendship and concern for China; in short, the gospel transparently seen in the lives of its messengers.

Christians know that all these needs can be met in a loving relationship with our Father-Creator. Letting one's life speak louder than words produces receptive hearts the world over. In this regard let's take a leaf out of China's history book and see the godly character of one man.

The Boxer Rebellion of 1900 which was instigated by the Empress Dowager Cixi (1834-1908) had at its heart a rebellion against European influence. European and US legations were besieged. An international force captured Beijing on 14 August 1900 and pressured China into paying a huge indemnity. The order in many provinces by the Empress to kill all missionaries was countermanded by some governors but not the governor of Shanxi, resulting there in the most brutal massacre of all the provinces. The situation is similar today. Religious policies emanating from Beijing are carried out in a less than uniform manner at county and provincial levels, depending on the attitudes of the local authorities.

In Shanxi, 159 missionaries and children died, the worst massacre occurring in Taiyuan. Some were beaten, then burned to death or beheaded. Many young Chinese converts or their loved ones died after enduring hideous torture. One pastor, tied to a pillar, spent the night preaching to bystanders until an angry mob tore his heart out. This violent attempt to destroy Christianity failed completely, just as the attempts by the Communists in 1926 and 1928 also did. Church history repeatedly teaches the same lesson about the spiritual power released by persecution. By 1906, the Shanxi church had more than doubled in number.

Thirty years later the church followed St Paul's instructions to settle cases within the church, instead of by a civil court. Mr Hu, the leader, had as a young believer in 1900 seen his children killed and his pregnant wife slashed by Boxer swords. He and other victims later confronted their attackers in court seeking justice.

'How should this man who murdered your children be punished?' the judge asked. Hu pleaded for time to consider his answer. Being illiterate, he asked someone to read him the Sermon on the Mount which provided him an answer.

'Set him free! I forgive him!'

Astonished, the court pressed on him a large indemnity. Hu reluctantly accepted and distributed it to destitute people in the city. Hu is an example of how the Boxer Rebellion elicited the best in the Chinese Christians. Such faithfulness resulted in Hu becoming the leader, teacher and judge of legal disputes in his church.[1]

---

[1] Lyall, L., *God Reigns in China* (Sevenoaks: Hodder & Stoughton, 1985) p. 26–7

To 'preach Jesus' without the totality of the biblical message and history may leave more questions than answers in the minds of hearers. Jesus walked on the earth *only* 2,000 years ago. China's history dates back to the time of hunters and gatherers, *c.* 5,000 BC. The legendary Xia dynasty existed *c.* 2205–1523 BC and documented history started during the Shang dynasty, *c.* 1523–1028 BC.

China has had approximately 4,500 years of unbroken civilization (Chinese astronomers calculated the length of a year to be 365¼ days in 444 BC); to begin by asking Chinese people to believe in a God-man who lived 2,000 years ago leaves a lot of implications unspoken. Looking at the issue from the point of view of someone who knows little or nothing about Christianity, many questions would arise. Did God come into existence when Jesus was born? Where was he before that? If he existed before Jesus, and if he is all-loving, why did he disregard the people who lived and suffered prior to that time? Like all of us, they yearn to know a Creator who has always existed and hence holds history in a firm and unchanging grip. That is the kind of God to believe in!

Long before Confucianism, Taoism and Buddhism flourished, and 2,600 years before Jesus lived, the Chinese people worshipped such a God – *Shang Ti*. He was called 'the heavenly (above) Emperor'. Expression of adoration and supplication was through the annual Border Sacrifice of young, unblemished bullocks at the border of the country. As the emperor took part in the service the following words, recorded in the statutes of the Ming dynasty, were recited:

> Of old in the beginning, there was the great chaos, without form and dark. The five elements (planets) had not begun to revolve, nor the sun and moon to shine. You, O Spiritual Sovereign first divided the grosser parts from the purer. You made heaven. You made earth. You made man. All things with their reproducing power got their being ... All living things are indebted to Your goodness, but who knows from whom his blessings come to him? You alone, O Lord, are the true parent of all things ... He sets fast forever the high heaven, and establishes the solid earth. His government is everlasting ... Your sovereign goodness cannot be measured. As a potter, You have made all living things.[2]

This sounds remarkably like a collection of passages from Scripture. Compare it with Isaiah 64:8. Is Shang Ti the same Supreme Being who appears in Genesis? This monotheistic adoration was unusual as most ancient people groups were polytheistic.

The simple beliefs of the people were altered tragically by heresies and eclecticism. During the Zhou dynasty (1066–221 BC) religious leaders emphasized his majesty and holiness, over mercy and love, and later taught that only the emperor was holy enough to

---

[2] Legge, J., 'The Notions of the Chinese Concerning God and Spirits' (Hong Kong: Hong Kong Register Office, 1852) p. 28 in Nelson, E.R. & Broadberry, R.E., *Genesis and the Mystery Confucius Couldn't Solve* (St. Louis: Concordia, USA, 1994) pp. 20–1

worship Shang Ti – once a year. Common people were then forbidden to worship their Creator. This spiritual vacuum was filled three centuries later by Confucianism, Taoism and Buddhism. The veneration of Shang Ti was corrupted by Taoist heresies resulting most probably in the ancestor worship still conducted today.

Originally the emperor acted as the high priest between man and God. His spirit was believed to continue this mediating role after death. At first emperors, then later national heroes and family patriarchs were honoured as spirit intercessors who could grant favours. For example, Qin Shi Huang-di came to power in 246 BC and declared himself the first Emperor of (a united) China. He is known for building the Great Wall, roads, an ambitious canal system, standardization of weights and measures, and for his terracotta army which went to the grave with him (seen today in Xian).

Under the sway of Taoist superstitions, he permitted corruption of the Border Sacrifices by erecting four more altars to the white, green, yellow, and red 'Tis' (heavenly rulers). The first imperial sacrifices to these 'Tis' occurred in 166 BC, marking the tragic transition to polytheistic worship. The chief of censors at the time vehemently opposed the move. However, the practice continued for more than twelve centuries.

In AD 1369 historians studied the ancient records and found the heresy. The emperor of the Ming dynasty (1368–1644) consequently abolished these rituals and returned to the worship of Shang Ti as practised by the Zhou.

The sacrificial rituals were transferred to a site in Beijing. Today, tourists flock to the impressive Tiantan Park where three sacred edifices reflect the dedication of the Chinese to the one Supreme Being. The Hall of Prayer for Good Harvests (*Qinian*) – completed in 1420 AD – is mounted on a three-tiered white marble terrace surrounded by balustrades. The cone-shaped roof is in three tiers covered by 50,000 blue tiles. No nails were used in construction of the circular wall, supported by 28 wooden pillars hewn from single trees. No joists were used on the ceiling, which is supported by four huge pillars.

The smaller Temple of Heaven Imperial Vault houses the memorial tablet inscribed with 'Heavenly Sovereign Shang-Ti'. Further south is the triple-tiered, white marble Altar of Heaven surrounded by balustrades.

The yearly ceremony happened on the winter solstice (*c*. December 22). Although the populace were forbidden to watch the procession, it must have been a spectacular sight. The emperor, the 'Son of Heaven' travelled from the Imperial Palace (Forbidden City) to Tiantan Park accompanied by a vast retinue of princes and high officials. He first meditated in the Imperial Vault, while musicians and singers recited prayers. The emperor then moved to the Hall of Prayer for Good Harvests. The next day he returned to the Imperial Vault, thence to the Altar of Heaven to perform the sacrifices. Three offerings of wine and silks, gems and food were given while musicians, singers and dancers performed songs of praise, and then the young bullock was burned.

Due to the infiltration of Confucianism and Taoism and later Buddhism, Shang Ti was largely forgotten as the one and only God. However, ancient Chinese writing preserved the knowledge of the origin of the human race. The *language itself* bears witness to the original beliefs of the Chinese.

Tradition states that Chang Jie who lived during the legendary period, was the inventor of the Chinese language (presumably not a single-handed effort). The earliest characters were drawings of everyday items. Remarkably, the 'pictograph' (picture word) and 'ideograph' (idea-in-writing) system was in use by *c.* 2,500 BC. Pictographs were combined into ideographs and later developed into characters.

This century, Pastor Chong Heng Kang, reflected his people's love of antiquity, especially the study of the Chinese language. His co-author of a work on linguistic apologetics describes an astounding revelation: 'Something that he had observed in a footnote of a Mandarin textbook used by a missionary came to mind. The character meaning *boat*, had been analysed as follows: a *vessel*; *eight* and *mouth* or *person*. A comment followed that, interestingly, Noah's ark, the first great boat, had just eight passengers.'[3]

Through the detailed study of the ancient writing forms by Pastor Kang and associates, we know that some of the subjects were the creation of the first man and woman, the original relationship between God

---

[3] Nelson, E.R. & Kang, C.H., 'The Discovery of Genesis: How the Truths of Genesis were found Hidden in the Chinese Language' in Montgomery, J.W., *Giant in Chains* (Milton Keynes: Nelson Word Ltd., 1994) pp. 173–4

and people, how sin began and God's remedy. These notions are reiterated in ancient teachings – which refer to the first man and woman as being intelligent, created beings resembling the Creator God, who made people, all life and the universe. Over the centuries, their historical connections have been lost and modifications have resulted in the modern simple script – a 'shorthand' version of the early pictographs.

While discovering the original ideas behind the ancient characters, comparison with Old Testament accounts produced startling results. For example the characters for:

- *Righteousness* combines a lamb + (over) 'me'. (Through the spilt blood of the lamb over me, I am made righteous.) The character for 'me' comprises a hand and the knife used in animal sacrifices. The whole story then is 'I use a knife to make a sacrifice of a lamb. His blood covers me and makes me righteous.'
- *Sacrifice* comprises four parts: an oxen + sheep that are without blemish and killed with a knife, used to make sacrifices. So the ancient Chinese knew the biblical concept of blood sacrifice.
- *Create* can be used especially to describe the creation of man: God + dust or earth + mouth or breath + action + walking or moving man. God blew upon the earth with the breath of his mouth and through this action made man, who would both speak and walk.
- *Law* comprises: mouth + tree + God.
- *Pattern* or *example* comprises: Tree + lamb + eternal + water.

Were the people who settled in China part of the diaspora following God's judgement on the Tower of Babel? All people groups are descended from Noah's lineage. By counting the genealogical years recorded in Genesis and correlating them with the dates of other events, scholars have theorized that the Tower of Babel incident may have happened approximately 40 years before Chinese history records the first dynasty (Xia).

From the similarities between these and several dozen other ideographs and biblical references, researchers like Pastor Kang, Ethel Nelson, Richard Broadberry and others have postulated that the earliest Chinese had a knowledge of God's dealings with the Hebrew people.

Without knowledge of the biblical story, the characters would have been nonsense.

If the above theories were true, one grieves that the early emperors, for all their ferocity, lacked the wisdom or moral courage to destroy the false teaching of religious leaders. China's history of the nation would have been incalculably different. What would the nation have been like if the people, as a whole, had later readily accepted Jesus as the fulfilment of the sacrificial system at the time he was first preached to them? Some today know of Shang Ti but few recognize who or what he was in the Chinese culture thousands of years ago. If they did, perhaps the following conversation need not have taken place.

James Hudson Taylor, founder of the China Inland Mission recounts his conversation with a former Buddhist.

'A few nights after his conversion he asked how long this Gospel had been known in England. He was told that we had known it for some hundreds of years.

'"What!" said he, amazed. "Is it possible that for hundreds of years you have had the knowledge of these glad tidings in your possession, and yet have only now come to preach it to us? My father sought after the truth for more that twenty years, and died without finding it. Oh, why did you not come sooner?"

'A whole generation has passed away since that mournful inquiry was made; but how many, alas, might repeat the same question today? More than two hundred millions in the meanwhile have been swept into eternity, without an offer of salvation. How long shall this continue, and the Master's words, "to every creature", remain unheeded?'[4]

Despite the violence of the Opium Wars, rebellions and natural disasters, China entered this century with a population of over 400 million. Land was becoming increasingly precious as more and more people wanted to own and/or rent it. Land was already subdivided into tiny plots due to the tradition of inheritance to sons. Land-owners charged exorbitant rents. Peasants who supplemented their incomes through cottage industries now found they could not compete with the new manufactured goods. Peasants drifted to the cities to find work. Powerful warlords

---

[4] Taylor, J.H., *Hudson Taylor* (Minneapolis: Bethany House Publishers, USA)

China's Dancer

took local government into their own hands and supported their huge armies through taxing the peasantry. Foreign imperialism still loomed as a major problem in the nation.

Against this backdrop emerged a man of remarkable insight into his country's needs. A medical doctor and a baptized Christian, Sun Yat-sen (1867–1925) was born in Guangdong Province. He hoped the Qing government could be peacefully persuaded to establish reforms in politics, education, health and agriculture. The Qing were not amenable to changes. Sun Yat-sen was the instigator of the successful overthrow of the last emperor of China in 1911.

He formed the Guomindang (GMD), or Nationalist People's Party. Advocating the 'Three People's Principles' – Democracy, the People's Livelihood and Nationalism, he earned the title 'Father of the Nation'. He provides us with a reminder of the lack of support from 'Christian' nations: 'We have lost hope of help from England, America, France or any of the great powers. The only country that shows any sign of helping us is the Soviet government of Russia.' Unfortunately he died in 1925.

During the 1920s, the competing political influences came from: the GMD, the Russian Comintern, the Communist Party, warlords, foreigners and the official government. The Chinese Communist Party (CCP) was formed in 1921 in Shanghai with Mao Zedong later becoming its leader. The first uneasy alliance was formed in 1924 between the GMD under Jiang Jieshi (Chiang Kai-shek) and the Communists to defeat the warlords. But this was shattered in 1927 when GMD soldiers massacred Communist supporters in Shanghai.

Following the atrocity, Mao formed his Red Army (People's Liberation Army) and tried unsuccessfully to gain control of Hunan Province in the 1928 'Autumn Harvest Uprising', losing over 40,000 men. In 1930 another 2,000 died. Mao persuaded his comrades to accept that the revolution would have to rely on the peasantry for its survival. 'Whoever wins the peasants will win China,' he stated in 1936.

In their isolated mountain base in Jiangxi Province, Mao and his followers endeavoured to persuade villagers to seize land from their landlords and to form their own self-governing councils, thereby trying to win over the masses to Communist ideology.

He warned his followers that 'the army must become one with the people so that they can see it as their own'. They had to abide by the following rules:

> Speak politely.
> Pay fairly for what you buy.
> Return anything you borrow.
> Pay for everything you damage.
> Don't strike or swear at people.
> Don't damage crops.
> Don't take liberties with women.
> Don't ill-treat captives.

Mao taught them guerrilla tactics:

> The enemy attacks, we retreat.
> The enemy camps, we harass.
> The enemy tires, we attack.
> The enemy retreats, we pursue.

It is no wonder that the peasantry were supportive of these new ideologies after the horrendous corruption and exploitation by the warlords and Jiang Jieshi's GMD. Mao recalled that 'Revolution is a drama of passion; we do not win the people over by appealing to reason but by developing hope, trust and fraternity. In the face of famine, the will to equality takes on a religious force.'

In 1934, in response to the GMD's extermination programs, the Communists precipitated the historic 'Long March' through a vast area of Central China. The 86,000 trekkers covered over 9,000 kilometres, crossed 12 provinces, 18 mountain ranges, 24 rivers, occupied 62 cities and broke through enveloping armies of ten different warlords besides defeating or avoiding forces from the government. Combat met them daily.

Trudging through the Snowy Mountains was an arduous task: 'As we climbed higher and higher we were caught in a terrible hailstorm and the air became so thin we could hardly breathe. Men and animals staggered into chasms and disappeared forever. Those who sat down to rest or to relieve themselves froze to death on the spot.'[5]

A remnant of only 4,000 eventually staggered into Yanan, Shaanxi province, in 1935–6.

Mao Zedong, as the dominant leader during the Yanan period (1936–45), experimented with

---

[5] Smedley, A., 'The Great Road' *Monthly Review*, 1956 in Childs, R., *Leading the Chinese Revolution: China 1921–49* (Auckland: Macmillan Company of NZ Ltd, 1987)

Communist solutions to the problems in the region. Women were given freedom to vote, to choose their marriage partners, to be educated and to be paid for work. They produced armaments and grew food for the Red Army. On co-operative lines, armaments, steel and textiles were developed. New schools and universities became mediums through which the Communist message could be transmitted as well as avenues for teaching necessary technical skills. Theatres, choirs, film studios and cultural clubs were set up.

All people aged eighteen or over, were eligible to vote for village, county and provincial councils. Land reform was Mao's biggest tactic to win loyalty. Land was taken from absentee landlords and redistributed to peasants, and debts were either lowered or waived. Using irrigation and conservation techniques, large areas of wasteland were brought under cultivation.

But major problems remained in the country. In order to alleviate economic problems at home, Japan had ambitions set on the Northwest of China. In 1931 Japan invaded Manchuria and in 1937 troops moved aggressively against the rest of the nation even as far south as Guangzhou. A second alliance between the GMD and CCP was crucial if China was to realize freedom. The Red Army kidnapped Jiang Jieshi in Xian to force him to see co-operation was necessary. In the National War of Resistance against Japan (1937–45) the Communists were now seen as respectable allies of the United Front, a change from their label of 'bandits and traitors'.

In December 1937, 50,000 Japanese troops were let loose on the population of Nanjing. Some historians put the death toll of the massacre as high as

300,000 men, women and children – many died by beheading.[6]

Women were raped and men were used for bayonet practice before execution. Store houses were stripped and burned and the city later put to the torch.

The Communists were no match against the better trained and equipped Japanese; however, their strategy was to resist attacks and instigate social and economic reforms to win popular support. The Red Army activity in rural areas convinced the local people that the Communists were the true defenders of the Middle Kingdom. Communist regions became self-sufficient in food, clothing and equipment. Ingenuity was used to make weapons – cannons were made out of elm logs and tin cans, and land mines out of teapots.

Although there was some co-operation between the two forces, this was soon shattered in January 1941 when Jiang Jieshi ordered his forces to slaughter more than 3,000 members of the Communist New Fourth Army. Subsequently, both sides acted independently with a view to what was likely to happen to China once the common enemy has been defeated. When events brought the US into the war, both the GMD and the CCP celebrated with a holiday. They knew that the US would declare war and defeat their enemy. America gave the GMD three billion dollars' worth of aid, mostly military. In 1945 after the dropping of the atomic bombs, Japan surrendered.

Now the stage was set for the two contenders for power to battle it out for the right to lead the nation which had the biggest population on earth. Civil war

---

[6] See Chang, I., *The Rape of Nanjing* (New York: Basic Books, USA, 1997)

raged for the period 1946-9 despite American efforts to mediate between the opponents. During the war the CCP had gained enormous recognition and territory, and by 1945 nearly a quarter of the population – 100 million people – lived in 'red' areas. Between 1947 and 1949 the peasant armies gathered momentum, advanced on cities, and found little resistance. By contrast, the GMD lost a lot of support because they could not control the rampant inflation which hit the urban areas more severely than the rural ones, exacerbated by corruption at every level of government.

On 1 October 1949 the People's Republic of China was proclaimed. The GMD leadership fled to Taiwan (formerly Formosa).

'Our nation will never again be an insulted nation. We have stood up,' said Mao Zedong in 1949.

Still, not every heart was red, so the CCP spent considerable energy over the next few years legitimizing its power.

The immense task before the Party after 1949 was to reconstruct and modernize within a socialist framework. The Consultative Political Conference acted as a parliament. This body prepared the Common Program which announced that the nation was a democratic dictatorship of four classes: working class, peasants, petty bourgeoisie, and national bourgeoisie. Petty bourgeoisie included trades people and owners of small shops. National bourgeoisie consisted of wealthy but patriotic people, who had not collaborated with the Japanese or other foreigners. Class labels were attached arbitrarily and were dependent on the subjective opinion of others; what was considered patriotic behaviour by one was considered treasonous by another.

Furthermore, class labels were not only attached for life, they were also hereditary. The children from bad class backgrounds (e.g. landlord class) faced serious problems when they applied for jobs, wanted to marry or sought an education.

This restrictive, indelible attitude towards class status contrasts with the way the Lord dramatically lifted the self-esteem and status of the Dahua Miao (Big Flowery Miao) – a minority group of Guizhou and Yunnan provinces. Han Chinese traditionally despised them and by Qing times they were slaves of the landed Yi minority. In former years, the feudal lord would have mounted his horse from the back of a stooping Miao.

The Miau became fervent converts of the teachings of Christ, brought by China Inland missionaries, and gave up their conflicting customs willingly, including their loose sexual practices. The mass movement of 1906–8 saw thousands throw off their amulets – worn to ward off evil spirits. This movement spread to Yunnan province. By 1909 between 4,000 and 5,000 Miao in Sapushan area were professed Christians.

The missionary Samuel Pollard invented the Dahua Miao script out of traditional symbols and designs on their clothing.

'This, their own script, was the object of great pride among the Miao. Only if one realizes what it means in rural China to be able to read and write can one appreciate this pride.'[7]

---

[7] Beauclair, I. de, 'The Ta-Hua of Kweichow Province' in Stevens, K. M. and Wehrfritz, G. E., *Southwest China: Off the Beaten Track* (London: Collins, 1988) p. 107

Talented Miao were educated at the mission schools in Shimenkan and Zhaotong and at the West China Union University in Chengdu.

'In this manner, within two generations, the Dahua Miao almost became the sustainers of culture in Guizhou. The Communists immediately placed educated Dahua Miao into leading positions involving the organizing and administration of minorities.'[8]

By 1949, 90 per cent of Miao attended churches in the Wuding area north of Kunming, Yunnan and substantial attendance figures also existed among the Wuding Yi and Lisu minorities. The story of Little Stone Village in Wuding is typical of this turbulent time. The villagers suffered greatly for their faith during the fifties and the Cultural Revolution when leaders were martyred and all churches closed down. They were told to choose between God and Chairman Mao. Persecution in remote mountainous parts of Yunnan continued after the death of Mao, but Christians remained firm despite their prison sentences.

In 1979, under Deng Xiaoping, churches re-opened across China and conditions improved but it wasn't until 1982 that officials investigated the persecution of the Miao Christians. They declared them blameless and released them from prison.

After this time,

'An observer of Miao Christian communities reports that their life is their faith. The gospel has been integrated with their simple lifestyle to such an extent that there

---

[8] Ibid., p. 107

seems no sharp division between "sacred" and "secular". Their faith is expressed in gentleness of spirit and warmth of hospitality... The Miao church has survived the severe testing of persecution. Will it now be able to face this insidious threat, as a simple tribal culture imbued with the gospel faces the inroads of modern materialism and secularism?'[9]

The 1950 Marriage Reform Law raised the status of women. The currency was stabilized and the army engaged in large-scale construction tasks such as building dikes. Private and nationalized industries co-existed. Co-operatives were encouraged and land was re-distributed.

Under the First Five Year Plan in 1953, cities like Xian underwent accelerated industrial development. Collectivization of the economy was introduced in 1956. Small groups of businesses became co-operatives, the government took over capitalist enterprises and high inflation raged. The Hundred Flowers Campaign allowing freedom of expression of opinion was short-lived when Mao realized the breadth of discontent.

After 1949, Mao improved life for most Chinese but then began to destroy much of what he had established. The 1958 policies of the Great Leap Forward divided the populace into communes and making backyard steel became a national obsession. A slogan of the time read: 'Overtake England in steel

---

[9] Lyall, L., *The Phoenix Rises* (Singapore: OMF, 1992) p. 84, 88

production in fifteen years.' New agricultural and environmental practices created massive problems for the next growing seasons. This mass experiment, yoked with natural disasters, hastened a tragic famine. According to official sources, eight million people died from causes traceable to the Great Leap Forward. The unofficial estimate is more than double this. The party's rationing system prevented many deaths that the famine might otherwise have caused. Not surprisingly, loyalty towards the CCP diminished as people favoured pragmatism over ideology.

The pragmatic side of Deng Xiaoping, which China was to experience dramatically during the eighties, was aired at this time in his famous comment: 'It does not matter whether it is a black cat or a white cat, so long as it catches mice.'

Production had returned to the levels prior to the Great Leap Forward by 1962 when policies were modified to allow householders to own small plots of land and decide what crops to grow. Liu Shaoqi the Defence Minister, advised that an educated expert elite should guide government policy. Mao wanted equality and feared elitism would spread out of control. These fears precipitated Mao's last disastrous idea – the Cultural Revolution (1966–1976).

During this season of darkness, books were burned and historical records destroyed. The only acceptable guideline for life was 'The Little Red Book of Collected Thoughts of Chairman Mao'. He closed all secondary schools and universities. One million students attended rallies in Tiananmen Square in Beijing to worship him. He commissioned these 'Red Guards' (numbering in the tens of millions) to save the

Revolution. The young people were from the acceptable classes – workers, poor and lower middle class peasants, soldiers, party officials and revolutionary martyrs.

'Smash the old and bring in the new!' he urged.

Mao demanded they attack the 'Four Olds': old ideas, culture, habits and customs. The Guards 'struggled against' millions of people accused of capitalist tendencies. Evidence for such deviation from the party line frequently comprised nothing more than owning western books, singing western opera or believing in God (deemed as superstition.)

> 'A girl "remembered a really freezing day when she and her friends made three of the teachers from their school kneel on the ground outside without their coats or gloves. . . the leader of their group . . . told them to beat the teachers. We found some wooden boards and the pupils started hitting the teachers. We kept on till one of the teachers started coughing up blood . . . We felt very proud of ourselves. It seemed very revolutionary." '[10]

Deng Xiaoping, former General Secretary of the Central Committee, was condemned as a 'capitalist roader' and paraded through Beijing in a dunce's cap, ridiculed for his love of bridge and sent to work in a factory.

They scoured museums and destroyed anything even vaguely akin to the 'four olds' and ransacked and closed mosques and churches. They searched the

---

[10] Ross, S., *China Since 1945* (Hove: Wayland Publishers Ltd, 1988) p. 36

homes of Christians and burnt any Bibles and religious literature found there and beat or even killed their owners. Others were imprisoned for many years. The church went into hiding during the Revolution in order to survive. Law and order gradually returned after Mao stepped in to stop the headlong rush into civil war. But the Revolution did not end officially until Mao's death in 1976.

The government during the 1970s strove to end China's isolation from the rest of the world. In 1971 China was admitted to the United Nations and in 1972 President Richard Nixon visited China. In November 1973, Australia's Prime Minister Gough Whitlam visited China to meet Mao Zedong and Premier Zhou Enlai.

The ten wasted years of the Cultural Revolution gave birth to a whole generation of young people, dispossessed of an education who, after the madness had ended, had no opportunity to gain technical employment or contribute to the desperately needed modernization of China. The revolution produced massive problems in education and agriculture. Industrial production had declined and the foreign and traditional influences on culture had been drastically cut. But, from the fires of persecution, the church emerged divested of its links with the West, strengthened and more capable of relating to the next generation of potential believers – coming now from all walks of life.

The world was rocked by the shocking news of the massacre of students in Tiananmen Square on 4 June 1989. Following years of promising economic development and opening to the West, a return to the 'political power grows out of the barrel of a gun' mentality of the Maoist era seemed unbelievable. It is estimated 3,000 people died and between ten and thirty thousand more were arrested, a hundred of whom were later executed.

Since 1977 until his succession by Jiang Zemin, Deng Xiaoping had been the most influential man in China. To stimulate the economy, Deng aimed at 'Socialism with Chinese Characteristics'. He advocated political reforms, closer co-operation with the West, the one-child policy and the 'Four Modernizations'.

The objectives of his reform program were to:

1. institute a contract responsibility system in agricultural areas;
2. revive individual businesses in urban areas;
3. decentralize a substantial amount of authority to state enterprises;
4. reform the irrational price system.[11]

In 1992 the Fourteenth Party Congress stated its intention to establish a 'socialist market economic system'. By mid-1993 economic growth rates were surging ahead. Prices soared and people bought gold and invested in enterprises. The government grappled with a record deficit in 1993 and inflation reached a massive 27.7 per cent in October 1994. These statistics underscore the difficulties of a centralized economy changing to a market economy, albeit with Chinese

---

[11] Dreyer, J. Teufel, *China's Political System* (London: Macmillan Press Ltd, 1996, 2nd Edition) p. 147

socialist characteristics, and the attendant fluctuations between falls and successes.

Though the economic growth in the past two decades has been startling, this has caused a dangerously widening gap between rich and poor and between different areas within the PRC. The closure of inefficient state-run enterprises for economic reasons has caused the unemployment of a substantial slice of the labour-force and the ramifications of the social cost will be felt for years to come.

'The production of useless or substandard goods continues to be a problem for China. What to do about producers' disproportionate concern with making short-term profits to the detriment of economic efficiency and the production of high-quality goods, is of great concern to the leadership. So as well is the development of distinctive economic systems in Guangdong and parts of Fujian. Though stunningly successful, they show dangerous tendencies to evade Beijing's control.'[12]

What will be the role of the Chinese church in alleviating the social problems and enormous changes in the nation in the challenging times ahead? The last two hundred years have shown that she has survived wars, revolutions and persecution and, instead of dying, has increased numerically and spiritually beyond all expectations. The historical negative associations of Christianity with foreign domination can be broken down only by the mass example of Christians – both western and Chinese – living in New

---

[12] Ibid., p. 161

Testament obedience and humility to the teachings of Christ. How much freedom will the government permit in the registered and unregistered churches in the future? Shao Zongwei mentioned the guarantee of religious freedom under the constitution in his article 'Religious Freedom Stressed' in the *China Daily*:

> 'The number of Christians in China had increased to 10 million by the end of (1997), a high ranking Chinese official said yesterday in Beijing. . . "The remarkable increase since the founding of New China in 1949 is eloquent proof that Chinese Christians can run their own church better than the foreign missionaries did in old China," said Ye Xiaowen, director of the State Bureau of Religious Affairs . . . "Chinese citizens' freedom of religious belief is guaranteed by the country's Constitution. They are entitled to the right to believe or not believe in any religion. However, both believers and non-believers must comply with the laws of the country . . . The Chinese Government maintains that every country should respect the characteristics of other countries . . . while opposing any interference in the internal affairs of other nations under the pretext of religion. It's requirement that religious organizations and sites for religious activities must be registered with the government is not meant to confine the development of religion in China. The major purpose is to protect normal religious activities and safeguard the legitimate rights of sites for such activities," he said.'[13]

To clothe and feed 22 per cent of the world's population on 7 per cent of the world's arable land is an

---

[13] Shao, Zongwei, 'Religious Freedom Stressed', in *China Daily*, June 27, 1998

outstanding achievement by any government. The Middle Kingdom has been criss-crossed by thousands of kilometres of railway tracks and highways and industry has developed rapidly. The task of overcoming the environmental hazards of the country – as evidenced in the massive floods of 1998 – certainly needs all the wisdom, skill and prayer that the country can muster.

Whatever the long-term impact on China of the economic meltdown in Asia, it is clear that 'the CCP under its ageing leadership nevertheless remains in place. Its existence so far has prevented the emergence of an alternative system. However, the system is at a critical juncture. Large numbers of people are uncomfortable with the status quo. Yet there is no consensus on what new direction to take.'[14]

[14] Dreyer, *China's Political System*, p. 339

5

'A suite of well-furnished rooms'
— Accommodation —

'The College provides a suite of well-furnished rooms together with a gas stove, kitchen utensils, a refrigerator, a washing machine, telephone, water heater etc.' (teaching contract)

My mother brought me up with the notion that before a guest arrived in your home, you should clean the house, make the bed, put out linen and in these and other ways, try to make the person feel welcome. The Foreign Affairs Office personnel were obviously not brought up by my mother. The above quote is the way the teaching contract described my flat, but looking around the place, I couldn't see any resemblance whatsoever to what was written in black and white. (If the flat was not up to standard, I could theoretically have cancelled the contract and gone home.) Although faxes had assured me that the College had made preparations for my arrival, they did not extend to the accommodation. I arrived jet-lagged after 1½ days travelling via Kuala Lumpur and Guangzhou, and nothing prepared me for what I found. I couldn't foresee on my first dismal night that I would later see an analogy between the transformation of the first flat and the move into the second, and what was happening in China, outside my front door, where the Chinese people were racing to embrace in home and business all the high technology science can manufacture.

The lounge suite comprised a wooden three-seater, two single chairs and a matching glass-topped coffee table. At the end of a tiring day spent standing on concrete floors in the classroom, you want somewhere comfortable to relax, but you can't 'sink' into wood. The chairs, made for smaller people, were low to the ground.

The couch, coffee-table, refrigerator and circular, collapsible table were all fighting for space. Numerous rickety stools ensured that one did not linger at the dinner table too long. The medium-hard bed was blissfully comfortable by comparison. One frequent visitor could not understand my preference for my bedroom over the lounge, no matter how many times I explained. Red and green electrical wiring was not enclosed in wall cavities but ran along the walls, disappearing into mounted wooden power-boards. The whitewashed walls were rejecting their covering only to reveal a bland grey undercoat. In many places chunks had long since fallen out, exposing crumbly sandstone-coloured cement.

The chief features of the flat were two air conditioners, one in the lounge and one main bedroom. I was drawn irresistibly to this concession to western conveniences. In the bedroom was a wooden desk and chair, a small chest, bookcase, wardrobe with doors I couldn't close, more stools, a three-foot iron safe on casters next to a large double bed draped with a mosquito net. The wooden casement windows on either side of the room were slowly rotting away and best left shut. Wooden bars ran vertically in front of the windows to keep intruders out, or was it children in? Lengths of unmatching pink material were crudely pegged to the windows to keep the sun and prying eyes out.

I was reluctant to investigate all the linen in a cupboard for fear that vermin might jump out; anyway, it didn't look fit to be used. Then Mr Lu airily remarked one day that there were curtains somewhere. So I searched in earnest and found amongst the junk, eight-foot drops of tastefully embroidered curtains for all the windows. They made the world of difference to the appearance of the room. The fluorescent orange rope retrieved from around my boxes, used for threading them on, really added that extra touch of elegance to the interior design!

Also in the cupboard were a couple of mosquito nets. As I washed them out, ready to go up in Jeanette's room, I thought, 'Here we go again.'

According to the proverb, necessity is the mother of invention. The first few weeks reminded me constantly that I was my father's daughter. He has always been very 'handy' and consequently has fixed everything from household appliances to Radio Australia transmitter stations. It always seemed a strange twist of divine providence that such a practical person should be given four daughters, instead of a tribe of sons. Dad never seemed to notice the irony and taught us many of the practicalities of home maintenance just as he would have, had he been blessed with boys.

All this went through my mind one evening in the first week, when a gentle tug on the mosquito net sent dust and the bodies of ancient insects cascading on to my bed. I should have washed the net then and there, but my immediate problem was how to get it back up in place before nightfall. Even when I stood on the bed, the hook in the roof for the net was far out of reach. Then I spied the plastic handle on the stout tub of '*New Victory Super Mega Mass 2000 with its new richer taste*' (I assumed it was a healthy drink of some sort). I took off the handle and cut some orange cord. I made a loop, balanced it on the end of the curved handle and reached for the hook. Success! I tied the other end to the net frame and hoisted it up to the required height.

How important was the flimsy mosquito net, one might ask. The first two months were the worst of the whole year as it seemed everything was working against my ever enjoying my new role and residence. Getting the net securely hitched was a psychological victory because my bed then became a sanctuary from the discomfort of the rest of the flat. Arranging the drapery each night gave a sense of psychological, if not physical, protection against the insects and 'long-legged beasties and things that go bump in the night'. I felt terribly violated the night a rat ran across the edge of my pillow but, at least, I had the net between me and it.

On the plus side, the flat was of reasonable size except for the bathroom and kitchen. The view from the balcony stretched for many kilometres on a good day, taking in the park and a farm in the foreground. The flat was on the top floor of the last block at the end of the alley on the perimeter of the College grounds, so I was as distant from the centre of campus activity as I could be. Nevertheless, I was startled several times a day, starting at six in the morning, by the strident sirens blasting from the girls' dormitory. The first morning I heard it I thought China was being attacked by 'foreign devils' (Westerners). On the very first teaching morning I was ejected out of bed by fire-crackers going off in the stairwell at 6 a.m. I thought a bomb had hit the place.

The kitchen was outside the flat near the front door. If there had been a fire, it would have been contained there. This happened once in a kitchen two storeys down and gave everyone a shock, not least of all the hapless owner of the gas bottle. Our cookhouse was only about five by seven feet in size and doubled as the laundry. A tiled concrete bench supported two gas burners and at one end was a sink with a hole roughly cut out of the tiles. Rat dung, failed traps and powdered cement littered the floor under the bench. Warped narrow shelves for crockery ran along two sides and the whitewash from the crumbling, mouldy wall fell on to the plates. There were hardly any serviceable pots and pans, but lots of broken ones and a rusty electric oven. We had to buy most of our own kitchenware.

Jeanette's bedroom was large but had only one window facing the park and a door which led to the balcony. A water-stained desk and upright chair faced the window. A deep yellow cupboard sat in one corner, stuffed with unsavoury, stained linen, pillows and quilts. Standing along one wall was a hard, lumpy bed and diagonally across the room a thick string of raffia was slung, presumably to hang clothes on.

The fourth storey flat had been empty during the long summer holidays. Weeks of windy weather had blown quantities of dust through the rotting casement windows and the three-inch gaps under the four outside doors. Years of weather and vermin had eaten away the wood. The concrete floors were slowly being worn away, leaving a powder which required frequent sweeping. Students mentioned that they had been commandeered by one of the previous occupants to help him spring-clean the flat in readiness for me at the end of term. It was a kind thought but unfortunately it had all been in vain.

The cramped bathroom housed a toilet, sink, and a shower nozzle connected to a hot water service. The water from the sink and shower ran straight on to the tiled floor and into a drain. The hot water, heated from the kitchen gas bottle, refused to work properly most of the time and deposits from the heavily silted water clogged the nozzle.

Getting anything fixed in the flat was a major headache. I had arranged my flights so that I would arrive a few days early because I thought I would need time to learn about the teaching routine and the ways of the College. Instead, one meeting was all the orientation I received in the way of teaching, and most of the rest of my time was spent trying to motivate people to get things fixed or waiting around while workmen did so. The toilet, most appliances, lights – almost everything didn't work. I was prepared to live in the same standard of accommodation as the other teachers; so I investigated. My flat was a hovel compared to others I visited.

I wrote home: 'The college looks ancient but the oldest building is only a few decades old. Amidst

the deteriorating buildings are new, sparkling tene-
ments for staff and students and a new campus is being
built next to my place. Fire-crackers have been continuously let off as professors celebrate their move to new
residences.'

Clinging to the vague contingency of Jeanette's
arrival boosted my incentive to make the place as
comfortable as possible. I wanted to do the College a
favour in a way too. It became increasingly obvious as
more inadequacies came to light that, if the place was
not fixed up properly, future western teachers would
quickly head for home, disillusioned. I had no way of
knowing at the time that my thoughts would be so
prophetic.

It seemed logical to my western mind that if repairs
needed to be done on the flat, then during the holidays
was the best time to do them. But it was holiday time for
everyone on campus, not just the students and teachers.
The Chinese typically make preparations after the person arrives, rather than before. Perhaps the habit is a
sad reflection on the unpredictable nature of living in
China. The College may not have believed that I was
actually coming until I stepped off the plane.

The scores of adult lizards had the decency to recognize the new ownership of the flat and most left. The
cute inch-long babies remained. If I left a paper or
something else on the table overnight, in the morning
I'd be surprised by a baby crouching on the underside
of it, eyeing me suspiciously. Then they'd show off
their heroic parachuting trick to the floor.

The worst thing about the flat were the rats.

The nightly rat parties sent me into a shock which
partially paralysed my ability to do anything effective

against them. I didn't realize for a few weeks that I was in shock. I had fallen very quickly into a state psychologists call 'learned helplessness', wherein unconsciously I thought that nothing at all could be done about the rats. I tried every night to block up the gaps under the doors; they either by-passed the blockage or ate through it. Rats eat everything – including plastic – and stop short only at metal. Over time we collected umpteen biscuit tins, bottles and other containers for foodstuffs and cutlery and kept the lids tightly sealed.

Each morning I had to sweep up the dung and wash the floor. Fortunately they were feasting mainly in the spare room which was cluttered with surplus furniture, linen, fans, beds and things past residents had wanted to throw out but had lacked the courage to do so. The main attraction for the rats, I found out later, was a rice keeper. The contraption dispensed rice from the top into a tray at the bottom. The inner workings were complicated and difficult to pull apart for cleaning but I thought I had cleaned it sufficiently. I didn't realize until Jeanette looked at it two months later, that it still contained rice. The other complication was that the cement floor under the door was not even, so I feared that any barrier would not be flush with the floor and the rats would just squeeze under it anyway. My defeatist thinking on this may have been a symptom of the syndrome. Putting the rice store in the kitchen or on to the balconies would have just moved the rats' place of eating. There were rats in the kitchen anyway. Since the store was not mine I couldn't just ditch it, because it still worked.

One day the Lord suddenly jolted me out of my paralysis. I decided I had to demand, no matter how much effort it took, that the FAO do something constructive against the rats. The only time he listened and acted, was when I became a ranting, overbearing female. Polite requests were ignored, and he didn't see it as important enough to act on his own initiative. When confronted, he casually replied that he could get the carpenter to nail thick rubber to the doors. In a day or two a carpenter appeared and did a great job on all the external doors. Being flexible rubber, it became flush with the floor when the doors were closed and ended the problem – at least in the flat. I enjoyed my first good night's sleep and it was bliss to wake up in the morning to find the flat just as I had left it the night before. He put rubber on the kitchen door but cut a hole (the size of a rat), for the plastic outlet pipe from the air-conditioner. A few weeks later, rats ate through the pipe. Back to square one.

One night I was washing up in a tin basin in the sink. The hot soapy water fled down the sink hole, onto the tiled floor, along a depression to the end of the room, passing through a hole cut into a concrete upright on the way, down a drain and out into the open drains surrounding the building. The water this night disturbed a rat which staggered out of the hole at my feet, covered in soap suds. I kicked it out of the kitchen, slammed it against the wall, then smashed it with a bucket. Both the bucket and rat went out to the rubbish heap. 'How dare you defile my flat!' All the anger and frustration of the past weeks erupted. It was good my fighting spirit had returned. After Jeanette arrived we had further episodes with mice and rats in the kitchen and at different times had three holes in the wall concreted. Jeanette cleverly nailed the ring-top of a can onto the rubber on the door. The rodents bent it inwards and got in.

A night or two after the rat-killing episode, I saw a spider, sitting with splayed legs near the ceiling of the lounge-room. The colour and markings were similar to a harmless Australian huntsman; here the resemblance ended. I saw to my horror – the fat body and lon legs – the thing was the size of my hand, from finger to thumb-tip. The frightening part was not knowing if it was venomous or not. I told myself that size and appearance don't equate with potential harm. One of Australia's most common spiders – the daddy longlegs, with its tiny body and spindly legs, is one of the world's deadliest spiders, though its mouth is not strong enough to pierce skin, whereas the hairy-scary Queensland tarantula is harmless. Other scientific facts went through through my brain. There was nothing I could do to kill or coax it outdoors, so I closed the bedroom door and prayed according to the passage in Genesis 1:26.

> Then God said, 'Let us make man in our image, according to our likeness; let them have dominion over the fish of the sea, over the birds of the air and over the cattle, over all the earth and over every creeping thing that creeps on the earth.'

The first miracle was that I actually slept. The second was that I woke up an hour later, and found that the spider had vanished. Praise God.

We saw the spider's cousin a few months later in a shop window and, while trying to control our agitation, signalled to a salesgirl. She looked at us, then at the spider, then at us again, with a blank expression on her face, as if to say 'So?' We looked at each other rather foolishly and blushed.

I don't think it was poisonous.

The one thing I couldn't find was a rug for the floor. Pictures of the Australian countryside originally brought for teaching, served the dual purpose of covering a wall and cheering up the room. Buying tasteful linen for Jeanette was difficult in the first semester. I imagined Jeanette having weird psychedelic dreams if she slept in the fluorescent pink sheets which were all the rage in the shops in the city. (The market was flooded months later with pretty linen.)

During the first semester my accommodation improved because a stream of new appliances came one by one into the flat, to replace the dead or barely-working originals: boys struggled up the stairs with a washing-machine, portable oven, TV, VCR (I went through three until one worked!), lights, gas range, heater, pieces of large and small furniture, and even a new full-size refrigerator. I got a new rice-cooker; but no new hot water service.

Strangely all the originals were just stacked up in the spare room and elsewhere; everything had its counterpart. The day I suggested that two full-sized refrigerators were making the place over-crowded, Mr Lu obstinately refused to take anything away. Once again I couldn't understand what was going on. Later I spoke to George who casually said that we were going to move into another flat and they needed to keep everything together, to leave behind one 'set' for the new residents. I wondered what the new residents would want with appliances that were, at best, on the blink. A new flat! We tried not to get too excited in case it didn't eventuate for months, but we day-dreamed about clean tiles on the floor and real paint on the walls.

Many months before I went overseas I had a strange dream. I walked into a Chinese public conve-nience. No, it didn't smell. In front of me was an open concrete floor, then rows of cubicles. There was noth-ing else there and the floor was flooded with water except for one small triangle where I was standing. I knew this was where I was to live in China. The Lord was asking me to make a choice: was I going to accept this accommodation or not? Was I going to be obedi-ent and accept? Naturally, I hesitated but I agreed to accept it, if that was his will. The scene changed imme-diately. Next I was standing on a beautiful rich red carpet patterned in glowing gold and every other col-our besides. It looked warm and inviting, the kind of carpet chosen for stately theatre foyers. I was still in the Chinese convenience. The Lord wasn't changing my circumstances but he was making them better.

I returned to Australia during the semester break because of my mothers' illness and flew back to China a few weeks later. At the airport I was greeted by the smiling faces of Jeanette, Lyla and my student Felicity. They bundled me into the College van amid laughter and sighs of relief that I'd finally arrived. Consterna-tion filled me when Lyla said: 'Now don't blame the workmen for the toilet in the flat! You just wait and see.' They all laughed.

They had installed a new western toilet for me, this time in a tiny separate room. There was no door in sight! In the fullness of time wooden louvered doors were installed to open outwards. I wished that they had kept the Chinese toilet because the Asian system is understood by Chinese plumbers, but western ones are a mystery. During all the time of our residency, the toilets did not work properly, despite the efforts of several plumbers. When I saw a man bash a piece of metal he had taken from the cistern with a hammer, to make it bend when it wasn't designed to, I knew there was not a lasting solution in sight.

Although frustrating, in hindsight I am glad that these problems in the flat occurred because I can better understand the existing situation in China as a whole. A middle school (high school) teacher appeared one night and asked me to edit a thesis she had written about the problems within vocational training. China is trying to improve the expertise of its tradespeople such as plumbers and electricians graduating from vocational training schools. But they are hampered by a lack of money, trained teachers, equipment, and the community's poor perception of this kind of employment.

We were given two adjoining flats on the third floor of the block next door. We were the only occupants on this floor.

Jeanette and her team worked like Trojans to clean the two flats. Felicity found herself helping out both times, but she's such an obliging soul, she didn't mind.

Jeanette asked to be given at least two days' notice before the move. The FAO informed her that she would probably move on a Friday, but on Thursday afternoon, a group of students appeared at the door announcing that they had been told to move her furniture. Jeanette was horrified. The new flats were filthy after the builders had vacated them. It took many days of hard work to get them clean.

So I walked into a new, clean, light and airy flat with everything neatly arranged. She was so kind – my favourite biscuits were there, my Bible was under my pillow, soft drinks and boiled water in the refrigerator, hot water in the thermos and toiletries in the bathroom. The air-conditioners were installed in the main bedrooms. We each had bulky, ornate security gates outside our doors with a choice of three different bolts to use. At least this meant that we felt safe and sound at night behind such fortifications.

Unfortunately, like a bad penny, the hot water service for the shower followed me to my new flat – not that the lower altitude helped – *it still didn't work!* I would trot over to Jeanette's place to use her brand new, energy-saving and award-winning shower every night. The room was so small we had to dress outside the bathroom.

Each kitchen had its own concrete water tank which we emptied weekly. China has major water supply problems so disruptions were frequent. I later read that: 'The huge increase in the population of coastal China has resulted in shortages of surface water. Ground water has been used to make up the difference, thus causing a problem with sinking. In addition to causing structural damage to homes and businesses . . . coastal cities are more prone to flooding, particularly if the rise in sea levels that has been predicted actually occurs . . . In a 1993 report the

Chinese Academy of Sciences predicted that the coast-line would decline by 40 to 60 centimetres in the Pearl River area (Guangdong Province) and more along the coasts of Shanghai and Tianjin . . . Water shortages are common in major cities at certain times of year, and factories have had to close down production lines for lack of water. In Beijing during the 1950's, wells drew water from 16 feet below the surface; today the average depth is 160 feet, with many wells having become completely useless. The government has warned that, unless there is careful use of existing water, rationing will soon be mandatory. A 1994 report estimated that water shortages were costing the Chinese economy at least US$230 million a year. Environmental scientists noted that the country's water resources and farm-lands were not keeping up with the demands placed on them, and worried that the ecological underpinning of Chinese society was fraying.'[1]

Every night in this block, the water was turned off from around 11 p.m. until early morning. Often during the day the water and power would be off for a few hours. Cooking by gas was a bonus but I felt it was unfair to ask other people to carry full gas bottles up all those flights of steps.

One Saturday we wandered up to the girls' dormitory in search of Marilyn. The tiled building surrounds a large quadrangle on three sides, bounded by an imposing gate on the fourth side. Anyone entering the precincts is noticed by the female guard in her booth at

[1] Dreyer, *China's Political System*, pp. 248–9

the gate. The building is eight storeys high and massive. All eyes in the quadrangle and on all seven balconies, saw us cross the concrete, question marks etched on their faces.

We reached the seventh floor after much puffing and panting. There we were greeted, surprisingly enough, by a group of girls from one of my Practical English classes. Chatting and giggling enthusiastically – thrilled to have 'their' teacher on their own 'stamping ground' – they pulled us into their dormitory.

It was a narrow room covering the width of the building. Double bunks for ten girls lined the side walls. Small desks, like those in the classroom, formed two rows along the aisle. There were not enough desks for each of the residents to have their own. Fluorescent lights were fixed to the ceiling over the desks. At one end, a door led on to the balcony where wet washing was drying. Inside the door was a table and chair. Bags and suitcases where the girls kept their clothes, were placed on sturdy shelves. They didn't like this arrangement because the clothes smelt musty in the bags. Shoes were tossed under the beds. The only privacy each girl had was on her bed when she pulled the curtains together which were fixed in a make-shift fashion with brightly-coloured pegs to the bunk. Another girl from a nearby room, whom I didn't know, complained to me about the lack of privacy. What an understatement.

Whenever I ventured down one of the dusty roads on the campus, I would pass the back of the girls' dormitories. Suspended on coat-hangers, high up on every balcony of the building I saw clothes clustered together, fluttering, waiting for a breeze. Blouses, track-suits and dresses hung as reminders of the lives of their owners, themselves clustered together in dormitories, hoping for the fluttering promise of a bright future after college. The provision of only spartan accommodation was understandable because China does not have endless reserves of money to invest in education. The scale of the enormous building and the number of occupants, were a far cry from traditional family dwellings of north China. It was a shock to realize yet again how much Chinese society has been transformed since 1949.

'The house was built in the typical North Chinese style, around three sides of a quadrangle, the south side of the courtyard being a wall about seven feet high, with a moon gate which opened onto an outer courtyard, which in turn was guarded by a double gate . . . These houses were built to cope with the extremes of a brutally harsh climate, which lurched from freezing winters to scorching summers, with virtually no spring or autumn in between. In winter . . . howling winds which roared down from Siberia across the plains. Dust tore into the eyes and bit into the skin for much of the year, and people often had to wear masks . . . In the inner courtyard of the houses, all the windows in the main rooms opened to the south to let in as much sunshine as possible while the walls on the north side took the brunt of the wind and the dust . . . The floors of the main rooms were tiled, while the wooden windows were covered with paper. The pitched roof was made of smooth black tiles.'[2]

---

[2] Chung, J., *Wild Swans* (London: Flamingo, 1991) p. 43

When I wrote home about the first flat, mentioning it included the hi-tech air-conditioner and refrigerator, people would assume the rest of the flat was of the same standard as an Australian dwelling. When I wrote about the rats, rotting window-panes and concrete floors, they would assume it had been built many decades ago and that all the appliances in it dated from the same era. The fact was that both descriptions were true. This example underscores the situation in China, and other developing countries, where the latest twentieth-century technology exists side by side with much earlier technology or the manual equivalent. On the frequent occasions they notice it, the juxtaposition of the two strikes the Westerner as surprising. Perhaps the surprise is because there is no evidence of the intermediary technology. As we were growing up, we became familiar with the different models of technology at home and at work because, as they came on the market, older models faded out or disappeared into museums.

In Beijing years ago, I had lunch at a working persons' canteen. At the check-out was the latest cash register, similar to ones in any department store in Australia. The check-out girl, presumably distrustful of this modern gadget, calculated the prices on her *abacus* before putting the amount through the register. (The abacus was invented about 3,000 BC by either the Chinese or Babylonians.)

The College put in new western toilets in the second flats; below in the alley, mothers and baby-sitters encouraged their charges to use the open drains surrounding the buildings as toilets. Outside a row of ancient single-rooms, a woman usually washed fish under a tap. Nearby loomed a huge new tenement block for senior staff, sporting self-contained kitchens and modern windows tinted against the glare of summer.

Despite the warm and genuine *'huanying, huanying'* ('welcome, welcome') Chinese hosts invariably greeted us with when invited to their homes, I often felt a lack of warmth in the design and furniture of the interior. Not that this was irksome, since friends and fun are more important than furniture. But what was it that my senses were picking up? Was it a lack of items of furniture or possessions that I was used to seeing in Australia that was different? I knew wages didn't allow for much disposable income. But some of the homes had more possessions and of better quality than we had in the first flat. What was the missing ingredient? Or was it the result of my western aesthetic snobbery?

It dawned on me eventually that there was a lack of co-ordination of style, colour and pattern in their interior decoration, as my western mind understood such things. Possessions – furniture, soft furnishings and the like – appeared to be chosen solely with needs and functional purposes in mind rather than possessing also coherence of style with the rest of the decor. It seemed incongruous, because Chinese people are renowned for their artistry. The glowing silk embroidered robes of the nobility, pre-liberation, showed a keen eye for colour, movement and cohesive design. One marvels at the detailed paintings on the arches of the 37-metre-long Marble Boat (Qingyan Boat or Boat for Pure Banquets) and all the towers, pagodas, pavilions, bridges, corridors and temple at the Summer Palace, Beijing.

After my understanding of colour-sense had expanded to include the Chinese preference – green with blue, pink with red, I began to 'see' Chinese aesthetics. (Surprisingly, I liked my new curtains in the second flat with their large brown irises floating beside sage-green foliage.)

With a rich artistic tradition drawn from thousands of years of cultural endeavour, why were the homes so soul-less? I wondered if the ravages of the past few decades and especially the extremes of the Cultural Revolution had killed for a time the 'soul' of personal artistic expression in homes. Most of the homes I visited were built before the Cultural Revolution. Reconstruction of China post-1949 had little time, patience or money to spend on art, except where art-forms could serve a propaganda role for furthering socialism. Functionalism reigned supreme in the construction of office and apartment blocks. Were they a reflection of the starkness of the struggles of life and the pain of rebirth of a modern nation?

'During the decade from 1966–76, art schools closed, art journals ceased publication, and major art exhibitions came to a halt. Ink paintings in the traditional style came under especially sharp attack by the "Gang of Four", who condemned black-ink works as feudal, bourgeois, and counterrevolutionary. Artists and art teachers were sent from the city universities and museums down to do manual labor in the countryside or in factories. Most paintings and crafts during this period were group projects with political themes, often executed in the socialist-realistic style.'[3]

Something had been lost. Was what I sensed the out-working of a wounded culture?

Nowadays drab, concrete formalism is giving way to tastefully-appointed apartment blocks, splashed with bright colours on balconies and tiles. New, archi-tecturally-designed buildings reassured me that the Chinese were re-discovering their deep artistic roots. Most reassuring of all were the buildings which com-bined the elements of traditional Chinese arts with the grace of modern design. Sweeping balustrades found their inspiration in the imposing plazas and walk-ways of the Forbidden City and weighty carved male and female lions continue to guard the entrances to equally formidable twentieth-century office blocks.

I once enjoyed a meal in the home of a restaurateur, who lived some distance from my home. The white walls, delicate lights and sound-system were reminis-cent of Australian homes. There was more to it than that; there was '*a little bit of soul in there*'. Was the atmosphere in the home the result of this warm, gracious lady knowing the Lord?

The commonly heard word 'reconstruction' always elicits in me memories of Nanjing. The Japanese put the city to the torch under the 'three all – kill all, burn

---

[3] Kaplan, F.M. & Sobin, J.M., *Encyclopedia of China Today* (Sydney: Book Wise (Australia) Ltd., 1982) p. 335

all, destroy all'. Between 40,000 and 300,00 people lost their lives in the city. As I stood years ago on the ancient city wall looking in the direction of what remained of the 'old' settlement, I marvelled at the vast achievement of reconstruction of this modern city of 2,090,000 people (1990 census). The Chinese are down but never out for very long. Their whole history is one of destruction and rebuilding after the fires.

The Australian newspaper ran the article 'China sees Housing as shelter from Storm' (from *The Economist*), concerning major changes to housing in China. According to the article, Mr Zhu Rongji, China's Prime Minister, is looking for ways to energize the nation's economy. Substantial reforms to State-owned enterprises introduced to raise competitiveness between companies has resulted in huge unemployment problems. Added to this, is the Asian meltdown which caused prices to fall and growth to slip from 8.8 per cent in 1997 to 7.2 per cent in the first quarter of 1998.

Mr Zhu is pinning his hopes on a housing boom. From July 1, the fifty year practice of supplying flats at peppercorn rent to new people entering the State-sector workforce, ceases. This will affect 6 million people. Local governments and State enterprises have already started privatising housing. Economists point to the dilapidated state of much of China's housing stock, as evidence that a construction boom driven by privatisation is plausible in the near future.

'The China Analyst, published by the Bank Credit Analyst Research group in Montreal, says that $US80 billion ($129 billion) in new spending can be generated by housing reforms this year and $US150 billion next year. That would be a big stimulus at just the right moment.'[4]

Authorities have instructed the largest banks to lend almost $US12 billion against property, half of it in home loans. Many of the bank's bad loans are secured by unsold commercial and upmarket residential property developments, dating back to the early 1990s boom. A common sight, in cities where new office and residential blocks are pushing to the sky in ambitious construction projects, are the concrete shells of buildings lying derelict, abandoned long before completion. A casual glance at shop-fronts in shopping districts in many cities reveals that occupancy rates are not as high as developers may wish, especially in recently-built complexes.

An observer can't help but wonder what happened along the way to crush the hopes and dreams of those who set out with such great expectations to construct the buildings, and what the future will hold for the countless numbers of homeless beggars, especially the children, in every city, who clamour for money.

---

[4] *The Economist*, 'China sees Housing as Shelter from Storm', quoted in *The Australian*, June 2, 1998

6

'In Australia they speak Australian fruently'
— Teaching —

The students had arrived early and were sitting, staring fixedly, noting my every move while I was standing, waiting for stragglers. My classes were two hours long and no chair was provided for teachers. According to the writing textbook, the lesson topics in chapter one were 'co-ordination' and 'subordinating clauses'. I could not believe my misfortune. Subordinating clauses are difficult, pesky things which I chewed over and barely digested during the language course. Now here I was having to teach them on my first day. Obviously the students thought that they were riveting stuff because they sat riveted to their seats, mouths closed for two hours!

I read the text: 'In co-ordination, a connective word, such as "and", "but", "or" joins two elements together.' 'Could someone give me a simple sentence using "and"?'

Blank faces met me. 'Only a short, simple sentence.'

But wait, did I see a pen glide towards the paper? Across the room there was a slight shift in a chair. Is she going to grant me my small request? These are grade three students, the graduating class, why are they so unresponsive? (Grade three is the equivalent of third year at an Australian tertiary college.)

'Nice to see you,' a brave voice whispered.

'Well actually that is not a sentence. Should be: "It's nice to see you." ' I kicked myself, I shouldn't have squashed this tentative attempt. My heart sank and my mind ranged over the heated debates in literary circles about what constitutes a sentence: Is 'Good morning' a sentence? Does it really matter to the universe if it is or isn't. But I took the politically correct stance of my textbook, *A College English Writing Course Vol. 1*, the one my hand was clinging to, and squashed the first attempt at interaction. This was all so difficult for the students – and me.

'To be subordinate, means to be "inferior in rank". In a subordinate clause, one clause is dependent upon another . . . Take for example this sentence: "She talked on and on and on until I could scream!" ' How apt! Is this what the students were thinking about me? They just weren't grasping this new and exciting addition to their language at all.

'Any questions on this?'

'Do you understand what I have just said?' Silence. Then a vaguely murmured 'Yes.' Ah progress!

A bright spot came during the break when a few articulate students asked me some pertinent questions. Then came the second half. 'Turn to the exercises on page 12.' I gave them the answers to the first question. Then the second. Silence . . . then the third . . .

'How would we change these sentence fragments into proper sentences?'

'Leave out the full stop' someone answered. I relaxed a little knowing we were at last getting somewhere! 'And what else?' There was no response.

Eventually I dragged out of them the second part of the correct answer, so I thought the rest of the ninety-four questions would be easy. Not so. Somehow the repeatable formula 'drop the full-stop, add "and", make the capital a little letter' didn't come trippingly out of the memory cells with each question. Asking for volunteers didn't work. Asking an individual for the answers sometimes produced a shy, muffled response – occasionally – and even more occasionally – the right response. I thought gloomily that I would have to do a repeat performance of this chapter with the second grade three class after this one. Wonderful.

At the end of class, a tall girl with a refreshingly louder voice than the barely audible whisper of the others, gave me a post-mortem on the class. 'Perhaps we could move through the work a bit quicker because we know all this work. For years our teachers have carefully taught us grammar.'

(One look myself in the mirror after this first lesson showed how tough it had been. My shirt was untucked my hair had come adrift from its moorings, I could only laugh.)

From their reactions or lack of them, one would not have known they knew even 5 per cent of what I had been trying to teach them. During the next two semesters, there were some who came out of their shells and actually took an active part in the writing lessons, but the rest of the others just sat mute and rarely participated. By contrast, I quickly realized, this tall girl was in most attributes way ahead of the majority of the students. Every lesson with her involved lively debate about the subtleties of the English language. Students frequently gave 'my English is so poor' as the reason why they were afraid to participate in class. Unfortunately, like a muscle which grows in strength through exercise yet atrophies with disuse, oral language skills increase or decrease with the degree of activity. How did those in grade three, ever get to such a level, if they couldn't speak English?

'Once courses get going you'll have to find out what the school expects and what your students or teachers expect, all of which may or may not have anything to do with the course description or with what you want. Teachers need to learn which exams their students are preparing for, and how to help them both prepare for the graduation exams, and learn useful material beyond . . . Teachers need to remember that what they consider useful may not seem so to their students, or the department, or the department's party secretary. Students will need to learn what the school expects them to learn, as opposed to the teacher, as opposed to what they hope to get out of their studies . . . If you're at a small institution, you'll likely become a Jack or Jill of all trades, setting up the library and lecturing on topics you never realized you knew anything about.'[1]

---

[1] Weiner, Murphy & Li, *Living in China*, p. 8.

The daily routine for students

6 a.m.	Wake-up siren.
6–7.30	Morning exercises on the oval. Breakfast and preparation for classes while announcements are relayed over loudspeakers.
7.30–9.20	First morning class in two 50-minute sessions.
9.20–9.40	Second exercise session.
9.40–11.30	Second morning class.
11.30–2.30 p.m.	Lunch and afternoon nap.
2.30–4.20	Afternoon class.
4.30–6.00	Dinner, sport, recreation and homework.
7.30–9.20	Evening class for some students.
11.00	Lights out in dormitories.

Some students have classes on Saturday mornings. On weekends there are adult classes for working people from outside the College. Morning exercises are compulsory and organized on a roster basis because the oval could not hold all 4,000 students at once. The taped instructions for the exercises are played over the loudspeakers and backed with military music. The same tape is played every day, so the students quickly learn the routines. We did not take up the suggestion to join them for the early exercises. It must be an impressive sight: several thousand students spread out in lines on the dirt oval moving rhythmically to the beat of the lively music and 'yi, er, san, si'. We did see the mid-morning sessions though, as we wove our way across the campus. Numerous classes spread out in lines along every available road and path moving half-heartedly in the hot sun. Embarrassed students would giggle and stop their exertions as Jeanette and I passed by. We tried to commend and encourage their efforts, by imitating their actions but instead, just created mass laughing and disrupted discipline among the ranks in this serious business of keeping fit.

'I just want to give you the best'

My predecessor wrote about the students: 'They are very friendly and always willing to help. They're also inquisitive. I like them very much though. Students are highly motivated to learn but many just aren't used to feeling the pressure I had at College. i.e. they don't usually get very much homework and they tend to be given a lot of mercy when it comes to deadlines. No behaviour problems though . . . most of them have chosen to study English . . . Good luck, you're not only fighting the British English the kids learnt in middle school but also the American English we've been trying to pound into them.'

The English Department gave me several Oral English classes in grade two (the equivalent of second year tertiary students in Australia). They were a mixed bunch in a couple of ways. Most had come straight from middle school to College and were aged from about 18 to 21 years. Some were streamed into teaching (the 'Education class') and would be at College for two to four years. Others were Practical Oral English two-year students who theoretically would become secretaries, clerks or translators in business. With a scant two years of Oral English, the unpromising economic future destined most of these to become teachers, usually back in their hometowns or villages.

One Oral English class comprised older students who had already been teaching for years in their own hometowns. They had come to College for two years of training and most would return to their schools after graduation. Why, I puzzled, did they do this in reverse order? Many were not as motivated to learn Oral English as the younger ones in other classes. Perhaps they questioned how much value speaking English would be when they returned home. 'We don't have many opportunities to practise our Oral English because we don't often meet a foreigner' is a common cry from students (and the reason for our own popularity).

I had the two grade three classes for English Writing in the first semester and 'Introduction to Britain and America' in the second. By the second semester they had loosened up a lot and trusted me much more. They were keen to learn as much as they could about overseas, but sometimes the details became a little muddled as can be seen in some answers in the examination paper.

'About 18BC English had built 13 colonies in North America Atlantic Coasts.'

'What important document written in 1776 changed the American colonies into States?' 'Uncle Tom's Cabin'.

After Jeanette arrived there was a reshuffle of responsibilities and I gained an Oral English grade one class for the remainder of the semester. On weekends we taught a further group of students in what Jeanette and I dubbed the 'adult' classes, merely to distinguish them from the full-time ones. I gave a monthly Writing class to graduates and weekly Oral ones to a different group of working people during both semesters. For the first semester I taught almost 280 students and for the second nearly 240 per week. Two classes had about twenty students each and the rest, almost forty each. Getting to know the names of so many black-haired, brown-eyed people was a major task. No, they don't all look the same. All of them had English names given or chosen in their first year at College which made life easier for us than remembering Chinese names.

Following an unpromising start to my teaching efforts, I wondered dismally if all my classes would be just as unsuccessful. How was I going to teach them to speak and write English? With the difficulty of getting *any* English out of them, the idea of improvement in their skills seemed like a far-off dream. As the semester progressed though, these problems were whittled down to a size that I could cope with. Fortunately the students came to the conclusion that I wasn't a monster after all, and that all hell wouldn't break out if they spoke up in class. Later in the term I tried to make them scared of me if they didn't speak up. The plan was foiled because by then the ice was broken well and truly and they just giggled at my mock ferocity as if to say 'we know you're a softie!'

Also, as time went by the heavy hand of censorship didn't fall from the Dean of the English Department as I feared; but rather, signs of appreciation of my teaching methods came my way. Teachers from the College and outside schools sometimes silently crept into my classes in order to see how I taught. So I began to relax and to expand into creative areas and to reduce my reliance on textbooks. The students appreciated the mixture and would come alive after they had ploughed through the stodgy text exercises during the first half of the class. Certainly the textbooks were not all bad, but they were written by teams of writers who surely didn't have a creative bone in their bodies. I was privileged to have almost complete freedom to teach what I wanted to and how I wanted to do it. I was told I could skip chapters of the textbooks if the students were progressing well or even overtake the work which some classes did, and move on to the later books in the series.

In this respect I was enjoying a freedom teachers back home would give anything for. At first I felt at a disadvantage not being a qualified classroom teacher, but in hindsight I realized that it was an advantage because I came expecting nothing in the way of resources and convenient classroom set-ups, so was not disappointed or complaining, 'But they don't even have such and such . . .' It put me on my mettle and I had to think laterally about achieving learning outcomes. Some things worked and some things – well – we won't do that again! I loved making up visual aids, always appreciated by the classes because they were different and colourful. They were too polite to comment that my freehand maps of the USA and Britain were a little lopsided.

My goals were to make the lessons as interesting as possible and to engage the majority of people in active participation. While enjoying the lesson, they lost some of their self-consciousness, leaving space for their language skills to bubble to the surface. Natural curiosity took over and I was often submerged by a myriad questions about any topic related or unrelated to the subject at hand. From their point of view, I was captive to their class only once a week, so they wanted to ask all the questions floating around their heads since our last meeting; important questions like, 'Miss Belinda, did you know Madonna is going to have a baby?'

The teacher wrote: 'Oral classes are pretty much as flexible as you and the students can make them and you can do almost anything you think will help improve the students' English.' Any lesson which included lots of pictures, maps, diagrams, magazine articles, story-books, belongings – anything at all to illustrate a point of vocabulary, stimulate discussions and be a springboard for multi-staged exercises, were certain to capture attention. I wanted to produce listeners and scholars, who were eager to respond to the material and to show a way to provide for their classes once they were out teaching.

I learnt the hard way the value of teaching 'whole language' – writing, reading, speaking and listening – together in the one lesson. While devising lessons, my creative thinking would veer towards writing for an Oral English class. When preparing for a Writing class, I would think of inspiring topics for discussion. I gave up some of the battle to conform and compromised by giving the lesson a majority share of its intended content – oral for Oral classes, writing for Writing, but used the other elements as well. 'Whole language' lessons, by incorporating each of the four elements were more captivating and closest to the way language is used in everyday situations.

'You're looking at eyes and you share in a life'

The lessons on the names of clothes were very popular, especially because I supplied dozens of pictures and an over-sized calendar of western models I had found in the flat. As I unfurled the calendar, male students who always sat at the back, arose en masse from their seats and stayed in rapt attention for the next two hours. Questions flew around and one of the back row asked, 'What are hot-pants?' (Hot pants with or without a short skirt were the latest fashion with the girls.)

This lesson highlighted one of the problems in their understanding of the west. In any body of knowledge about a subject there were glaring gaps in the basic information. For example, the most fundamental word in a vocabulary on female clothes is 'dress'. About the most peripheral is 'hot-pants'. But 'dress' was a new concept to many of them and I had to repeatedly demonstrate its meaning (even though dresses were popular attire.) They frequently confused 'skirt' with 'dress'.

They possessed only limited knowledge of basic facts and one or two quirky bits as well, which led them to skewed interpretations of what the West was like; the 'rose-coloured glasses syndrome' was common. Their understanding of Australia was an example of this. Their general knowledge was scant, but everyone knew that Sydney was hosting the year 2000 Olympic Games. (Although Beijing lost the bid, I found only enthusiastic support and no animosity at all.) Most knew that Australia had a small population living on a huge land mass. This puzzled them because they didn't know that much of our land comprised desert, rimmed by only a few areas fit for agriculture and settlement – and that we have high unemployment. (My understanding of China is anything but encyclopaedic.)

'Do people speak English in Australia?' the textbook asked.

'Yes, they speak English fruently. They also speak Australian fruently,' a bright grade one replied.

'Chicago is now located in the middle of Lake Michigan.' Now you know.

I showed my video class 'Man From Snowy River'. They 'oohed' and 'ahhed' at the right moments and took fright when it became scary. They found the language hard going and I had to explain what a 'muster' and other terms meant and give a synopsis of the story every so often. They can't be molly-coddled by clearly enunciated teaching videos all their College days. Seeing the glorious Aussie landscape brought a lump to my throat. Jeanette was teaching next door, heard the film soundtrack, wandered in and gave a 'thumbs up' to the film, much to the amusement of my class. *Her* students were intrigued as to what was happening during the video, so she gave explanations every so often – 'that's the wild horses coming' etc. With windows everywhere, every sound carries.

English lessons became without intention, opportunities to 'fill in the gaps' and replace their misconceptions with truth and facts. We passed on information which might be useful for those who would later be working alongside Westerners. It was important to provide as realistic a view of Australia and other western countries as we could. I was painfully conscious nonetheless with everything I said, of the chasm between their comprehension and mine.

Another issue we had to consider, given the almost limitless range of English vocabulary, was what would be the most useful words? What do they really need to learn for their future employment, especially the teachers-to-be? What did we want their future pupils to learn? Would learning what a vest was really advance the cause of education?

'Could you teach us about Australian customers?' they often asked. They meant customs. So we discussed special events that were dear to the heart of Aussies and matters of etiquette and tradition involved in such things as going to someone's place to dinner.

'How much did you pay for your watch?' one of the boys asked. Because it has a large face and is decorated with gaudy colours, it often became the focal point of conversation and was convenient to use as an example in a lesson. I told him how much it cost and didn't think any more about it. The next week, he escorted me back to my flat, carrying some heavy books. On the way he sheepishly said: 'Last week I asked you how much your watch was. My teacher has just told us that we should not ask foreigners how much they pay for things. I'm sorry.' I was amazed by his courtesy. We then had what I hoped was a constructive discussion about when it was permissible to ask such a question without causing offence, and when it was not. He reflected a common earnestness to learn the 'right way' to interact with foreigners. Formally in class and informally outside, Jeanette and I were often drawn into similar conversations which were important to further mutual understanding and respect between our two cultures.

My previous experience with students was limited to talking to hand-picked ones on half-day excursions, while travelling on rushed two-week tours. Teaching students sitting in lines in sterile classrooms away from the glitz and excitement of the concert tours, was a very different situation. I had to change 'hats' from dancer-performer to teacher, though not stifling the performer in me to the extent that lessons became dull and lifeless. They could not learn English if the lessons were boring. I thanked God for the years of stage experience he had given me because they provided me with confidence, the ability to think on my feet and creativity to make up innovative exercises.

The students themselves turned the indifferent classrooms of concrete, glass and grey painted wood into rooms of industry, humour and communication between our two cultures. The warmth of the welcome at the start of each class, chatting during the breaks and the incurable giggling and questioning, somehow softened the harsh appearance of the surroundings. I quickly became less sensitive to the inadequacies of the facilities, as we all concentrated on the task at hand. That is, until I walked between the rows reading a book, and fell into a deep depression in the concrete floor. Jeanette said she once teetered on the edge of a hole, almost lost balance, then jumped lightly across it. 'You would have been impressed with my jeté, Belinda.' (A jeté is a leap in ballet.)

If, while standing between the rows, I looked tired or footsore, a nearby student would tell me to sit down on her stool and tell another to move over. I really appreciated these little touches of concern.

The physical setting in some ways hindered the learning process. But despite these numerous obstacles and a meagre one Oral class per week, I was amazed to reflect over the year, on the great improvement in the standard of Oral English in the English Department.

Each classroom was huge, scaled to seat over fifty people packed together, though thankfully, rarely used to capacity in my classes. The classrooms had louvered windows on two sides which did not close and allowed in noise from other classes, several construction sites in the College grounds, blasts from fire-crackers several times a day, sirens, people yelling and once, a pig screaming in its death throes. (We were near the dining rooms.) I developed powerful lungs after numerous difficulties using a radio microphone made me abandon the idea in frustration.

I wrote home: 'The cicadas are extremely noisy at present in response to the hot weather and so teaching is often difficult over the noise. Had a brilliant video class yesterday – between the cicadas chirping and the sound distortions on the tape, the students really learnt a lot.'

The students wanted me to stand in the middle of the front row when speaking to everyone, because it was the prime spot acoustically. I grieved that their hearing was not as sharp as it should have been for their young age. In Chinese society there is a staggering tolerance to noise. The sirens marking the times of the day, I'm sure can be heard in the next city. Speeches, karaoke music and live performances were almost always pumped out at a volume beyond what is needed or desirable. Nowhere did I find an understanding of the causal relationship between exposure to loud noise over a long period of time and deafness. One day I walked into the classroom set up with television for teaching by video. The students were snatching a look at a midday soap-opera before the start of class. They didn't notice me because it was at full volume. After motioning for silence, I gave them an uncompromising lecture about protecting their ears. I never heard such a volume of sound again.

Not only did their dulled hearing impair their ability to learn, but seeing the blackboard had its own problems as well. Sunlight turned the blackboard shiny, when viewed from the sides of the rooms, making reading from it difficult. Students moved their desks around as far as they could in order to see, but there were limitations. I wrote very large letters on the board but some still complained they could not be seen clearly from the back of the room. To complicate the situation, many of those with poor eyesight, were too shy to move down towards the front, even when bidden to, preferring the problem to the embarrassment of being singled out. They tolerated poor eyesight and the lack of glasses to an extraordinary degree and were tight-lipped about reasons why they were not buying glasses. Perhaps finance was an issue. They preferred swapping glasses with each other.

The common practice of dictating from the board, then sharing notes, was an attempt to circumvent these problems. Written notes developed a life of their own. My simple sentences underwent a mysterious metamorphosis as they flew from notebook to notebook while the student who could see the board, copied them down for students who could not. The more they were copied, the greater the mutation, until . . .

'NY is brought down by the Mississippi Created the M Dalta Every year the land floods, leaving largest harbour in the world.'

'Today cattlemen are in co-operative associations which decide how many sleep.'

That was a double muddle: a change from 'cattle' to 'sheep' to 'sleep'.

The most pickled pot-pourri of eloquent penmanship was: 'Thanksgiving Day is a riligion's day, it comes to a long time. In a city, there is always planting good crops, but one day, coming lots of the bad. The plants was growing dead, people had no ideas. Suddenly, a cloud of seagulfs came, they ate out the bad and help the farms out out of the hard. So people remember this day and thank for God.' Who knows?

The definition of an awning shows poor sight or note-taking: 'canvas covering (against rain or sun) for example a ship's deck or before door or widows.'

I encouraged individual note-taking, but was fighting a losing battle against copying each other's notes because of the poor facilities and these entrenched practises of studying which literally go back thousands of years.

It was so satisfying to gauge just how far the students progressed during the year. The textbook suggested pronunciation drills: 'beat, bet, bait'. These were valuable in some ways perhaps, but when I started yawning more than the students, I knew there had to be a better way. So I taught them Australian and translated Chinese poetry, more for pronunciation than for understanding of meaning (They looked up the meanings for homework.) They drilled me for the meanings of words they could not find in their dictionaries. The poems were much more interesting to us all. The pièce de résistance was learning 'Clancy of the Overflow'. Their improved diction amazed me as did the very tricky Oral comprehension on the life of A.B. 'Banjo' Patterson. There wasn't a prouder teacher at the college that day! They learnt the meaning of a giant pat on the back.

In each classroom, a large imposing desk was perched on a dais in front of the blackboard. From this position, commanding both the blackboard and the class, the teacher traditionally maintained control and taught the lesson. The class dynamics changed dramatically whenever I moved from the desk to anywhere else in the room. On the dais, I was accorded all respect and subservience by the students who sat docile and mutely fearful, staring up at me. On the other hand, in the aisles, the formal atmosphere was broken and they responded with the sentences, dialogues or whatever else, with much more alacrity.

Questions addressed to the class frequently went unanswered until I stepped off the dais and 'joined the ranks'. 'Do you understand?' I'd ask ad nauseum. Silence or a universal 'Yes' would greet me. If I asked the same question off the dais, I was more likely to get a truthful reply. While standing on the dais, it took months of repeated effort to get them to admit they did not understand. At last the day came, I asked the question from the dais and heard a faint voice say in quavering tones: 'I don't understand.' I nearly kissed her!

I learned that their silence came less from an ignorance of the right answers, and more from a reticence to speak. If they gave the wrong answers, they feared losing face in front of the others. I could well understand because I was reticent to speak Chinese in case I got it wrong. I might say something rude!

This reaction phenomenon to where I stood in the room was common to every class I taught, even the weekend classes. It was a remarkable demonstration of the power of body language and the influence of room design and furniture placement upon human behaviour. I wonder if Australians are less influenced by these considerations because we have a less rigid system of respect for authority, as expressed in body language. Also, my movements while teaching would have determined how the students came to perceive me over time. If I had chosen to remain characteristically standing stiffly at the front during each lesson, they would have thought of me as much more authoritarian than I really was. As a consequence, their reluctance to engage in verbal interaction would have retarded their language acquisition.

I chose another course, knowing from the American teacher's letters that behaviour problems would be minimal if I appeared only a mild authority figure. Sitting on chairs and tables, walking around the room, joking and getting each one to talk brought us closer and helped convince them that I was engaging with them in their struggles. The effort paid off. The days I saw closed up, scared students relax and giggle and pour out their own sentences, made all my sacrifices and homesickness worth the pain. When they realized that they need not be afraid of me, teasing and playful quips started coming out. Replying to the textbook question: 'What will you be doing tonight?' Sally grinned cheekily and said: 'I don't have anything to do tonight. There may be a good film on and perhaps Miss Belinda may invite me to her flat to watch it!' Cheeky. The Dean was not concerned with my behaviour.

I taught a lesson entitled 'Climbing Ayres Rock' after an article of the same name, which I hoped would be informative, stimulate conversation and writing and be a bit of fun as well. In the preamble to talking about what to wear on the climb – hiking boots, shorts, T-shirt and hat – I asked Jocelyn to draw a person on the board. I knew Jocelyn's fame as an artist because she had drawn a pretty 'welcome' picture for Jeanette's arrival.

In asking her to draw, I wanted to affirm her artistic abilities and encourage participation in the topic. Either I didn't explain myself clearly, or she didn't understand, but instead of a simple unadorned figure, the artist quickly added all sorts of features: a ball-gown with flamboyant puffed sleeves, diamond neck-lace and hair piled high upon her head. As this blackboard beauty took form, I dithered about how to carefully say 'That's not what I wanted,' without embarrassing her in front of her classmates. Students hate being singled out for a task at the best of times. Everyone had a good laugh, including our Rembrandt and I hope she was not too embarrassed, since she was such a quiet and shy person. Fortunately whenever the class laughed at a student, they were laughing 'with her' not 'at her'. It was their irrepressible sense of fun that spontaneously erupted, rather than a determined effort to humiliate the red-faced person.

They were trained to stand when spoken to by a teacher. I wondered if their slowness to rise to their feet indicated what they thought of the practice. Standing up was less common if I asked a question standing in the aisle. I yearned to lessen their humiliation at failing and hence losing face as much as possible. With horror I pondered what humiliating experiences must have happened in their young lives for them to be so afraid of being humiliated again. Unfortunately, most of my classes were in Oral English, so I had to open their mouths and hearts one way or another, in order for them to progress. Usually talkative people achieved the best results in learning Oral English; quiet ones by nature had to be very motivated to press on.

What I was dealing with was more than just their learning a skill. Improvement in language meant improvement in self-confidence and esteem. Encouragement did wonders for flagging egos and I gave it freely and reaped abundant harvests in return. Criticism in Chinese education seems more the norm than encouragement. These people needed to get some confidence. A crying need among the student body was for recognition of them as individuals, and belief in their ability to succeed in their studies and life in general. Separated from their families and friends and others to give them support, they seemed to be glad of any help, support and guidance that we or anyone else, could offer. Our hearts really went out to them. But there were so many people all wanting to be seen as 'special' and loved that we were constantly overwhelmed by the size of the need.

> *'Living every day, by a heart and a mind.*
> *With reasons better than feelings'.*

Possibly because of this yawning void in many lives, giving names to those without English names, always touched them deeply, perhaps because it was an occasion to be treated as an individual. In all my travels around China, I have never once found any reluctance or hesitation when I offered to give an English name to either student or older person.

In traditional Chinese society, maternal relatives were not part of the clan, so women lacked a family name or surname, being referred to instead as someone's daughter or wife. Their family names was gradually forgotten. Boys had three names: one was used exclusively at home; one denoted their generation in the clan; and the other was used in public. When males turned twenty-one, an adult name was also conferred. Which gender would have had the healthier sense of identity? (As I write this, on the radio a man is quoting horrific figures of female suicides around the world, commenting that there is a disproportionate number of deaths amongst Chinese women compared with women of other nationalities. One can only speculate what is the reason behind this strange and tragic phenomenon.)

The day of giving names at the start of College life was a memorable time of fun, laughing, teasing and bonding between teacher and student.

I wrote in a letter to my niece: 'Stephanie, today in class I had to give English names to almost all my students, whom I met for the first time . . . I named one girl Stephanie and explained that my niece was taller than me and says: "What's the weather like down there Shortie?" They were amazed that someone could possibly be taller than me and thought it very funny.

The class is named after my friends and family. My imagination was running thin towards the end because there are forty in the class.'

Giving a name is important for everyone because a name is important to the Lord. He taught me this concerning my name and through an experience in China.

Years before while in a city in Jiangsu province, I talked with a lively group of male university students who wanted my autograph. I asked this one and that one what their English names were, then came to two lads who didn't have English ones. I asked if they wanted me to give them names. 'Yes please,' they enthused. I stalled for time while I shot a quick prayer heavenward for inspiration, then named one David and the other Daniel. Suddenly, I couldn't sense what was happening around me, all my senses ceased to function. I was transported in time and space as the Lord powerfully impressed on my heart that he would use these men in mighty ways for the Kingdom in the future. I knew beyond a doubt that these lads would become in years ahead, leaders in a huge move of God over China. Overawed and a little shaken by what I experienced, I slowly came back into the present and saw and heard this jovial bunch laughing and teasing the lads about their new names. They hadn't noticed any change in my behaviour, but I knew that two lives would be changed dramatically when God said the time was right.

I knew they were in the right environment because within the hour, I met another lad who gave me an insight into what God was doing there. He talked about his philosophy studies. I asked if he believed all he read about existentialism. 'No, because actually I am a Christian.' I told him I was too. He broke out in a grin and said, 'That means you are my sister!' There were a number of others there that night who were Christians.

Roadblocks to Reform

'My topic is: "How to be a good teacher after graduation". ' I stifled a yawn because this was the third, or was it the fourth student to speak on this topic for the Oral examination? The sentiments of the first few sentences concerning reforming the education system sounded familiar to me. Then particular phrases and even words sounded like those used by previous students.

'In this way I want to become a competent and capable teacher.'

I said: 'This is sounding just like what other students talked about. Why don't you make up your own talk and not copy others?'

(Ignoring me) 'I must try to develop students' initiative.'

All year I had been encouraging, cajoling and even insisting that students think up their own topics to speak or write about. I did not want them to copy other classmates' ideas or copy verbatim out of books. (It is somewhat suspicious getting an almost flawless piece of work from a student who is usually at the lower end of the spectrum.) I had a degree of success at times and enjoyed original pieces written by students who understood that I was giving them permission to be as creative as they liked. My insistence on originality was not just for educational purposes, but to set them free from the treadmill of blindly reproducing other people's words and philosophies. Old habits die hard in China though and I had to give constant reminders to 'use *your* own imagination, not someone else's'.

'Students sit quietly and are spoon-fed teachings which they would never question,' said the English-language *China Daily* concerning the influence of Confucian thought on education. I admired the Chinese preference for learning language by rote: students could reproduce passages of any length almost word perfect. (I wish I could be that diligent with learning Mandarin.) After all, they were well-practised at learning Chinese characters by memorization, one at a time. But understanding what they were writing or speaking was another issue. Today, in the freer atmosphere of the classroom, Chinese teachers themselves complain that students are afraid to open their mouths. The next generation may not be so reticent since they are from one-child families. I had to be vigilant about asking them to explain words and concepts in their own way, otherwise they would regurgitate the written definition without enough comprehension.

Educationalists in China recognize the need for massive reforms to their teaching methods and my College was especially receptive to any innovations their foreign teachers wanted to introduce. A teacher-centred ('Chalk and Talk') method of teaching, though useful for past generations, has restrictions for what is required in today's world because it stifles individual initiative. So the argument goes. But introducing creative, interactive and student-centred teaching methods, though desirable, would be greatly hampered by the huge numbers of students. I heard budding teachers talk about classes in primary and secondary schools which had 40–50 students. These figures were for the top-ranked schools. Further down the scale, are schools with 60–70 students per class per teacher. Conditions are so cramped that some students must sit outside the classroom door. A shy, quiet student told me about her teaching practice at a school in a town, which was within the jurisdiction of the major provincial city. She had to teach English to a class of 82 students!

Another girl, also shy and unassuming chipped in: 'I had to teach a class with 86 students.' So, if these are the numbers in cities near major provincial centres, what numbers do schools have further out in poorer, rural areas? *China Daily* reported that 80,000 children were unable to go to school at all in Guangzhou because there were not enough schools to cope with the numbers of children. I will never complain about my classes of 40 students again.

One of my colleagues at the College commented that teacher-centred methods also put a lot of pressure on the teachers. Ruth, one of my former students is now teaching in a village school 30 kilometres from Guangzhou. She wrote: 'I not only teach English but also music, nature, PE, health. Luckily, my main spirit is put into teaching English as my headmaster told me that it's a main subject. I also teach different grades. I have 20 lessons a week . . . I feel that I have big pressure. Most of my students are good. But there are some naughty boys whom I teach English in Grade 5. They speak a lot in class and don't listen to (your) lesson. I must try my best to control them and (get them to) follow me.'

In a second letter she said: 'This term I teach more classes than last term as one of my colleagues left my school suddenly. I need to concentrate on my work. However, I also go to further study by my own. I bear everything with perseverance. In fact, the longer I teach, the tireder I feel. Though I try my best . . . I fail. Every day, I must criticise student's homework six times. I must have morning reading lesson every morning and have assistant lesson every afternoon. By this way, I hardly can breathe. I often need to deal with naughty students. It cost me much time.'

By contrast another former student wrote: 'the situation is very bad . . . now I only have eight periods every week, so I have plenty of free time . . . I still continue to study the business English.'

A teacher-centred method of education, where the students must be silent unless asked to stand and speak, is more practical though than a student-centred method. The latter naturally lends itself to small classes, plenty of space, availability of resources, moveable furniture and all the things in short supply in these large schools.

The reform of the education process is hampered in countless ways. Reform will not be uniform throughout China, but will start with the more favoured schools and spread to other schools as the population and conditions improve. My colleague at the College casually remarked that when he studied English at a prestigious foreign language college in Beijing, that his largest class had sixteen students in it. Needless to say, he is now an almost flawless English-speaker.

7

'Only education is high; all else is low.' – *Confucius*
— Education in China —

Traditional Chinese teaching urged people to seek explanations; consequently they excelled in science. The world has been richer for their inventions, such as the umbrella, wheelbarrow, kite, abacus, water clocks, sundials, magnetic compass and fireworks. They used waterwheels to drive mills and heavy hammers. They worked metal in bronze, iron, and steel and steel rudders on ships were used from the first century BC onwards. (They were not used in Europe until the twelfth century.) Paper was invented in AD 105 and printing on paper started 500 years later. The Chinese were the first to use paper money.

Traditional education

Education was necessary for boys wanting to join the civil service. Officials held great power in governing China. Some worked in Beijing, others in provinces which were divided into smaller districts and counties with lesser officials in charge. Mandarins were government officials who administered the laws of the land on a regional and district level. They were outsiders, assigned every three or four years to districts other than their home districts. They lived in large, multi-roomed homes in walled compounds with numerous servants and armed guards at the gates. Mandarins were not required to protect the people or intercede with the government on their behalf but to see they stayed peaceful and orderly, paid their taxes and performed public duties. Many over the centuries were capable individuals who devoted their lives to earnestly trying to improve the social and economic infrastructure of their districts. Most of the mandarins though, were more concerned with protecting their own reputations and positions, through emphasizing traditional attitudes and practices. As the local law enforcers they were investigator, prosecutor, judge and jury. The accused were thought of as guilty until proven innocent.[1]

> The son of the family was of supreme importance to his family . . . He was sent to a good school. The goal was for him to pass the examinations to become a mandarin, an official, which was the aspiration of most Chinese males at the time. Being an official brought power, and power brought money. Without power or money, no Chinese could feel safe from the depredations of officialdom or random violence. There had never been a proper legal

[1] Mente, B. De, *NTC's Dictionary of China's Cultural Code Words* (Illinios: Lincolnwood, USA, 1996) p. 134–5

system. Justice was arbitrary, and cruelty was both institutionalized and capricious. An official with power was
the law. Becoming a mandarin was the only way the child
of a non-noble family could escape this cycle of injustice
and fear.'[2]

The famous Chinese poet Bai Juyi illustrates this
parental emphasis on learning:

> For ten years I never left my books;
> I went up and won unmerited praise.
> My high place I do not much prize;
> The joy of my parents will first make me proud.
>
> (Untitled)

To become an official, a young man had first to pass
exams held every three years. The examination system
existed for 1400 years from the Tang dynasty (AD
618–906). Candidates who passed went on to take
provincial and then national exams. Candidates had
to learn all of the five classic Confucian books by
heart. Confucian teachings were used because they
were seen as the basis of good government and personal behaviour. In 124 BC the Imperial University
was set up to teach Confucianism to future government officials. (Confucius is the westernized name for
the teacher *Kong Qiu* who earned the title *Kongfusi* –
Great Master Kong. Ironically he didn't achieve his
goal of becoming an important court adviser but
his teachings were compiled by his followers.)

On the relationship between a ruler and his people,
Confucius taught that 'If you desire what is good the

[2] Chung, *Wild Swans*, p. 28

people will become good also. The character of the ruler is like the wind and the character of the common people is like the grass; and the grass bends in the direction of the wind.'[3]

The Confucian Golden Rules:

- Fathers show love for your sons. Sons, you show respect and humility in return.
- Older brothers look after your younger brothers. Younger brothers you must be humble before your older brothers.
- Husbands treat your wives with respect. Wives you must be obedient.
- Elders you must show consideration. Juniors you must show respect.
- Rulers you must be benevolent. Subjects you must be loyal.

Passing the exams did not guarantee a job – for every successful candidate 3,000 were disappointed. Less than one per cent of the Chinese population passed. A successful candidate still needed the support of a senior official, upon whom his career depended. In the fifteenth century, there were only 100,000 imperial civil servants in China.

In *China Men* the Chinese-American writer Maxine Hong Kingston mentions her father's (referred to as 'Ba Ba') attempt, when he was fourteen years old, at passing the qualifying test for the last imperial examination ever given in China.

---

[3] Bloomfield, R, *China: Tradition and Change*, (Auckland: Longman Paul Ltd., NZ, 1993) p. 11

'An official led Ba Ba to a cell, where he asked him to undress. The official looked over his naked body for notes written on the skin, combed through his long hair for hidden papers, cut open the seams and hems of his clothes.' He was kept in a cell until dawn, then was led to the testing room for the oral examination. 'Ba Ba stood with his face to the wall and his hands clasped behind him . . . He recited by heart from the Three Character Classics, the Five Classics and the Thirteen Classics by Confucius' disciples.'[4]

For three days he wrote essays and poems in different styles and types of calligraphy but, after the ordeal, scored only well enough to become a schoolteacher.

An advantage of the system was that for a few commoners there was an opportunity for upward social mobility without reference to wealth or birth. One Song dynasty (960–279) statesman argued that astronomy, law and political economy should be examined as well and criticized the dependence on memorization. To traditional education, mastery of the classics was more important than practical subjects. Philosophy was valued as the basis for a government career and poetry was deemed the most intellectually demanding and aesthetically rewarding endeavour.

---

[4] Mann, M, *Library of Nations: China* (Amsterdam: Time-Life Books, Holland, 1990) p. 77

Education in the modern era

> *'People are the most valuable resource.'*
> (Chinese Communist Party slogan 1950s)

The Chinese educational authorities have had to grapple with issues common to every country such as how much weight to give to instilling society's mores, and how much to learning work-related skills – cultural classics vis-à-vis technical subjects? In addition there are pertinent issues peculiar to China. How should resources be divided between urban and rural schools and universities, the poor and the wealthy, Party members' children and ordinary ones? How should curriculae be written? How much time should be allocated for political study versus academic study, and how much value placed on 'red' verses 'expert' advice, classroom learning and labour projects? The pendulum has swung to extremes in both directions since 1949 over many concerns. Education defined as 'both the transmission of cultural norms and expectations and as training in specific job-related skills' is an enormous undertaking for any society.[5]

The PRC in 1949 was faced with limited finances, a lack of trained teachers and the task of transforming many existing beliefs and practices. With such restraints, the party had to decide whether to provide education for the masses, as a basic standard, or invest heavily in a highly-trained elite. Tackling the teaching of history was a sensitive question. Totally to disregard

---

[5] Dreyer, *China's Political System*, p. 211

all tradition would leave the country without a national identity. How should tradition be blended with the emerging socialist culture?

Revamping the educational system involved rewriting textbooks so that the Communist Party, socialist ideology and Mao Zedong's thoughts were portrayed favourably and the evils of capitalism analysed. The value of collective behaviour was stressed from the earliest years onwards. A goal of providing schooling for all, including children from the poorest peasant families and factory workers, was set in motion. Adults could attend literacy lessons in their spare time. Normal schools were built to train more teachers. The strong Soviet influence in the system could be seen in the emphasis on mathematics, technology and science, both as pure subjects and as applied science in technical schools.

> '*Learning is as necessary to a nation as
> water to a fish*.' (Chinese proverb)

An important development was the revision and simplification of the Chinese language, making it easier to learn. The government encouraged the phonetic system Pinyin so as to standardize the pronunciation of characters in every province. It also pushed for the use of what Westerners call 'Mandarin' or the language of the official class. The Communist Party, in reaction to this official class, termed it *guoyu*, the national language, or *Putonghua*, meaning ordinary speech.

Writers of print media were urged to use characters from lists of frequently-used characters, in an effort to eliminate a vast number of complicated, but seldom-required characters. Some complicated characters comprising many strokes, were reduced to a few strokes. The standard for literacy was set at recognizing 1500 characters (for peasants) or 2000 (for workers and urbanites), to read newspapers and journals, keep simple accounts and write basic statements. The literacy rate of 25 per cent in 1949 more than doubled by 1955; an impressive achievement for a developing country.

The formal education system was divided into six years primary school, three years junior middle school (high school), three years senior middle school and six years of university. A variety of vocational schools were run under the tight supervision of the ministry of education in Beijing. Of concern during this early period, was the tendency of students to work so hard that they risked ruining their health, a reflection on the traditional Chinese stress on diligent study.

The Great Leap Forward aimed at broadening and levelling the educational system. In 1958 there was a massive increase in the number of children attending schools. Consequently there was a shortage of teachers and resources, and standards inevitably fell. People complained that education had become 'elitist' and 'bourgeois scientific objectivism' also came under fire. Some research projects were cancelled since their aims were considered too far from the nation's primary goal of improving productivity. Intellectuals were sent to the countryside to labour alongside peasants, in order to reduce the city dwellers' arrogance and to lessen the perceived divide between rural and urban areas.

According to Mao Zedong, writing on Education, 'The lowly are the most intelligent, the elite are the most ignorant. In the countryside the schools and colleges should be managed by the poor and middle peasants.'[6]

Schools were closed so people could concentrate on steel-making. Young people from peasant backgrounds were given preferential admission to colleges and the ideological part of courses was expanded. Education was geared to serve the interests of the working class and hence integrated with productive labour. Slogans of the time dictated that every student be both 'red' and 'expert'. But 'redness' was more highly regarded, resulting in academic standards falling as politics took prominent place in the curriculum.

Recognition of the disaster of the Great Leap Forward meant a return to the teaching standards of pre-1957, so academic excellence was again valued. Key schools were established, usually in urban centres, with better-trained teachers and resources, for the most promising students. By 1966 the country had over 116 million students in primary schools, and 14 million in high schools, compared to 24 million and one million respectively in 1949.

The debate on education during the Great Proletarian Cultural Revolution (1966–1976) revolved around the need to suppress bourgeois and feudal attitudes in the system, so that 'the revolutionary successor generation' could assume its role in the march towards Communism. One criticism of the education system was that children of poor peasant families had difficulty attending and continuing at school because

---

[6] Bloomfield, *China*, p. 14

the tuition fees were too high or the school too remote. Boarding fees were beyond the ability of parents. Age limits for each grade excluded late starters and expelled those who could not pass a subject within a certain time. A second criticism was that local circumstances were not included in educational policy-making. For example, vacations in tea-growing areas of Zhejiang were set according to a timetable planned to be in harmony with the differing needs of rice-growing areas in other provinces.

The examination system itself was criticized as was the course material for being too abstract, and placing too much importance on memorization rather than analysis. Students had little time to study the thoughts of Mao Zedong.

During the summer of 1966 small numbers of student groups, known as Red Guards, collected in Beijing. They attacked the 'Four Olds' – old ideas, customs, culture and habits. Mao lent them his full support, to the extent that by the last half of 1966 literally millions of students were travelling free of charge on trains, inciting political movements. Students, commanded to smash the old society, saw many teachers, educational administrators and researchers as exemplars of the old society and 'struggled against', humiliated, imprisoned, tortured or even executed them. Mao persecuted learned people, calling them the 'stinking ninth category'. Books bearing bourgeois thought were burnt. Many schools closed down and classes did not resume until 1968 and 1969.

When schools reopened, principals and other administrators were replaced by revolutionary

committees which reflected 'three-in-one' combina-
tions of 'revolutionary' teachers, students and local
representatives of workers or peasants. Students were
enrolled on the basis of recommendations, political cri-
teria and willingness to engage in productive labour for
several years before applying to a university. The
method again was biased towards the children of
cadres. Elementary schooling was shortened to five
years, junior and senior secondary schooling became
one four-year stretch, and university, three years. New
teaching methods and a simplified curriculum were
introduced. Illiterate but wise peasants were invited
to teach on growing crops and to assist in writing
textbooks, rather than to engage 'bourgeois expertise'.

Decentralization of education marked the Cultural
Revolution. Production brigades often ran primary
schools, and communes ran secondary schools in the
countryside. In city areas, street committees ran
primary schools and factories, secondary schools. The
advantages were that what was taught was relevant to
the economic realities of the area and tuition fees
could be abolished or adapted to the needs of the community, thus allowing more children to attend. The
curriculum integrated study with productive labour.
The examination system was replaced by tests, homework and an evaluation of the child's attitude toward
study and labour. The down-to-the-countryside
movement (*xiaxiang*) to combine students with peasants was stepped up but was greatly unpopular with
middle school graduates who found few opportunities
to escape to the city.

Universities began to reopen in 1970–2 and examinations were reinstated in 1972 when the government

realized how far academic standards had fallen. The tussle between 'reds' and 'experts' on educational matters continued for many years. A generation which would have assisted the modernization of China immensely was lost through the excesses of the Cultural Revolution.

Following the death of Mao Zedong in 1976, the arrest of the 'Gang of Four', and the ascendancy of Deng Xiaoping to power, educational policies and practices changed enormously. Deng Xiaoping's return ushered in dramatic changes to the education process, to assist in economic modernization; ideological goals were replaced by economic ones. Mathematics, science and foreign languages were elevated, political study and productive labour reduced. Intellectuals were once again given respect and importance, as was competition in schools and examinations. Old textbooks were revised and new ones produced. Teachers caught in the cross-fire of the Cultural Revolution were retrained and hundreds of foreign teachers recruited to lecture on developments in their fields.

Technical schools were opened. Ninety-eight of the 715 tertiary level educational institutions were designated *Key-point* that is, allowed priority in the choice of students and in resources, such as Beijing University and Guangzhou's Sun Yat Sen University. From kindergarten on, children were streamed into either ordinary or keypoint schools, resulting in little chance for a child from an ordinary school to enter a keypoint school later on. *Key-point* was also applied to some primary and secondary schools. Most were city schools, hence they excluded the 80 per cent of the school-age children who are from the countryside. The theory was that rural children would remain and participate in production in their hometowns. In urban areas, parents put tremendous pressure on their children to excel at school so that they would be accepted into college. Stiff competition engendered disillusionment amongst the ranks.

Some of these elitist policies have been phased out. Almost all middle schools now offer six years of education. Over 25 per cent of those sitting for the college entrance examination now pass. A modern form of elitism has arisen in the development of private schools for the children of the newly wealthy. The government made nine years of education compulsory for all students in 1985, though this ruling is not always policed at the local level. There are a variety of economic reasons for the excessive drop-out rate of school children, especially in country areas. The high number of dilapidated school buildings present dangers to children, especially during the wet season. Fujian province requested its counties and city districts not to build additional office buildings, auditoriums or hostels until their hazardous school properties had been renovated.

The drop-out rate also applies to teachers who often have to work under poor working conditions and with low pay. They would rather transfer to more promising business or administrative positions. The government has recognized these problems for teachers and has increased teachers' salaries in the past few years. Teachers now are concerned about the Government's policy change in 1998, from state-provided accommodation to home ownership. Many fear a huge percentage of their salaries will go into paying for accommodation in the future.

In urban areas, schools concentrate on preparing the brightest pupils for the demanding university entrance exams, resulting in average students being poorly catered for in the classroom. The state education commission has encouraged schools to cater equally for the needs of all the students rather than the top percentage.

Some work has been done to address these problems. Since 1989, Project Hope has enabled 540,000 rural dropouts to attend school. The number of dangerous classroom buildings has been reduced from 7.7 per cent to 2.66 per cent. Several provinces have devised plans to provide better housing for teachers and Sichuan brought in a new hotel tax to finance improvements in education.

'At the moment, the PRC is faced with a dilemma: An inadequate educational system is placing limits on economic development, while inadequate economic development sets limits on how much can be contributed to the advancement of education.'[7]

---

[7] Dreyer, *China's Political System*, p. 230

8

'You must tell us if you are going out'
— Security —

'Would you like to see a film tonight? It's in English,' Marilyn asked. I had only just met her that day in the first week, so I was a little surprised by the suddenness of her invitation. She suggested a male friend accompany us. As I was walking down Baby Alley to our rendezvous point later that evening, she suddenly jumped out at me from behind a leafy shrub. Our laughter stopped dead when Ramona appeared on the road.

'Where are you going?' she asked imperiously. Her face showed a mixture of concern and disapproval. I avoided a straight reply feeling almost as if I'd been caught smoking behind the shed at school. It wasn't any of her business I told myself. I was afraid of getting Marilyn into trouble and wrecking our friendship when it had barely started. We didn't stay talking to Ramona because I sensed a lecture was brewing. As we departed post-haste I felt like a child who had narrowly escaped a reprimand after a bout of naughtiness. The adult in me was annoyed at the implied restraint on my behaviour brought on by the questioning. After all we were only going to see a film in a theatre just down the road.

Marilyn wanted a male friend to accompany us. At the male quarters, Marilyn went through the gate without any hesitation. I queried if it was 'proper' to barge in on the hundreds of residents in the block. With a look of mild surprise, she said it was fine, perhaps puzzling why I asked such a question. Inside the gate, we crossed a wide quadrangle in front of the U-shaped building. The feeling of 'I shouldn't be here' started at the sight of men stripped to the waist washing under outdoor showers set into a wall. This feeling intensified as we climbed several flights of steps, passing rubbish and startled, quizzical looks from male students and now and then the smell of latrines wafting across our nostrils.

Marilyn made a few inquiries about her friend, but no-one knew his whereabouts. Disappointment made her reluctant to leave the premises; I couldn't wait to get out and resume my 'responsible teacher in control' mode outside the quadrangle.

> '*So it all begins, without an end*
> *You're out there walking the road.*'

The theatre was somewhat further away from the College than I had been led to believe; that didn't matter. My sense of adventure had returned at last, an exhilaration at being on my first reconnaissance trip down the streets of my adoptive city; a fledgling attempt to assimilate into the new community. It was so much better than just being on tour. The freedom was scary but exhilarating. We joined the throng of people in the hot, tropical air strolling fairly aimlessly amongst the street vendors plying their goods on the roads. Not many people were buying; window-shopping was more affordable. Marilyn took me to the most 'western-looking' shop, with prices to match. While I picked over piles of windcheaters and jeans on display, the shoppers looked at the main attraction of the evening – a strange person in their midst. I was pleased to sink at last into the anonymous darkness of the theatre.

The film was a 'teeny-bopper' romance from Hong Kong with English subtitles. The risqué bits brought on a repeat of the 'we shouldn't be here' feeling. The ending, the redeeming feature of the whole show, sparked thoughtful questions and observations from my escort on the way home. This was the first of many discussions about love and romance we were to have over the following months.

After the film, we met a pleasant Pakistani man who stopped to ask us a question about shopping. We all laughed that an English-speaking Chinese girl and her Australian teacher were speaking to an English-speaking Pakistani in a city in China! Meeting him felt both strange and comforting – holding out the vague possibility of further contacts with other English-speaking nationalities. I thanked God for mixing different people groups together and our ability to learn foreign languages in order to communicate cross-culturally.

The next day Ramona, having done her mental homework, declared to me that:

1. I shouldn't go out at night without telling the Department, and,
2. that the student I had been with the night before was definitely not in the English Department because Ramona knew everyone – all 460-odd – and she hadn't seen that girl.

The implication was that if she was an outsider by definition she was up to no good.

Fortunately I could play the innocent over her Chinese name and keep her out of trouble. I was quickly learning how things are run in the College. 'You must tell us if you are going out,' Mr Chen said in a fatherly fashion the same day. Ramona wouldn't have withheld any details of what she knew of the night escapade. The episode was a warning to me of how closely my behaviour was being monitored. Conversely I saw how much freedom, despite the monitoring, I actually had and how I should not entrust any confidential information to Ramona.

I giggled inwardly when I saw Marilyn in my first class, and remembered Ramona's certainty that she wasn't part of the English Department. In hindsight, I'm undecided whether I was foolish to go out with a total stranger or not. By seizing the opportunity I cemented a relationship for the future, at the same time as causing worry for those personally responsible for my behaviour. I wondered if they saw me as a borderline juvenile delinquent who must be watched and goaded to keep her on the straight and narrow. In my mind's eye I saw them fearing that their job might prove difficult in the months ahead.

One night Amanda, a friend from outside the College, rang me in great excitement saying that she had been given some tickets for the coming performance of a ballet company. A few days later her excitement turned to disappointment because plans had changed and she had to leave town for a couple of days and hence miss the performance. The ballet was to be a surprise for Jeanette when she arrived in China. Would I be able to get some teachers to go with us instead? Immediately two teachers jumped at the opportunity as ballets are an extremely rare occurrence in this part of the country. On the way to the theatre, the teachers tried their hardest to get me to divulge the identity of the benefactor. I politely skirted around an answer because I did not want any interference in this fledgling relationship nor were my friendships any of their business.

During the first three weeks I was at the College, the telephone rang constantly with both legitimate and bogus calls. Wanting to do the right thing and be polite in all circumstances, I answered each time. The illegitimate ones came at any time of the day, wrenching me out of bed in the early morning until any hour late at night. As soon as I'd answer, the caller would hang up without a word. I'd slam the receiver down. I was in a quandry: I didn't want to respond each time but I didn't want to alienate myself from the students or teachers. I suspected the FAO staff were keeping tabs on me, but had no way of checking. I told my classes about the strange calls and suggested that they visit me rather than ring.

My patience wore thin within the first week and resentment ate away my resolve to endure these games. One afternoon in the third week the telephone rang and the anonymous caller hung up as usual. I was absolutely furious. A minute later, George appeared at my gate.

'Did you just ring me and then hang up?' I said wagging a finger angrily at him through the gate.

Looking as startled as a lizard, he admitted his crime.

'*Don't you ever do that to me again! Do you hear?*'

'Um yes,' he said meekly.

He had rung this day, just to see if I was home to save himself a trip upstairs if I wasn't. He could have said he was coming up when I answered. The calls abruptly stopped.

It was a good thing there was a locked gate between George and me. It was good to feel power again over my circumstances and the multitude of people impinging every day on my 'quiet' life. The calls re-started, however, at odd times during the rest of our stay. We could never fathom what factors triggered this fluctuation in surveillance.

On one occasion the caller was one of my students

'Miss Belinda, I have a question to ask you. What is the meaning of the word "Democracy"? ' she asked innocently.

Tiananmen Square flashed through my surprised brain. I paused, believing there was a chance, given all the forms of surveillance around, that my phone could be bugged. I didn't want to launch into what might sound to the eavesdropper, like western pro-democracy rhetoric. One of Nehemiah's 'arrow' prayers brought inspiration. I gave her a dictionary definition and didn't elaborate much. Satisfied, she rang off.

An Australian girl living in Beijing once wanted to place a call to a city in another province. The operator said she couldn't. Was there something wrong with the line? No, the line was fine. The trouble was, the telephonist said, the recording equipment had broken down!

'If you're at a large school you'll become intimate with the Chinese concept of bureaucracy. At either sort of place you'll learn about the complex interplay between politics and expertise in China, between procedure and personality.'[1]

'The *danwei* (work unit) section directly responsible for foreigners at a school is the Foreign/External Affairs Office (FAO) – *waishi bangongshi*, or *waiban* for short . . . your waiban may be a single person assigned liaison duties, or a large office responsible for everything from preparing visa duties to hiring maids to swab the foreign toilets.

'Your waiban bears direct responsibility for you, suffers more than anyone else for your indiscretions, and wields great power over your daily life . . . many Westerners, unused to such control, come into conflict with their waiban . . . But most waibans . . . are reasonably professional, moderately materialistic, and hope to co-operate happily. Work from that base. Strive for cordiality with your waiban, if not warmth, and much happiness can be yours. Your friend the waiban can get

---

[1] Weiner, Murphy & Li, *Living in China*, p. 8

you theater tickets, be your guide and cultural interpreter
. . . Most waibans love to be asked for advice by 'their'
foreigners. By playing up to the Chinese system's pater-
nalistic tendencies you stand to gain . . . Avoid becoming
mortal enemies with your waiban. Your enemy the
waiban can move screaming babies to the room next to
yours, (order) workers to start construction projects by
your window . . . arrange the transfer of your favourite
teacher or refuse to extend your visa . . . troubles with
your waiban can taint your whole stay.'[2]

The College Foreign Affairs Office (FAO) staff ini-
tially comprised Mr Lu and George. They continued
as part of the English Department – teacher and senior
student and looked after the office part-time. From the
sight of the flat on the first night, I knew that my relationships in this area were going to be a struggle. How
to maintain a strong, caring Christian witness with
people who listened only when the 'ugly foreigner'
came out of me? There were endless numbers of
repairs to be done and hence lots of potential troubles
relating to the staff. Was the flat a reflection of their
attitude to me?

One glaring problem was their poor level of English, complicated further by their unfamiliarity with
the Australian accent. Printing what I wanted to say
and making lists of repairs proved more successful
than just speaking. I was particularly amazed at
George's below average grasp of the language. He had
been studying English at College for four years and
before that probably learnt written English for several

---

[2] Ibid., pp. 59–60

years at highschool. (Two years later George gained the role of Assistant to the College President.)

Once, Jeanette asked him to order a taxi to take her to a particular hotel. He thought she asked if he would take her shopping to buy some kites! To be fair, this happened soon after a couple of unsuccessful attempts at buying kites. In one such attempt, he had actually seconded the College car and driver for her convenience. So, he did try to do the right thing. Getting him to sit still long enough to fully understand what we were saying, was another matter.

We couldn't understand how he got the job of relating to English-speaking staff until we learned of his close connections with those who made the appointments. The qualification for the role was Party membership.

I saw at first hand a result of the system referred to in Australia as 'jobs for the boys'. Unfortunately, the person given the position is not necessarily the best qualified. To reduce potential problems, where we could, we enlisted the assistance of our enthusiastic fluently-speaking students, rather than the FAO staff. Knowing this unequal situation, made me double my efforts to improve their fluency. I prayed for opportunities in the future where their talents and hard work would be recognized by potential employers.

We tried to maintain a cordial relationship. Our struggles in relationships with the FAO left us constantly confused. When we couldn't induce any action after a reasonable request for assistance, we wondered what was going on. Was this lack of co-operation due to incompetence, laziness, poor communication or indeed a Communist plot against us because we were Australians? We seemed to be pawns not in a game where the rules were changing constantly but where the game itself changed with the wind, as the hidden game-plan of each opponent changed. At times, such as at dinners, they were friendly, courteous and we had some good laughs together. Co-operatively working on editing the odd English document was a pleasure. Sadly, if it wasn't for politics and China's unfortunate past history, we all would be laughing and chatting the rest of the time too, because there would be nothing between us to cause friction – no hidden responsibilities or agendas.

One night during the second semester, the phone rang while we were both in Jeanette's flat. I answered the call. Mr. Lu was angry because, according to him, I had arranged for a 'Bible' to be sent from Australia to the College, where it had been intercepted. Opening other people's parcels is not considered a crime. My name was not on the parcel, but he was positive that it was for me. Though upset by the severity of the interrogation, the Holy Spirit gave me a steady voice and clear thinking.

As the accusations heated up, I said: 'How do you know it has anything to do with me?'

'Because it came from Australia.'

His line of thinking was: the Bible came from Australia. Belinda is an Australian, therefore Belinda had it sent over.

'There are 18 million people in Australia – any one of them could have sent it.'

My inner prompting from the Holy Spirit was to deny everything and not open even a crack in my argument, whereby I could be incriminated. I was about to point out that logically if I wanted a Bible, I would have brought one from home. I didn't say it. With limited English, he could have taken what I said as an admission. It's rather ironic that the only time I found myself in real trouble, was for something that I hadn't done.

Whenever our problems with the FAO were not solved, we spoke to Mr. Chen who wielded enough power to unclog any impasse. (He became so used to my ringing during the 'fixing up the flat' era, that he once answered the phone with, 'What's wrong with the flat now?' He was a long-suffering man.

So, next morning, we poured out our troubles from the night before and added that our pay was late, we hadn't had many letters for two weeks and a stand/desk for my TV hadn't arrived. What game were they playing this time? Mr Chen saw it as a storm in a tea-cup, much to our relief. He even gave some new insight into the Government's poor view of bringing Bibles into the country. A day or two later, I arrived home after class to find a sheepish Mr Lu directing some male students to heave two low wooden cabinets up to our flats. Co-opted on their way to the Park, the reluctant lads bounced the cabinets off the walls as they progressed upstairs. Scratched and chipped, the cabinets nonetheless became symbolic of our victory over whatever forces of darkness tried to pull us down. Jeanette was given one too! We received our pay, and the 'Bible' which we requested to see the next day, never materialized. Perhaps it never existed. Was Mr Lu playing a game of 'let's catch the foreigners out' – but to what end?

The subject was not mentioned again by the FAO.

It was with mixed feelings that I met the Public Security Chief at the National Day banquet. It was a revelation to see face-to-face the man who pulled the strings to make the College FAO staff jump. He himself jumps at the direction of others above him, leading right back in the chain of command to Beijing. I wanted to be friendly. There was no point in getting on his bad side, but there was the impulse to say 'How dare you restrict me, keep tabs on me, don't you know I came here under great sacrifice, to help your country? The seven photos you have of me, does that mean seven people have files on me?' The less dramatic and self-pitying side of me replied: 'I know you're only doing your job; you're under orders too, can't help it. It's the culture after all; no privacy. I'm only here for a short time, you have to live here always.'

These conflicting roles of provider/protector/policeman of the authorities were most clearly spelled out in a conversation with Kathy.

Going shopping alone or going out anywhere alone was discouraged, but they could hardly stop us; not that we wanted to go far afield nor mix with nefarious people anyway. In second semester, Kathy arrived at my door on a day I had planned to go out shopping alone.

'Where are you going?' she asked, eyeing me curiously as I put on shoes and socks.

'Shopping.'

'Is Jeanette going with you?'

'No.'

'Are some students going with you?'

'No.'

'Do you want me to go with you?'

'No, don't worry, I'll be fine. Thanks anyway.'

The full import of what I proposed to do registered in a look of frozen horror on her face. She hesitated as though perhaps choosing her words for a lecture about being so foolhardy or preparing to read me the official edict from the Public Security Bureau concerning the movement of foreigners. But she caught herself mid-thought and bit her tongue. I was amazed that she still reacted this way after all our months of reconnaissance forays into the shopping districts. Secretly amused that I had 'won' my freedom, I also commiserated with her predicament. She was on friendly terms with us, but being part of the Foreign Affairs Office, was under orders to discourage such 'independence' in her charges – 'her foreigners'. The stress of this dilemma crossed her face in a second, graphically recounting the whole story of Chinese ambivalence towards foreigners throughout the centuries.

The Chinese are well used to being drawn into a system of spying on people. Keeping tabs on strangers and other irregularities is a practice that goes back into Chinese history much further than the Communist era. The *pao-chia*, or village headman, as early as 1741 onwards, had to keep records of the population growth in his village. Figures were recorded on the door placards of each household. He also reported on abnormal activities: burglary, gambling, harbouring criminals, illegal coinage, illicit sale of salt, gang activities or the presence of strangers.[3]

---

[3] Fairbank, J.K., Reischauer, E.O. and Craig, A.M., *East Asia: Tradition and Transformation* (London: Allen and Unwin Ltd., 1975, 2nd Edition) p. 241

We were trained in Australian cultural mores, ways of interpreting symbols and ways of doing things Aussie style. Going on short trips and reading a lot about China led me to believe somewhat naïvely that I had a degree of understanding of the culture. A few months as a resident burst my bubble about any such pretensions. Bafflement over the culture waxed and waned but never left us. Our limited ability to interpret the cultural symbols and Chinese behaviour caused us irritation and insecurity, but also made us dig deeper to unearth answers to our constant questions. We didn't know where the line was, over which we must not step, but thought if we inadvertently angered the authorities they would just send us home anyway.

In the meantime, we went ahead responding to directives the Holy Spirit gave us and left the consequences up to him. We ran the risk of being accused of going against our contract by praying for and with people and answering questions about biblical passages, but when needy people ask for ministry, what can one do but respond? It was tricky the night a lad, a total stranger, turned up at the flat asking if I had Bibles, while Lyla was there, talking to Jeanette. I edged him out onto the landing. Who knows how much she heard?

Surveillance was certainly stressful for us, but exciting nonetheless, and it was rather amusing that so much attention should be given to two very ordinary Australians. Yet ironically, we were treated like VIPs and showered with honour by the majority of people connected with us.

Ambivalence towards foreigners

The nation is in a dilemma concerning allowing foreigners into the Middle Kingdom. We are welcome to assist with reconstruction of the country but the Chinese have a backlog of negative feeling engendered by history and contact with the West. Modern Chinese must leap an historical and psychological hurdle in order to welcome us. They vividly remember the incursions 'barbarians' have made into their territory, trade and culture over the past centuries – and the ensuing bloodshed. They remember the humiliation that defeat in the Opium Wars brought the country with the shocking realization that their defences were not as strong as they had thought them to be. The Battle of Chuanbi which precipitated the First Opium War in 1839 (First Anglo-Chinese War) lasted only three quarters of an hour; the Chinese were easily beaten. Most Chinese consider 1839 as the beginning of their modern history, and their consciousness of the war remains acute. The war brought to a head centuries of both co-operation and tensions with foreign powers.

Paradoxically, humiliation also gave them a desire to learn and copy western technology and methods to further the country's development. In order to do this, they need to encourage Westerners across their borders for joint ventures, education and exchanges with counterparts in a multitude of fields. With people, come western ideas, habits, and ideologies, some of which run counter to Communist thinking and policy. Historical contact with foreigners, social influence, personal responsibility, traditional hospitality and protection, fear of theft and personal safety, all are factors which combine to result in tight surveillance of Westerners in China.

The local FAO/English Departments at the College were responsible for 'their foreigners'; so if an accident befell the foreigners or the law was broken, then these people were held accountable even if they had nothing to do directly with the situation. In extreme cases, theoretically, neglect of their 'personal responsibilities' might result in prison sentences. This policy may be the reason why foreigners may feel over-protected and cloistered by staff and students who exude tension concerning the guest's well-being and safety. One feels after a time of first rebelling against, and then getting used to such coddling, a welcome degree of security as well.

During the holidays I flew back to Australia because of my mother's illness. Jeanette was invited to the homes of various students who lived in other towns. The night before my departure, the Public Security Bureau refused her permission to travel outside the city because they said they couldn't guarantee her safety against Vietnamese bag-snatchers who had infiltrated China. Jeanette told a girl why she couldn't visit her town in the holidays.

She replied: 'But I'm sure if I explain to the men that you are my teacher, they will understand and give back your bag.'

Everyone warned us about the criminal element in the city. We didn't know how much were scare tactics and how much were realistic fears. They didn't want shopkeepers to cheat us and in every way wanted to show the best face of China. None of the dire predictions came true – possibly because we stood out in the crowd – no thief would be silly enough to try something on us surrounded as we always were, by so many staring people.

When crossing roads, our bevy of encircling body guards would suddenly grip our arms or hands or both and take charge. This caring attitude by the English Department was smothering perhaps, but we took comfort from the support as well.

The same policy of 'personal responsibility' extends to the care of equipment. Particular people can be held responsible for 'their' equipment, rather than the gear being seen as the joint property of the organization.

Laying aside considerations about safety, the Chinese culture has ingrained values of hospitality to visitors. Every detail of a guest's life must be looked after properly just as a Chinese guest would be. Daily activities are co-ordinated by a number of people.

Despite the troubles with the FAO, there were times when Mr Lu showed some understanding. 'Now you have enough room to dance in!' he said when talking about the lounge in the new flat he had redecorated for me.

Trying to communicate with home was a major hurdle. Letters run the risk of being tampered with and take two weeks to reach home on average. Our letters contained masses of 'sensitive information' from our families and friends like 'Guess which little bum-shuffle is walking now?' and 'The rabbit has had nine babies!' That last subject could have been inter-preted as highly suspect because in successive letters the numbers varied from four to nine (as more babies hidden by the mother in the backyard were discovered). Were the letters written in code? So faxes sent from the college were a welcome and faster alternative but enlisting the co-operation of the FAO was another thing. We were prepared to pay. They insisted on reading them – incoming and outgoing.

One day it was urgent that I should send a short fax quickly. I worked out my polite though firm strategy. They insisted on reading it, and an argument ensued. Mr Lu read it; I fumed. He dialled the telephone number, to see if anyone was home before sending the fax, then put me on the line. My niece answered. Seizing the better alternative to speak and not fax, I quickly told her to take down the message. I put down the receiver and fled the room in triumph. Jeanette dubbed the incident in the annals as 'Belinda's tantrum'. 'It wasn't a tantrum,' I protested, 'but it was close.'

Such tight surveillance is not a new phenomenon in China. Jung Chung in *Wild Swans* describes the 'containment' of her grandmother as a concubine, during which time her husband left her alone for six years.

'She was not the real mistress of her home, and she had to spend a great deal of her time buttering up the servants in case they invented stories against her – which was so common it was considered almost inevitable. She gave them plenty of presents, and also organised mah-jongg parties because the winners would always have to tip the servants generously . . . Throwing mah-jongg parties was a normal part of life for concubines all over China. So was smoking opium, which was widely available and was seen as a means of keeping people like her contented – by being doped – and dependent. Many concubines became addicted in their attempts to cope with their loneliness . . . Almost the only time she was allowed out of the house was to go to the opera, otherwise she had to sit at home all day, every day. She read a lot, mainly plays and novels, and tended her favourite flowers . . . Her other consolation in her gilded cage was a cat.'[4]

> '*I just want to give you the best*
> *And leave you with a love that never dies.*'

I walked into the classroom and put my books on the desk.

'Miss Belinda, may I make an announcement to the class?' asked the monitor.

'Yes certainly. What is it about?'

'The College President has banned the students from dating.'

I stood aghast as she read the message out in Chinese. The class listened, some giggled embarrassed, some became upset, the rest sat staring blankly and all had a look of acceptance, or was it powerlessness? I strove in my imagination to see the Chancellors of Sydney, Melbourne or Adelaide Universities making such a ban on their nineteen- or twenty-year-old fee-paying students.

A week or so later, dating came up in conversation with a man who, it transpired, had been given the delicate task of enforcing this edict.

'What will you do about it?' I asked.

---

[4] Chung, *Wild Swans*, p. 44

'I'll just tell the students to be careful so they don't get caught.'

His companion suggested: 'Sometimes girls get pregnant when this sort of thing happens.'

I shuddered to think of what might have precipitated this action by the President. I thought it over, trying to see every angle and point of view. Restricting access to friendships for adults, independent of their families, went against my grain. Jeanette brought me up short by saying, 'These students are a long way away from their parents. I suppose the President feels the weight of responsibility towards them like a parent does. He has to make decisions for their welfare; be it pleasant or bitter.' That's a point.

9

'Why don't you use chopsticks?'
— Cultural Differences —

'Zaijian.'

'Zaijian.'

I stepped from the brightness of the flat, stopped and stared at a strange sight. A patch of light flickered on the stairs as a pair of white shoes came down the steps towards me. High above the shoes, two lights about the width of a bamboo hat bobbed up and down in tandem.

'Ni hao'. Before I could find the words to reply, the lights disappeared downstairs, leaving me staring into darkness.

Anytime between seven and eight in the evening, the sound of a bell reverberating deafeningly around the buildings in the alley, signalled the arrival of the lady who would take away the day's garbage. I collected our bag of scraps and my torch and headed downstairs. The battery in my torch was running low and the light only feebly showed me the way down the dark steps. On the second floor a girl emerged from her flat, stood motionless in the dimness and stared at me for a long moment. I greeted her and continued walking.

In the alley, people were arriving with their bags and bins. I smiled at the lady with the unenviable task of shovelling the mess on to the wagon and carting it away. On the return journey upstairs, I wondered why the girl on the second floor had stared so. I was used to everyone staring at me, but not that intensely. Reaching the lighted flat, I laughed at the reason for her surprise. Wearing white runners, green pants and windcheater, with 'glow-in-the-dark' stars on the shoulder, all that she would have seen coming towards her in the blackness, were two white feet, two moving 'lights' in the air and a pool of faint light on the steps. The 'Ni hao' would have established that the apparition was in human form at least. All lingering thoughts she may have had that Westerners were strange people would have been locked into her mind forever. No wonder they call us 'foreigners' rather than 'Australians'.

Predictability

An Australian author mentioned that the Chinese accept the sight of a Westerner doing predictable things like swinging cameras and getting into tourist buses. They are amazed though by Westerners doing everyday chores like getting shoes repaired by someone on the roadside or buying a bunch of lychees. Having noted the reactions from passers-by who stopped in the street to stare at my strange behaviour while I conducted everyday transactions – I know there is some truth to the statement.

Unpredictability

'For many this is the first inkling of the vast unpredictability of life in China, which will soon extend to the availability of such sundries as electricity, water and transportation . . . Likewise, it is the rare teacher, foreign or Chinese, who can plan a semester's syllabus ahead. Who knows if textbooks will arrive or ditto machines work when they are needed? It may be unclear why you are at the school. The classes promised for you may not have been arranged. Your room may be without heat or electricity. The school may seem very honoured to have foreigners around, but may have done very little to prepare. Foreigners often become uneasy with this lack of predictability. With time, however, most come to see it as part of a larger pattern. How can anyone you depend on be predictable when the people they depend on are not? In time, you may become less predictable yourself.'

' "The nice thing is", points out . . . Jon Weston, "whatever you do here – getting lost, being delayed in travel, etc. – it is interesting and new. Sit back and treat it as a part of a plan." '[1]

'You come to my home to give English lesson to my students?'

---

[1] Weiner, Murphy, & Li, *Living in China*, pp. 7–8.

'You want an English lesson. What day do you want to have it?' I knew the answer.

'Today. You come now please?'

'No, I'm sorry not today.'

'But my students are waiting at my home.'

'No. I'm sorry. Please do not ring me early on a Sunday morning. This is my day off.'

'You won't come? My students will be very disappointed.'

'We can arrange another day.' The woman persisted, so did I.

Being woken early on a Sunday put me into a bad temper instantly so it was easy to refuse this request to provide a lesson – gratis – on my day off. I had dropped everything on another occasion to go to her home to teach her three gorgeous six-year-old girls. She had expected that I would continue to be spontaneously generous with my time and energy.

'Lots of people ask me for English classes,' I commented to a friend.

'Do they?' she asked surprised. Then it was my turn to be surprised by her ignorance of my predicament. In the first few months, being lonely, rather bored and fired with zeal for my challenging role, I accepted every request or demand for help which came thick and fast from students, teachers and strangers. After all, that was what I was in China for.

But I very quickly realized I was 'running on empty' – each request drained my emotional energy as I laboured to be understood in English (and they laboured to be understood by me). Resentment ate its insidious acid into my resolve to go the extra mile with each person who approached. Time and again I forgave those who inadvertently presumed upon my time, emotional energy and privacy. I was fast being worn down.

Fortunately the Lord's wisdom broke through the problem with the simple question:

'Did I call you to serve *everyone?* Who are you called to minister to?'

My mind was stunned by what my tired emotions had known for weeks. It was impossible to help every single person, obviously. I had to discern who were 'my flock' (students and significant others) and who were the authority figures over me. With everyone else, I could choose the degree of involvement I was prepared to give, instead of dancing to every tune everyone played. This defence mechanism sounded callous to my own heart, wanting to be all, and do all, for all who asked. But putting this attitude into practice lifted a great weight off my shoulders. A sense of more control over my life increased my emotional energy so that I could give more to 'my flock'. I began to feel happier. Around the time of this revelation the demands receded anyway, as the initial novelty of a new foreigner on campus wore off. Or had the Lord commanded the withdrawal after I had learnt the lesson?

My time on the catwalk

A severe bout of peculiar 'flu had lain me low for a few weeks. (I was still coughing when I returned home and had the last round of inoculations. The doctor cheerfully told me it might have been malaria.)

Reluctantly I went to the College clinic with Kathy. Walking home, we went into the 'flour shop' for a stock of tissues.

'Look there's a *guilo*.' Two middle-aged women stepped into the shop for a closer peek.

'Who is she?' they asked Kathy.

'She's a foreign teacher for the English Department.'

'Can she speak Chinese?'

'A little.'

I tried to ignore their inquisitiveness and continued to gather up the things I wanted to buy. I could understand the gist of what they were saying because Kathy spoke in Mandarin (*Putonghua*). Or had I heard the same questions umpteen times and knew what was coming next?

'Where does she come from?'

'Australia.'

'How long is she here for?'

'A year.'

All the time this was going on, the women stood staring in rapt attention at me. 'How to have a conversation without having a conversation.' I was the centre of attention but excluded from this Clayton's style of discussion.

'Look at her clothes. Did she buy them here or in Australia? How much did she pay for her blouse?' they asked fingering my blouse.

'Aren't they big buttons!' one said as she prodded each button down my front.

'Nice fabric.' Turning me around they exclaimed: 'There's buttons down the back too!'

I was amused that my green blouse which had entered my wardrobe's hall of fame because of its antiquity – I just couldn't bear to part with the faithful old thing – was seen as so stylish by these women, (ink-stain and all). They hadn't seen a blouse like that one before. Burning up with a high temperature and feeling weak, I didn't have the energy to do or say anything to change the situation, or even to get angry. I paid the shopkeeper and we walked out. Kathy had enough energy for both of us. 'Housewives! They've got nothing better to do with their time than gossip!'

> 'It was quite common,' the Empress' First Lady-in-Waiting said, 'for the foreign ladies to comment loudly upon the richness of dress of Court Ladies, and ladies-in-waiting, speculate on the probable price paid, and even to finger the rich materials, ignoring wearers of no account, while talking about the clothing in voluble asides to friends, who were just as interested, just as curious and just as inexpressibly rude.'[2]

As I got better at picking up the odd Chinese word or phrase and having learnt general information about the place, I could make educated guesses and join in the conversation. A reminder to those around me – people staring in the street – that I know some Chinese was helpful; to catch them out when they were talking about me dampened their enthusiasm to talk. I found

---

[2] Conger, S.P. 'Letters from China' 1909, quoted in Ling, *Princess Der 'Old Buddha'* (NY: Dodd, Mead, 1929, p. 231) quoted in Haldane, C., 'The Last Great Empress of China' (Constable 1965) quoted in Hibbert, C., *The Dragon Wakes – 1793–1911*, (Harmondsworth: Penguin, 1984) p. 392

it exceedingly irritating to be the centre of everyone's entertainment just by being there in the street.

The famed Chinese social critic Lu Xun (1881–1936) once wrote, 'Throughout the ages, we Chinese have had only two ways of looking at foreigners: either up to them as gods or down on them as beasts.'

Lu Xun may have exaggerated, but some of the attitudes he described still prevail. Foreigners in China live the best and worst of lives. Feted and made into buffoons, welcomed and kept at arm's length, they are both honoured individuals and pawns in the struggle of an ancient culture now both embracing and resisting westernization.

> 'Students and teachers feel these contradictions more keenly than most, for they enter into the deepest social relationship (teacher-student) in Chinese culture other than that of family. Yet they enter as outsiders. The cost is an experience as powerful in its joys as its frustrations. The prize is an understanding closer to the bone of Chinese life than any can claim, be they journalists, businesspeople or diplomats, who approach China only through official screens. Whether your time in China is a springboard to a career in Asia, an academic adventure, or just a lark, you are likely to find it an overwhelming experience which changes you, for better or worse, forever. Foreigners who have taught or studied in China tend to love or hate her. Neutrality is rare.'[3]

---

[3] Weiner, Murphy & Li, *Living in China*, p. 7.

Just before Christmas, a bright red invitation arrived asking us to attend an exhibition of works by a College art teacher. The delivery student said little about the contents of the invitation. Delighted to attend, we assumed we would just mingle with all the other art-lovers there and had no inkling that we would be expected to attend in any official capacity. A student escorted us to the show and directed us to a reception room where we met some of the teachers and dignitaries. After a time of chit-chat, we tagged along as everyone left the building. Outside were scores of mainly young people, presumably art students. The dignitaries milled around the entrance talking, then someone directed them into one long line. TV cameramen and photographers jumped out of nowhere. Our escort deserted Jeanette and me by disappearing silently into the crowd because he wasn't part of the official line-up. We thought we should quietly disappear too, believing we weren't part of it either. While we were trying to make our escape, one of the teachers spotted us, hurried over and coaxed us into position in the line. How embarrassing. No one had told us that we were going to join the official party at the opening ceremony. Now if we had been able to read the invitation . . .

Before I was given a VCR, I received a letter from home containing a suggestion that they send me a video of my parents' wedding anniversary to watch. I replied: 'Everything to do with us is everyone else's business. I bought a large cassette-player the other week with two students whom we didn't teach. One offered to carry it home for me because he had an appointment apparently at the College; we agreed and went on shopping. When we retrieved the player later that day, it was tied up in its box but the cord was out . . . The next day another student asked for his cassette tape back which he'd left in the player! Jeanette politely told him off for using my player without permission. I had words with said students the day after, but we're friends again. Do you get the idea that they have the idea What's mine is mine and what's yours is mine. So I think if others saw me watching a video in a classroom, even strangers, they'd just wander in and start watching too and ask a million questions and gossip. I even have people who join my classes without offering a word of explanation or asking if they may. If people stare at me through the windows of the classrooms, I go over to talk to them. They literally run away.'

Every day saw a minor collision of Chinese and western ideas. The results ranged from communication problems (which always sorted themselves out), amusing incidents, and an education for both parties. Just as Jeanette and I would grasp insight into the culture, the elusive butterfly of understanding would instantly flutter off on a distant tangent, leaving a trail of questions. There was no end of mutual bafflement as each side grappled with the implications of the other's culture. This sometimes rocky, but always fascinating, road is the only way to comprehension and mutual respect. Sweet were the times when 'Ahhh' and a toss of a head heralded a new understanding and the journey's end after one round of confusion.

One night some friends invited themselves to my flat, so I decided to make pancakes as a treat. They arrived just as I was stirring the mixture with a spoon.

'Why don't you use chopsticks?' Ramona asked quizzically.

I imagined myself still there at midnight trying to get the batter to the right consistency using a pair of chopsticks. Her expression showed confusion. A lifetime of Chinese culinary methods had enforced the notion in her that there was only one, not two ways of doing things. I saw the possibility of accidentally letting slip with a comment which could be easily misconstrued as an 'our western technology is superior' kind of attitude. I muttered a reply then changed the subject.

'Miss Belinda, I would like you to . . . talk, talk, talk'.

'Excuse me, to whom am I speaking?'

'Talk, talk, talk . . .'

'Yes, but are you one of my students or a teacher perhaps?'

'Talk, talk, talk . . .'

'Yes, but I can't help you if I don't know who you are!'

'Talk, talk, talk . . .'

'*What is your name?*'

I wanted to be polite, but that meant using roundabout ways of establishing the identity of the caller as well as complex English terminology which might not be readily understood. Often only by impolitely butting into the other person's flow of words and speaking directly would I get anywhere. The caller knew who he was and obviously knew me, but I had no idea who he was. This happened time and time again. No-one stopped to think that with almost 300 students, I might just have a little trouble recognizing the voice of one or two of them. My students laughed heartily when I re-enacted these conversations in class and quickly learnt to say:

'Hello Miss Belinda, this is . . . from your 95 Practical English class' or whatever.

Chinese history is littered with episodes of well-intentioned blunders due to misunderstandings about cultural norms.

'The first Portuguese explorers in China's waters accomplished little to prove Europe's cultural equality. In 1517 the Portuguese sent an embassy from the "King of Portugal" to the "King of China." On reaching Canton (Guangzhou) the mission fired a salute of cannon in proper Western style, which outraged the Chinese sense of etiquette and required an immediate apology.'[4]

With considerably more sensitivity to Chinese culture, Jesuit scholars of the same century became versed in Chinese culture, secured patronage of high officials and even gained court positions in Beijing. The most famous pioneer was Matteo Ricci (1552–1610). An Italian, tall and possessing a bell-like voice, he and his colleagues accommodated their message to the local scene. They took on Chinese identity as much as possible, such as wearing the

---

[4] Fairbank, Reischauer & Craig, *East Asia*, p. 244

robes of Chinese scholars and avoided all open connection with the Portuguese traders at Macao. Instead of preaching they learnt Mandarin, conversed with Chinese scholars about Chinese classic literature, and demonstrated prisms, clocks, and geographic knowledge.

Ricci was given an imperial stipend as a scholar. His successors applied their knowledge of astronomy to the revision of the Chinese calendar. The Son of Heaven was responsible to maintain a calendar which would accurately foretell the positions of the heavenly bodies and the timing of the seasons. Chinese astronomers had made an error of several hours in the prediction of an eclipse.

'The combination of Western science and Christian moral teaching attracted a number of outstanding converts, who were capable of collaborating in truly bicultural endeavours. The most famous convert was Hsu Kuang-ch'i . . . who became a Christian even before he passed the highest examination and entered the Hanlin Academy in 1604. With Ricci he completed the translation of the first six books of Euclid's geometry . . . He gave the missionaries an entree into high official circles and helped them to present Christianity through Chinese writings that had literary polish . . .

'During the middle decades of the long reign of K'ang-hsi the Jesuit mission at Peking (Beijing) reached the height of its influence. They once gave him . . . quinine, and were commissioned to survey and map the Chinese Empire using Western methods. Their position was that of courtiers to the emperor, performing the kowtow with complete servility like other officials, displaying knowledge with finesse, presenting gifts and making friends at court.'[5]

I carried around a vague sense of having failed daily in my efforts to understand, and assimilate into, the culture. The Chinese were so patient and forgiving of my constant toe-treading. Perhaps I wasn't that inept, but there was no way of knowing. The worst part in the assimilation process was being forcibly confronted with one's own imperfections; how far I was from the ideal person I wanted to be and way in which I wanted to relate to others. It was comforting to read about others' struggles adapting to a second culture with all its variable idiosyncrasies.

Dr Thomas Hale, a doctor working in Nepal wrote: 'Westerners working in developing countries learn many things about themselves they might never have discovered had they remained at home. The smoothly functioning wheels of Western civilization protect us from many of the grating encounters that are so common abroad and that so acutely test our character and spiritual resources . . . Our backgrounds, so oriented to convenience, do little to prepare us for the interminable delays, the unreliable transportation, the limited availability of so-called necessities and all the other challenges of living in a country like Nepal . . . They (new missionaries) have learned in theory at least, that the key to a successful ministry will lie in their ability to assimilate that culture and to free themselves from the attitudes and prejudices of their own. They have been warned about the inevitable feelings of superiority,

---

[5] Fairbank, Reischauer & Craig, *East Asia*, p. 246

paternalism, disdain, impatience and frustration that they are sure to experience and to which they previously may have considered themselves immune . . . In spite of (such preparation) I suspect that most missionaries during their first few years feel as we did – that they botched things up. Intensifying this feeling are friends back home who insist on setting them on a pedestal and making long excuses for their mistakes.'[6]

With time and education, I began to fit in better with everything around me and with the use of the odd word in Chinese, Chinese phraseology in English and deepening relationships with people, this feeling of 'botching things up' lessened and I felt more at home with my surroundings. It would be great to feel *really* part of the furniture – but that would be only after how many years?

I wrote in my diary: 'This morning I wanted to pray about the mid-autumn festival (early September) coming up on the weekend. This is when people appreciate the brilliance of the moon and sit outside to look at it. They also eat mooncakes. After warfaring, I read the passage in Ezra 8 about the people returning to Jerusalem from Persia and Ezra starting the process of re-instituting the proper worship of God. I was led onto the balcony and prayed in tongues for a long time, drinking in all sorts of details

---

[6] Hale, Dr. T., *Don't let the Goats eat the Loquat Trees* (Grand Rapids: Zondervan Publishing House, USA, 1986) pp. 65–6

of the surrounding area. It's a fabulous view. The Lord drew my attention to the state of the farms below. Only some of the land was cultivated, the rest was overgrown with glory-vine or something like that and many useful plants had been taken over by the vine. The Lord said that this was the state of the church in this city: a vibrant church had been choked by evil and many people had backslidden. I prayed that this weekend, as attention is drawn to spiritual matters, that many people would turn back to the Lord. Around each of the farms were brick walls – some had been broken down. Perhaps our work in prayer during our time here is to stand in the gap and be builders of walls.'

'Your Christmas is like our Spring Festival'

The first tangible indication Christmas was on its way came via a present from my family. Out of the hazy blue, floated a tiny scrap of paper from the post office informing us that a parcel was awaiting collection NOW. We knew that NOW meant NOW, otherwise we would incur the wrath (or pecuniary tendencies) of this august arm of the State bureaucracy and have to pay a 'fine'. The paper didn't reveal who the happy beneficiary was to be, so I snatched both our ID cards, money and a willing student, and headed for the post office. A taxi dropped us outside and we joined the bustling throng in front of the counter. The standard three yuan fee released a big Australia Post carton. My stomach leapt for joy when I saw peeping through the slit made by the Customs Inspectors, tinned tuna and fruit in jelly and packets of sauces – *cheese* sauces no less! I couldn't wait to get home to see what other delights my thoughtful family had sent. In delectable delight Jeanette and I mulled for a long time devising a scheme to ration the groceries over the remaining months in China. The sauces were welcome to spice up our vegetarian diet.

In the library, I was delighted to find a highly condensed version of Charles Dickens *A Christmas Carol* produced by a western publisher. For a few weeks leading up to Christmas, I read it to an Oral English class in the last ten minutes of each lesson. They sat motionless and silent as the descriptions of Scrooge and the formidable ghosts marched off the pages of this great piece of literature. Better still, they understood the gist of the action and Dickens would have been pleased that they readily agreed with the story's sentiments.

I told a class that we were given three days off work to celebrate the occasion. Whenever I wanted the message to sink in to everyone, I spoke it as well as wrote it on the board. Cheering broke out at the announcement. As a joke I added:

'So this means that the next class after Christmas will be four hours long to make up the lost class!'

'Surely you are pulling our leg, Miss Belinda?'

'Oh yes of course I am.' I thought nothing more of it.

As I climbed the stairs to my first lesson with them after Christmas, I became enveloped by some of this class.

'Are we really going to have a four-hour class today?'

'Oh yes,' I said unthinking. The students trudged up the steps in silence. In class they were responsive but in a slow, 'we must do this because our teacher says we must' kind of way.

'What is the matter with you all today, you're all so quiet?'

Silence. Then the spokesman for the class slowly stood up.

'Miss Belinda, are we really going to have a four-hour class today?'

'Oh, of course not. Did you think I was serious? Of course I wouldn't do that to you.'

There were cheers from everyone, and I understood the moral of the story – don't joke with a class about important matters like missing out on dinner! More seriously, I learnt the sad lesson that the trust between us could be disrupted at any time by the sobering fact that they were so used to unpredictable things happening to them, some most unfair, that they would believe anything. Even faith in the good intentions of their teacher could be shattered in a moment. Australians are incurable jokers and our sense of humour does not carry cross-culturally at all, so it was best to resist the urge to tease them.

Christmas captured the imagination of people around us. They saw the decorations cheering up the city and were hooked into the 'Santa Claus mentality'. They equated the festival only with eating lots of delicious food and spending time with family. Some tried to identify with the occasion by saying that it was like their Spring Festival. I balked at that, feeling sad that they didn't understand the reason for the season. Beyond the tinsel, there was a deeper curiosity or yearning to be met; a deeper need that wanted to be filled. This was evident in the frequent question at

English Corner: 'What do you do on Christmas Day in your country?' I went through the routine, including going to church, and without fail, the next question wasn't about food or family but about church. I had to be careful at such a public gathering because what I said could have easily been misconstrued as proselytising. English Corner is not the place to preach. So I kept my answers, though informative, light and personal, rather than directional for their lives. They soaked in all the insights.

There was also a steady stream of students excitedly giving us cards and gifts. Some were presented from individuals or groups of friends and others came from whole classes. I was touched that they wanted to spend what little money they had, on us. They had cemented the concept of 'ownership' of both of us firmly in their minds, even though only forty of them were taught by both of us. Cards were often to both or we each received one from the same person. One lass made cards by laminating autumn leaves to create a stained-glass window effect. We hung them on string from every fixture in the lounge and the overflow fluttered on the walkway windows.

The neighbours knew we had been given some Christmas cards.

Inquisitive as ever, visitors peered at our cards from Australian friends.

'The cards are taped up. I can't read them.'

'Yes I know.' I felt mean sealing them, but some contained letters talking about the Lord, our ministry in China or were very personal in content and I didn't want the messages relayed through the gossip lines or to FAO people to accuse us of going against our contract. '*Party B shall respect China's religious policy and shall not conduct activities incompatible with the status of an expert.*' I regretted not including in my circular to friends information about what *not* to write and that they should refrain from writing a letter on greeting cards.

> '*So you're lonely, but not ever alone.
> It's only for a while.*'

An Australian Christmas Day conjures the tastes and aromas of plump roast turkey, ham on the bone, plum pudding (with our genuine threepences and sixpences) topped with a brandy custard and Christmas cake as rich as the pudding. Australians question the wisdom of cooking traditional British fare in the often blazing heat of December, but the custom shows little chance of modifying at least in our family.

Christmas is a time of sending season's greetings to friends and relatives and feeling afresh the poignancy of enormous distances between oneself and loved ones interstate and overseas. Celebrating Jesus' wonderful birth with the family in church services and feasting reminds me of the precious value of others' lives and how precious and imperative the gospel message is to all mankind.

With all this in mind, Jeanette and I approached Christmas with mixed emotions. I wrote home courageously: 'Don't worry about us at Christmas because I'm sure we'll be blessed in a different way even without our loved ones near us.' The honest truth was, we feared that missing our large, rowdy families would escalate into bouts of tearfulness on the Day. We were used to making Christmas Day big, bright and bouncy for our 'hungry hordes'. How do we do that, in a foreign country – for two?

The Chinese love every opportunity in life to celebrate and the teachers and students slipped right into the Christmas spirit weeks before, with frequent cheerful pronouncements like, 'We're going to give you a present.' The size, shape and number of proposed presents and activities changed every couple of days, as ideas excitedly passed between all those eager to do their best to make us feel loved and special on this important occasion. Their thoughtfulness was truly overwhelming. Jeanette and I secretly thought: 'A silk scarf would be lovely.' Ever practical and envisioning weighty presents, we thought of the trouble of bringing luggage home. To our consternation senior teachers quipped: 'Last year we gave the foreign teachers a turkey – a live one! They didn't know what to do with it. It ran all over the flat. So funny.'

During Christmas week we heard puffing and panting at the gate. Some muscular lads had struggled all the way up the steps with a perfectly-shaped conical pine-tree vigorously growing in an exceedingly heavy pot. The tree was about 180 centimetres high.

'Take the tree inside,' reverberated around the buildings from a teacher standing on a balcony across the alley. Speechless for a moment at the sheer size and generosity of the gift, we hesitated as the lads gathered strength for another move of their cumbersome burden.

'Take the tree inside.' After a quick conference about the size of our little lounge-room relative to the size of the tree, we said to the boys: 'No don't put it inside, leave it here.' They were relieved.

'*Take The Tree Inside!*'

'No we want it left here.' Our lungs weren't as well-trained in the art of balcony-yelling as the teacher's were.

'*Take it inside now.*'

'No, *we don't have enough room inside. It looks lovely here. Everyone can see it.*' The lads had been looking one to the other, like spectators at a ping pong match, not knowing which one to obey. After a few protestations and gesticulations; pointing of fingers and flapping of arms, the teacher finally understood our drift.

'*Leave it there,*' he said.

Our last lung-full expired with a show of our profuse appreciation.

The neighbours knew we had a Christmas tree.

Overjoyed, we set about thinking how to decorate it. In the lead up to Christmas, various people had given us gifts of small, tasty mandarins. These, as well as toffees, Jeanette tied on to the tree with lengths of wool. The neighbourhood children loved to pick them off the tree when they came to visit and also clandestinely, reached through the gate to get them. We bought several metres of silvery wrapping paper and some of the girls enjoyed cutting them into decorations. Jeanette taught us how to make angels.

The generosity of the English Department knew no bounds. On Christmas Eve, Mr Chen, a number of teachers and the FAO staff put on a party for us – at our flat. They arrived bearing cartons of apples and oranges, party delicacies, and a chicken was put in the fridge. Swirls and curly-cues of cream in pastel colours danced all over a cake and Santa Claus grinned from the top of it.

At a loss to know how to cook party fare without the necessary ingredients, Jeanette had settled on making some peanut brittle. We thought we'd be able to buy rice paper to set the mixture on to, but to no avail. So she used writing paper instead, which left a soggy residue in the mouth. The teachers didn't eat much of it. Perhaps we didn't press them enough times to eat. Chinese people accept food and drink only after a number of offers.

The night was filled with singing and dancing in our cramped little quarters, not that the teachers minded, they had a great time. They graciously gave us each a heavy jade carving mounted on a piece of polished wood. We were truly touched by such expensive offerings. In the midst of all the singing and laughter, I heard the phone ring. To my surprise a Chinese friend of three years standing from Jiangsu Province was on the line. We chatted away for a long time, through the din of the revelry. At an early hour, by Australian standards, all the party goers departed en masse.

The neighbours knew we had had a party.

Next morning we awoke prematurely to the strident cacophony of leaden sledgehammers crashing into the walls of two or three flats below. Everything vibrated with the impact. Jeanette and I were bewildered by the poor timing of the 'renovations'. Why did they have to crack up cement anyway? We dared not even ask the obvious question: how long will we have to put up with this?

'I've looked at the chicken. It's still got the head and legs on,' Jeanette yelled. I could see we were soon going to be in tears, so while Jeanette wasn't looking, I gingerly unwrapped the fowl. There it was, plucked but intact. Before I could become squeamish, I grabbed the sharpest knife, closed my eyes and hacked off the neck and legs. The next problem was how to make stuffing without adequate quantities of breadcrumbs. Jeanette made an ingenious concoction including cooked rice, oranges and cashews. Our nerves were well and truly jangling because of the noise by the time we sat down to eat the cooked chicken and vegetables. Photos of our dinner together betrayed our brittle attempt at Christmas cheer.

In the hamper were individual plum puddings and packets of custards. We savoured every morsel – they tasted all the better knowing the love and sacrifice which went into sending them. The puddings and custards were the best Christmas present any ex-patriate could get. They made me miss my family even more and I fought back the temptation to imagine them going to church together, eating a fine dinner and playing games in the afternoon, or as my nieces invariably remark, their dads going to sleep!

With no chance for a siesta after dinner, we sat on the balcony and knitted and cross-stitched. The racket was not as loud outside as it was inside, so gradually we began to relax and our natural good humour made a comeback. The substantial cake which promised to be much too rich with all the cream, was very delicious – in small slices.

For the first time in my life I collected mail on Christmas Day. On the way as I walked between groups of students strolling along, I had an odd 'impression' (or was it a vision?) of them being locked away in glass cages of deception against the truth of the gospel. Their impassive faces staring at me were blinded from seeing the light of truth. The cage was a formidable barrier between them and me. Their slow steps were moving them closer to an unseen and sinister destiny. By the time I arrived home I was almost in tears, moved by the reality that countless millions of Chinese were going to hell because they hadn't an opportunity to hear or respond to the Word of Life. It is so tragic that the day set aside to celebrate what ushered in the greatest events in man's history, is just another working day in the Chinese calendar.

I was aware at this season that the basis of traditional Chinese life was a belief in harmony and balance. It affected the food people chose to eat, times at which they did things and the way they planned their buildings. Mr. Chen explained the concept of harmony between people. When problems were brewing, he said, it was important for one party to do all they could to be good to, and therefore placate, the other party in order to avoid further difficulties. I saw the merit in this thinking and we appreciated his exertions in living up to this notion. This custom contrasts with the western notion of 'talking the problem out'.

The Chinese belief in harmony between people is linked to a belief that every place had its own natural spirits. Some spirits dwelt in the mountains, rivers, rain, wind – others were around the house – in the stove, the well and vegetable garden. People tried to keep on good terms with the spirits and sometimes honoured them with gifts and included them in feasts and rituals. They believed the souls of the dead returned just as the caterpillar of the silk moth changed its form during the insect's life cycle. Many accepted the Buddhist idea of rebirth.

We did not have any visitors over Christmas because Jeanette told the English Department that we wanted a quiet Christmas together. Our contract stated that we were entitled to three days off per year to celebrate Australian public holidays. Mr. Chen insisted we take all three days off together. He said he would get into trouble with the College President if we took them at three different times during the year. With the hammering going on, we might as well have gone back to class on Boxing Day rather than endure three days of hammering. We decided to take our mail (and Jeanette's gift of a huge block of Australian chocolate) into the park. It was a welcome surprise to find a quiet nook under a tree without people standing, staring at us, while we were reading and munching. We also visited the art exhibition at the museum. Without the jostling of the crowds on opening day, we appreciated what the artist was trying to convey, especially in the oil paintings of the fisher-people. They offered a 'window to the soul' of a fishing community, bearing the labours of this demanding occupation, and surviving in this oft-times troubled society.

10

'You are barbarians!'
— Historical Look at China's Conflicts with the West —

Shock waves reverberated throughout Chinese society as a consequence of the Opium Wars (a series of clashes with Britain and France between 1839 and 1860). The wars brought into question the notion of the superiority of Chinese culture. As a result of their history, in the hearts of the people, are mixed feelings about their own country. They are exceedingly proud of being Chinese and the progress achieved in reconstruction since 1949. However, at the same time, they emphasize how far 'behind' China is and how superior in their opinion, western nations are in comparison, especially in technology. One can't help but be amazed at their massive accomplishments in reconstruction, given the wars, civil disturbances, natural disasters and political turmoil of this century.

Contact with the West

The Chinese knowledge of western countries and their inhabitants remained sketchy and full of misunderstandings during the Ming (1368–1644) and Qing (1644–1911) Dynasties. The lore of Ming times when Europeans first set foot in China and Cheng Ho sailed to the west, was copied, errors and all, and presented as 'accurate' information concerning the much later Europeans of 1800.

> 'In the Kwangtung provincial gazetteer, edited under Juan Yuan in 1819–22, the account of the Spaniards in the Philippines was sandwiched in between Quilon (in southern India) and the Moluccas, and dealt with the Ming period only. Portugal was stated to be near Malacca. England was another name for Holland, or alternatively a dependency of Holland. France was originally Buddhist, and later became Catholic (it had become a common belief in China that Christianity was an offshoot of Buddhism). Finally, France was said to be the same as Portugal. One is left with the impression that the scholars were not interested in learning about the West.[1]

'You are barbarians, you are not fit to trade with the mighty Chinese people!'

This was the Emperor's dramatic response to the Portuguese penchant for brawling, drunkenness and disrespect for Chinese customs and laws, following the arrival of their ships *c*. 1514–16. Expelled from Canton (Guangzhou), it wasn't until mid-century that they were allowed to officially settle permanently in Macao. The bad behaviour of the Portuguese retarded the efforts of subsequent Spaniards, Dutch, English and Russians to make contacts in China. The first

---

[1] Fairbank, Reischauer & Craig, *East Asia*, p. 448.

English ship appeared in 1626. In 1637 Captain Weddell, a merchant venturer imposed his will on officials at Guangzhou by bombarding the Bogue Forts guarding the Pearl River (*Zhujiang*) estuary. Towards the end of the next century, the English began to trade in the only permissible port, Guangzhou. During the next sixty years the Anglo-Chinese trade gradually became institutionalized into 'the Canton System'. The traders were permitted to do business only through the 'Cohong', a guild of powerful Chinese merchants whose primary duty was dealing with foreign trade, mainly in tea and silk.

British commerce with China was based on their experience in India. The British East India Company (BEIC) was a private association with extensive capital resources. By its royal charter, it acquired expansive governmental powers abroad and in some regions monopolized the national trade. It built armed outposts, navies and cargo fleets and exercised jurisdiction. As both a merchant company and a governing body, the BEIC ruled in India until 1858. A triangular trade between England, India and China began in response to the British public's demand for tea. The eighteenth-century tea trade became a huge investment for both sides and stimulated further developments: the British attempted to monopolize it at home and to finance it through trade between India and China, and the Qing court attempted to regulate it at Guangzhou and profit from it at Beijing. Concurrent with European enterprises, were those of the Chinese merchants who plied their trade throughout Southeast Asia. Westerners merely moved into the business channels already developed by these merchants.

The movement of Europeans in Guangzhou was restricted to the 'Thirteen Factories' along the Pearl River. They were not permitted to enter the city proper, and Chinese people were forbidden to teach them to speak the language, although this law was relaxed over time. They communicated in a trade Pidgin-English comprising Portuguese and English, but using the Cantonese word order. Once the tea crop had been shipped downriver, the westerners had to return to their villas at the Portuguese settlement of Macao, where their families were required to remain year-round. Some however, were happy with this connubial arrangement:

'George Chinnery (a renowned painter and somewhat of a character of his time) claimed that he had chosen to live in Macao because of its proximity to Canton, where no women were ever allowed. He had had the misfortune to marry a wife whom he described as "the ugliest woman I ever saw in my life." Whenever his wife threatened to join him (from Calcutta) in Macao he fled to Canton, exclaiming once on his arrival there, "Now I am all right. What a kind providence is this Chinese Government that it forbids the softer sex from coming and bothering us. What an admirable arrangement is it not?" '[2]

---

[2] Yorke, G.J., 'The Princely House, A Manuscript History of The Early Years of Jardine, Matheson & Co. in China' MS. 23 in 'Jardine, Matheson & Co. An Historical Sketch' (Privately printed by Jardine, Matheson & Co.) quoted in Hibbert, *The Dragon Wakes*, p. 375.

The British had few civil rights. They were horrified by the severe Chinese laws to which they were subject, especially the punishment by execution of anyone causing the accidental death of a Chinese person. There were many disputes over the administration of justice. These restrictions greatly irritated the Europeans who preferred to have their own representatives in Beijing rather than to deal with the Cohong. The British requested trading privileges, but in the face of Chinese opposition, merchants continued to harass their own government into more trading concessions from the Qing government.

Private enterprise, the 'Country Trade' that existed in India, was later extended to China. British entrepreneurs from the 1780's onwards became nominal representatives of other European governments in order to control the BEIC. This became an established custom. James Matheson, for instance, was Danish consul and Thomas Dent was Sardinian consul. Dent, Matheson and other 'private English' at Guangzhou acquired fleets, formed insurance companies and carried on banking operations. These private traders were friends and relatives of merchants in agency houses in India. These houses in turn, like those at Guangzhou, dealt in London – the hub of Britain's world-wide economic expansion. Similar growth of commercial interests occurred on the Chinese side. Guangzhou was the outlet for silk and cotton textiles, produced by handicraft industries on farms in the south. China benefited from the introduction of maize, sweet potatoes, peanuts and tobacco. Cotton textiles were made from raw cotton imported from India, called 'nankeens' (named after Nanking), the centre of this industry. The main market for textiles remained the Chinese domestic, rather than export, market. Tea and silk consignments came from Central China. The 'Canton trade' became important as a centre of growth in the accumulation of capital, the creation of commercial mechanisms and an articulate commercial interest; all of which became vitally relevant to Chinese policy considerations.

Decline of Manchu (Qing) government

During these centuries of trading with western powers, albeit at arms length, the Qing government had extremely serious internal problems that threatened the stability of the whole nation. The previous (early Ming) period saw peace and prosperity for the populace. Later emperors though, were isolated from their subjects' needs because of elaborate court etiquette and custom. The Qing dynasty was Manchu (from Manchuria, *Dongbei*). They ruled 550 million Chinese though they themselves numbered only 10 million. Manchus enjoyed special privileges such as their holding half the civil service posts. Even if Chinese candidates passed the examinations, there was no guarantee they would be granted a position because bribery to secure placement was rife amongst court officials.

The land was feeling the pressure of the increased population. The blame for government corruption and inefficiency was placed on the shoulders of the Emperor's advisors, by peasants who frequently rebelled.

An example of the extent of corruption in the court is shown by the official, close to the ear of the Qianlong Emperor, He Shen. His personal fortune, gained from corruption and extortion, was confiscated after the Emperor died in 1799, and was estimated at 800 million taels (ounces of silver) when the annual revenue of the whole empire was only about 40 million!

Added to this, nomadic tribes raided the country, especially in Manchuria. The Manchus were blamed for serious natural disasters too. These were taken as portents that Heaven was displeased with the emperor's rule. In 1887 when the Yellow River (*Huang He*) overflowed, killing 900,000 people, astrologers predicted the fall of the Qing dynasty.

Unbelievably, the Manchus refused to concede that reform was desperately needed.

Qing administration in every aspect had become less effective at a crucial time when internal problems were increasing. These two developments produced a downward spiral, of the kind Chinese history had so often seen before. This time, because of new factors from abroad, the process was to culminate in the nineteenth and early twentieth century in an unprecedented crisis for the traditional system of government and society. The Industrial Revolution had created enormous changes in the European economy. Markets in other countries for manufactured products needed to be found in order to maintain economic growth. As China was mainly an agrarian society, the traditional attitude towards trade was one of contempt.

In 1793 King George III sent an embassy led by Lord McCartney to Emperor Ch'ien-lung asking for fewer restrictions on the British. Amongst other things he requested permission to trade at Ningbo, Tianjin and other northern locations. Despite the profusion of McCartney's expensive gifts, such as clocks, telescopes and even a hot air balloon (complete with balloonist), his attempts failed. The unsuccessful mission reinforced the fact that the balance of trade would remain in favour of China.

'As your ambassador can see for himself, we possess all things. We set no value on objects strange or ingenious and have no use for your country's manufactures,' replied the Emperor.

The BEIC was restricted by its charter to export a proportion of English woollens and cloth but the poor prices fetched, didn't cover the cost of freight and production. Tea had been paid for in Spanish silver. When Spain became an ally of the United States during its War of Independence, the British lost their market to buy Spanish silver. Britain needed a commodity which the Chinese would buy in large amounts to balance the score.

This void was filled by opium. By the third decade, opium sales were rocketing and instead of silver flowing into China from Britain, it was flowing out in massive amounts.

The Rise of Opium

The origin of the opium trade between India and China lay partly in the growing popularity of opium-smoking in China. The opium poppy was introduced in the early eighth century by Arabs and Turks. The Chinese opium was of inferior quality compared with the

Indian variety. Opium had always been eaten raw as a medicine against dysentery and other ailments. What encouraged the spread of the drug was the new fashion of smoking that followed after tobacco-smoking had arrived in China from the USA via Manila in the seventeenth century. Millions of Chinese had smoked opium in moderation over the centuries without any apparent harm to their health, including the Empress Dowager Cixi. But as internal difficulties increased, many Chinese now sought temporary relief from the worries of life through opium addiction. Opium alleviates hunger pangs and smokers quickly became addicts.

The Country Traders who managed the opium trade, along with their legitimate trading in rice, raw cotton and chiming clocks, had no legal right to remain in Guangzhou year round, but several evaded the restrictions in order to remain.

By imperial edict, the selling and smoking of opium was prohibited in 1729 and its importation or domestic production in 1796. Prohibition of the drug itself promoted corruption among the officials and soldiers concerned. In 1799 an imperial decree condemned the opium trafficking: opium was exempted from the 'free interchange of commodities' permitted with foreign nations in Guangzhou. 'Foreigners obviously derive the most solid profits and advantages . . . but that our countrymen should pursue this destructive and ensnaring vice . . . is indeed odious and deplorable.'

But in practice, official connivance grew as the drug trade grew. Yamen underlings and soldiers (groups representative of contact between the government and people) were especially notorious smokers. Fear was added to greed as the opium distributors linked with secret societies and forcibly opposed officials who would not accept bribes. Lower officials in league with the trade passed on their profits to those above them, right up to the court.

The imperial edict posed a problem for the BEIC. To the Company its vast tea trade was the first priority and the tax on tea provided the British Government with an equally vast revenue. (By 1830, the Company was selling thirty million pounds' weight of China tea annually, at a net profit of £1,000,000. One year the tea tax provided a tenth of the British government's entire revenue.) But the Chinese were prepared to pay cash for opium. In the year of the imperial ban representing four thousand chests, representing twenty times the medical need, had been imported.

The sailing orders of the BEIC's Indiamen were rewritten to prohibit carrying opium, but the Company knew what happened to the opium sold at auction in Bengal. Chests of Patna opium, each containing forty balls of crude opium, a thick juice enclosed in a shell of dried poppy petals the size of an apple dumpling, were auctioned for four times the cost of production. It was bought and shipped by local British or Parsee Country Traders who trafficked between India, China and the East Indian Islands. This speculative trade created intense competition. The opium was landed near Guangzhou as contraband, from 1780 to 1793 at Lark's Bay near Macao, a safe place away from Chinese or Portuguese spies. Their smuggling boats, well armed and manned by sixty to seventy oarsmen would take delivery of opium chests, each weighing approximately 133 pounds, from the foreigners' receiving ships. By the 1830s 1–200

Chinese ships were taking deliveries from about 25 foreign ships in waters off the Guangzhou coast. Meanwhile, in its local negotiations with authorities, the Company was able to wash its hands of all formal responsibility for the illegal drug ring.

The revenue went some way to balance the silver sent to pay for silk and tea. The value of copper coinage fell dramatically. Peasants used them for everyday transactions, but taxes were paid in silver. As silver was becoming increasingly scarce, its value increased, resulting in peasants paying steadily higher taxes. This meant less prosperity, more unrest, and a greater likelihood of rebellion.

> 'The chain of vested interests in the drug traffic had grown too weighty to be broken by mere good intentions. With a tenth of its revenue coming from a tax on China tea, the British government had a strong motive for making sure tea arrived from Canton without interruption. But the purchase of tea was financed by silver procured by the sale of opium. And opium-growers in India bought Lancashire cottons. And the opium was put on the market by a company which owed its very existence to a British Parliament where all these other vested interests could exert a contrary pressure, if the Company yielded to competition, and let itself be forced out of the opium business.'[3]

The Company smugly stated: 'Were it possible to prevent the use of the drug altogether, except strictly for

---

[3] Beeching, J. *The Chinese Opium Wars* (London: Hutchinson & Co. (Publishers) Ltd, 1975) p. 34

medicine, we would gladly do it, in compassion for mankind.'

Compare this to the rhetoric of Gladstone, the Prime Minister, who called drug trafficking 'the most infamous and atrocious trade'.

Robert Morrison, the translator of the Chinese Bible, wrote in 1828: 'There is a great trade in opium here, the Chinese having become excessively addicted to it. And there is only one Christian merchant in Canton who conscientiously declines dealing in the pernicious drug. He is an American. The East India Company, as a body, don't deal in it, but their Captains do.'[4]

A few years later the firm Messrs Jardine and Matheson was selling 6,000 chests annually, at a profit of £100,000 in opium alone.

The Chinese government was incapable of stopping the trade. To get rid of the problem, superiors tried to push the trade out of their jurisdictions. In 1821 Governor-General Juan Yuan forced the receiving ships away from Canton to nearby Lintin Island. Britain had become dependent on the opium trade and the trade had become entrenched in China as an ever-increasing smuggling system which corrupted the court. The opium trade was added to the Canton trade from which the imperial household had become used to receive income for over a century.

'We treated their "chops", their prohibitions, warnings and threats as a rule, very cavalierly . . . We disregarded

---

[4] Hibbert, *The Dragon Wakes*, p. 84.

local orders, as well as those from Peking and really
became confident that we should enjoy perpetual impu-
nity so far as the opium trade was concerned . . . We often
spoke of (the Mandarins') forbearance and wondered at
the aid and protection they extended to us; in fact they
considered us more as unruly children.'[5]

When the BEIC monopoly of trade ended in 1834,
other British traders were able to compete in the market. There was a desire in Guangzhou to renew efforts
to encourage the Chinese to open up the nation to
further trade in legal imports manufactured in large
quantities in the West. Britain therefore needed official
representation of all British traders to negotiate with
the authorities and to oversee their own merchants in
Guangzhou. The new Superintendent of Trade, Lord
Napier of Meristoun, was given instructions in 1833 to
go and live in Guangzhou, announcing his arrival 'by
letter to the vice-roy', and to represent the interests of
the merchants.

As Lu Kun, Viceroy of Kwantung in July 1834,
reminded the British:

'The great ministers of the Celestial Empire are not permitted to have private intercourse by letter with outside
Barbarians. If the Barbarian headman throws in private
letters, I the Viceroy will not receive them or even look at
them . . . Even England has its laws; how much more the
Celestial Empire.'[6]

---

[5] Hunter, W.C., 'Fan Kwae at Canton Before the Treaty
Days 1825–44' (Shanghai: 1911), quoted in Hibbert, *The
Dragon Wakes*, p. 109
[6] Ibid., p. 90

The Viceroy nicknamed him 'Laboriously Vile'. It is interesting to ask in hindsight if both sides were not suffering from the same ailment. The Viceroy wrote an indignant letter to the Emperor who, equally angry that the 'barbarians' should consider themselves as equals, refused to accept Napier's letters.

On 22 August three powerful Mandarins arrived in Guangzhou from Beijing and informed Napier that they would be calling on him next morning at 11 a.m. At 9 a.m. a group of Chinese people arrived bearing ceremonial chairs. Three were placed facing south, the direction in which authority, (Mandarins) was customarily required to face. Other chairs for the Chinese merchants were placed in two rows at right angles to the first row, running along the western and eastern sides of the hall; one of these rows unfortunately had its back to a portrait of King George IV.

There were no chairs for the English. Lord Napier was predictably furious. He ordered the chairs to be rearranged so that none should have their back to the King and he would sit in the place of honour, flanked by two Mandarins and the third would sit across the table beside his secretary and assistant, Superintendent John Francis Davis. The Chinese were understandably appalled by this arrangement and tried to persuade him to change his mind. No, he would not bend. The interview would be conducted on his terms. Although this was China, the discussions were to be held in an English factory and national pride was at stake.

The Mandarins did not appear until past one o'clock, the traditional 'late' time a person in authority should arrive when meeting a lesser personage. Napier informed them that their tardiness was 'an insult to His Britannic Majesty which cannot be overlooked a second time'. Needless to say, Napier received a cool reception from the Mandarins and failed in his attempts to increase trade, but succeeded in alienating the English even more from the people of the Middle Kingdom. Furthermore, Napier circulated a proclamation identifying the interests of the Westerners with those of 'the thousands of industrious Chinese who must suffer ruin and discomfort through the perversity of their government'.[7]

Outraged, the government suspended all business transactions and employment between both nationalities until the date of Laborious Vile's imposed departure. Napier decided instead, to show them British power. On 7 September two frigates were ordered to enter the Pearl River and sail up to Whampoa Island. The Bogue Forts (40 miles downstream, guarding the mouth of the Pearl River) opened fire and the ships retaliated. Two sailors were killed and six wounded, and the ships *Andromache* and *Imogene* got through to Whampoa. The 'Napier fizzle' had an even sadder conclusion as Napier died of fever soon after in Macao.

Under the influence of the new Foreign Secretary, the Duke of Wellington, the attitude of the British government changed to one of conciliation. Many such as the Messrs Jardine and Matheson strongly opposed this policy.

Today in the city of Dongguan, Guangdong Province, visitors are greeted by the formidable and unsmiling statue of Lin Zexu erected outside the

---

[7] Collis, M., *Foreign Mud* (Faber, 1946) quoted in Hibbert, C. ibid., p. 98

Opium Wars Museum. In 1838 Lin was appointed High Commissioner at Guangzhou with instructions to act against the drug trade. He ordered 20,000 chests of opium to be surrendered and destroyed. Trade ceased when merchants became prisoners in their own factories. Lin demanded that the foreigners sign agreements promising they would never bring in opium again. The British government representative in Guangzhou took responsibility for the opium held by the traders and surrendered the cargoes. The insulted British argued they were entitled to compensation. A force was sent to blockade Guangzhou and fighting erupted on November 1839 in the Battle of Chuanbi. The first Opium War had started.

> 'Elliot gave way; the signal to engage was hoisted; and the *Volage* followed by the *Hyacinth*, bore suddenly northwards across the front of the anchored Chinese fleet (of fifteen war junks and fourteen fireships), their guns blazing. Within three quarters of an hour, four men-of-war junks had been sunk and the rest so badly damaged that there could have been no possibility of their withdrawing into the river had not Elliot reminded Smith that this had been the whole purpose of the action. So, with one sailor wounded aboard the British ships, and with only some slight damage to their rigging, the fight was broken off.'[8]

The main British fleet arrived quickly and proceeded to blockade all the major ports of the coast. Once it reached Bei He near Tianjin, (dangerously close to Beijing), the emperor was rattled enough to send a reprimand to Commissioner Lin and order the

---

[8] Hibbert, *The Dragon Wakes*, p. 134

governor-general at Tianjin to parley. The forces with-
drew southwards with the promise of negotiations at
Guangzhou.

Elsewhere fighting was fierce. An example of the
odds against the Chinese forces was the attack on the
Brogue on 7 January 1841. Six hundred Tartar troops
– the elite corps of the Manchu dynasty were killed
and a hundred became prisoners. Thirty British soldiers were wounded, mostly by accidental explosions
at Fort Chuanbi. Fort Tycocktow was blasted to
pieces and 1,461 men of the Royal Navy were
involved against 3,000 Chinese troops.

In 1841 Britain coerced the negotiators to accept a
draft Chuanbi Convention in which Hong Kong
would be ceded to the British, trade at Guangzhou
re-commence, and direct and equal discussions would
be established between British and Chinese officials.
The emperor was furious at the demands, and hostili-
ties were resumed by the destruction of Guangzhou's
outer defences.

By 1842 several major coastal ports and ports
along the Yangtse River (*Chang Jiang*) had been
occupied. The Chinese government decided to negotiate only when British ships threatened Nanjing. The
Treaty of Nanjing (1842) was the first of a series of
notorious 'unequal treaties' which increasingly
angered the Chinese. They were giving away rights
and privileges without receiving anything in return.
Under the treaty terms, Hong Kong was ceded
outright and it became a trading port free from any
regulations. Other treaty ports were Xiamen,
Fuzhou, Ningbo, Shanghai and of course Guangzhou. Compensation of 21 million Mexican dollars

for the destroyed opium and the cost of the war was paid to Britain. The Cohong was abolished and import duties imposed on foreign goods.

France, Holland and America also signed treaties with China allowing freedom to trade. The treaty between Britain and China included the 'most favoured nation' clause whereby Britain would share equally in all rights and privileges that China might grant to any other country. The 'extra-territorial' privilege exempted all foreigners from Chinese justice. Foreigners were henceforth to be ruled by their own law and officials. They gained access to the land's interior and were allowed to promulgate Christianity without obstruction. In reaction, terms of agreement were occasionally ignored.

China's doors were forced open against her will. Curiously, opium was not even mentioned in the treaty.

'The opium question was not, in fact, the ultimate cause of the war, which really resulted from the strong conflict of attitudes of the Chinese and Westerners. The Western nations could not accept the claim of the Chinese emperor to rule the world, and demanded relations based on equality.'[9]

The most important consequence of the war was the revelation of the political and military weakness of the government. The peasant armies behind the 1851 Taiping Rebellion, took advantage of this. Despite the

[9] Haw, S.G., *A Traveller's History of China* (New York: Interlink Books, US, 1995) p. 152

immense size and power of the Taipings, they were defeated ten years later. During this time the French and English wanted to open up inland China for trade along the major rivers. They made diplomatic representation to Beijing in 1854. In 1856, while the Qing Court was entangled with the Taipings, these foreign powers launched the second Opium War.

The *Arrow*, owned by Chinese living in Hong Kong, was suspected by Chinese officials of having pirates on board. Officials carried off the entire crew of twelve members. Britain demanded their return on the grounds that the ship was in British territorial waters. Britain demanded that the Chinese refrain from violating British territory. Failing to get a satisfactory reply, Britain declared war.

The fighting reached a climax with the sacking of Beijing itself when Anglo-French forces seized and looted the city, forcing the Manchu Court to surrender.

The Treaty of Tianjin (1858) and the Beijing Convention (1860) expanded the scope of imperialism in China. Eleven trading ports were added to the original five – on the Chang Jiang, in north China, Taiwan and on Hainan Island. Exempted from transit taxes, western ships were allowed on certain inland rivers. At long last the foreigners were permitted diplomatic representation in Beijing, enabling then to deal with the central government directly. The opium trade was legalized.

France, Russia and American forced China to sign similar treaties. In effect Russia obtained the whole region north of the Amur River. The French forced recognition of their control of Annam which had once been a vassal state of China. In 1898 the French gained the Leizhou Peninsula, south of Zhanjiang, and now other areas in Guangdong Province and Hainan Island were within their sphere of influence. The Germans showed interest in the Shandong Peninsula.

Hong Kong

Of this part of the British Empire, Lord Palmerston, the British Foreign Secretary, commented to Captain George Eliot, Superintendent of Trade in Guangzhou, 'You have obtained the cession of Hong Kong, a barren island with hardly a house upon it.'

The British were looking for an island where they could live under their own jurisdiction. Hong Kong, before their arrival had a small population and was of minor importance economically. Though only thirty square miles in size it has one of the world's best deep-water harbours. It is separated from the mainland peninsula of Kowloon. Unfortunately an unhealthy climate meant fever was common. Because of its original size and steep cliffs, the island was not of much use in the 1840s. By the Convention of Beijing in 1860 the southern part of the Kowloon Peninsula and Stone-cutter's Island were also ceded to Britain. Surprisingly, from this time onwards a substantial number of Chinese migrants were attracted to Hong Kong, happy to live under British rule. In modern times the island has been enlarged through reclamation projects in the harbour.

The transformation of Hong Kong in such a short span of time, has been breathtaking. The Hong Kong that China gave to Britain is unrecognizable compared with the Hong Kong the nation received back in 1997.

11

'My duty and my pleasure'
— Friends, Students, Associates and the Outside World —

During my first week I had my meals in the canteen, as the guest of the college. The students ate their meals with relish, stared at me but kept their distance in case I did something threatening like greeting them. But one day, a bright friendly face approached and changed the view I was beginning to have of the students. Being genuinely interested in getting to know me, she sat down. It was such a pleasure to converse with a friendly soul speaking reasonably good English – American twang and all. Marilyn re-appeared as one of my grade two students on my first day of class.

Over the next few weeks she visited often and shared many concerns that college students worry about, the world over, like being disappointed by a boyfriend. What clouded her mind the most, however, was her father's current affair with a 'concubine'. She spat the word out. Unbeknown to her, distressed by all she had told me, I prayed over the situation and asked the Lord to bring conviction to the couple's hearts. A week later, I carefully broached the subject. Marilyn was all smiles. She had just heard from her mother that her parents had made their peace and the 'concubine' had left. When I asked her how it had happened, she said that she thought that the woman's conscience had caught up with her. Praise God.

> 'Behold, He who keeps Israel shall
> neither slumber nor sleep.' (Ps. 121:4)

But a myriad of fears gnawed at her own peace. Marilyn remembered how once when she was little her father took her to see a criminal being executed. During middle school a classmate was caught for smuggling and was executed. Is it any wonder her life was full of fears?

Westerners in China play the role of welcome confidantes in a milieu of tight surveillance of one another. Being only peripherally connected to the community, the Westerner has no vested interest in passing on information to authorities. People carrying burdens, in the absence of other adults to safely talk to, would willingly share their grief with us. The Chinese government in times past has discouraged their people from prolonged contact with foreigners for fear of the Chinese being indoctrinated with unwanted political ideas. But all the confidential talks we had, revolved around issues much closer to home and far away from politics. We heard about the universal problems people have the world over: naughty children and the like, and saw most clearly problems that China alone must tackle. Their sharing brought me closer to people who became very dear because they trusted me. At the same time, my Australian identity stood out all the more starkly to me, because in a few months' time I was going to leave all these people and their problems behind. It was easy to feel guilty about being born in Australia.

The students were quietly proud to have 'their' own western teachers and did not mind showing 'owner-ship'. Our students were always thrilled to talk to us, whether on the campus or down the street. They told us what they wrote to their parents about us (at least the complimentary passages!) and wanted to have photographs taken arm in arm with us. I doubted that we were the attraction per se, but there were so few western people in this part of the province, that we were a novelty. Chinese society for thousands of years has respected scholars and teachers, based on the Con-fucian ideal of 'duty' to parents and other authority figures. Children are taught this respect from an early age. A western teacher coming into a college, sails on the crest of the wave of such respect.

We were never short of students willing and able to help with any predicament, big or small. Although taught it is their duty to help, their cheerfulness in doing so shows that it truly is 'their pleasure' which is the most common response to our grateful thanks. Take this particular day for example. I wrote in my diary: 'The English Department door was locked when I arrived, so I couldn't retrieve my radio to do my "Karaoke bit" in class, that is speak via a radio microphone. (My voice, in the beginning didn't carry well across 40 heads in a non-acoustically designed classroom situated near other yelling teachers and a construction site.) I went to the classroom and asked Elly to go to the office later, when I thought it would be open. She slipped out silently and when she re-appeared with the radio, Nigel, a monitor jumped up and carried a desk over to place the radio on. I was grateful for his assistance without being asked. At the end of class, the radio vanished unbidden back to the Department office. Anita, efficient as always, said she couldn't shop for us tomorrow because of the exams coming up, but had arranged for Pauline to do it instead. Pauline is a fourth year, whom I don't teach, but I see her a lot. Just at that moment, Pauline stood respectfully at the door waiting to see me. After apolo-gising for getting into a muddle over last weekend's shopping arrangements, (which wasn't a problem at all), she said she would come vegie-shopping with us tomorrow and also on Saturday, if we wanted her to. During class Sally, the female monitor, gave me some copies of photos which were taken while on the previ-ous weekend jaunt. This included an entourage of about a dozen students! At the bottom of the steps of the building, Sally clucked over my bout of flu. "You take care of yourself, you don't look like yourself today!" '

Most Saturday shopping sprees down the street included one or more students coming with us. Their devotion was remarkable since they rarely had any-thing to buy themselves. They took as a matter of course that they would carry our purchases for us. We wouldn't let them until we were overloaded. Then on the hottest days, I would pause to buy us all a drink,

which I thought would be the least I could do after
their traipsing around in the heat without a complaint.
An argument usually ensued because they would insist
on paying for everyone. Sally, especially was always
quick to whip out her purse before me. Eventually I
insisted enough to stop them using up their meagre
allowance. Sally let slip the reasoning for this generosity. She was told as a child that she should never 'take'
anything from a teacher and leave the teacher out of
pocket. If she did, the gods would punish her. She
laughed and knew that it was erroneous thinking. I
talked about how the Lord sees her.

Unfortunately poor pay in recent years has eroded
the desire for students to become teachers themselves.
But as far as I could see, the respect for teachers has
remained intact.

> *'Women have long hair and short intelligence.'*
> (Chinese proverb)

Relating to the few boys in my classes took a special
effort but the rewards were there. I felt sorry for them,
because they did not have much confidence in their
skill. They often told me that girls are much better at the
language than boys. This attitude did not presage a
good start to a College education, dominated as they
were 4:1 by girls. The friendship groups were strongly
single-sex. In the classrooms this translated into a
lay-out where all the girls sat at the front of the class,
with the keenest at the very front. The males typically
sat in a group at the back. This gave them ample
opportunity to drift into Chinese instead of English.
Practice is the key to language fluency. The back of the

class was the worst area for hearing me and seeing the blackboard. The attitude current in most male groups was not conducive to hard work. (The exceptions were the three or four males in the Education class. At least one of them passed the extremely difficult national Band Four English examination in May 1996.) This slackness contrasted sharply with the attitude of one or two of the groups of girls who took diligence to the point of over-work. Success in studies rested to a large extent on the consensus of the group, working either for or against study. The attitude of and adherence to the group is much more important in Chinese society than individual aspirations.

It was a never-ending battle to get the ones who were struggling to sit at the front, where they could see and hear. Splitting up the male groups was almost impossible. The best course for me was to pour more time and energy into their efforts, to keep up discipline, especially regarding homework, and in fun, to reward loudly every success. They lapped up the special attention and quickly learnt that they could not get away with laziness. They became serious about their studies and practised pronunciation exercises with enthusiasm. My goal was to replace the attitude of slackness and poor self-image with diligence and an individual sense of potential. The 'Gang of Eight' in a Practical English class gave me no end of problems in this process, but the effort paid off. I could not help liking the lads and laughing at their buffoonery.

Early in my first semester half the Gang were co-opted to help the teacher in distress. The incident helped me enormously in getting to know the students. My old washing-machine had died on me.

I wrote home, describing how I had been greeted by four male students from one of my classes, all dripping with sweat but very pleased with themselves nonetheless for having lugged up four flights of steps a brand new 'Little Swan' washing-machine. After much discussion, trial and error, and general hilarity, we worked out how the thing operated. Their English was imperfect, but they could read the dials in Chinese. My Chinese was sparse, but I know how machines work; so between us we made a great team and were all the wiser for the exercise – and the clothes got washed. I was so pleased I had done my 'Language and Culture' course. There is so much truth in the things we were taught. I often found myself in a position of dependency on others and this was morale boost for my students, giving them affirmation of their culture and way of doing things and cements friendships. I didn't mind being dependent on them.

Having a good rapport with the students made dealing with difficulties in their behaviour a painful and disappointing experience. I needed to *'be as wise as a serpent and harmless as a dove'* (Matt 10:16) in handling puzzling dilemmas. It was vexing to find students lying about why they must have time off from class, why they haven't done their homework, why . . . why. I received so many notes saying 'I must go home because my mother is seriously ill' that I ceased to react to such notes emotionally. If they wanted to play games, it was their future they were playing with. I realized that I had been duped around the time called colloquially 'Tomb-Sweeping Day'. That may not be the best translation of the official title, but it does describe the activity by believers in ancestor worship. Family members sweep the graves of deceased relatives and leave food prepared for the occasion. It's a weekend for families to come together. Students from various grades told me about the forthcoming event.

I was presented with a number of notes saying that they were ill or their grandfather was dying or other tragedies had suddenly occurred, necessitating time off from college at the end of the week. Sometimes the bearers of these notes were class-mates who were quite open in their ridicule of these excuses. Being still rather naïve about the wiles of students, I was shocked by the alleged dishonesty in seemingly honest, hard-working souls and by the casual 'dobbing in' by class-mates. It would have been much better if they had been honest and merely said that they wanted to go home. But perhaps it was, to all concerned, a very small matter and one which wouldn't ruffle the feathers of strong class-mate friendships? Who knows? Better to lie and save face, than to tell the truth and risk losing face?

In the absence of any substantial evidence, from then on I treated notes with a casualness which might have seemed rather callous to those in genuine need. But I was in the dark, as usual, unable to find the truth, yet unwilling to appear suspicious by asking too many questions and thus threaten the trust I had built up carefully over the months. I longed for them to trust me enough to speak candidly. Perhaps they had learnt while young that honesty does not pay or that there are other considerations beyond honesty.

For the second semester, I was faced with teaching 'Introduction to Britain and America' to two grade three classes. This was quite a challenge because I was neither British nor American, but it proved rewarding nonetheless. For assessment, I set a short essay on American geography: not a difficult task. Following weeks of warning, the deadline arrived and most people handed their papers in. One girl convinced several others that the deadline wasn't actually a deadline and that I would just talk about the essay on that day. I had said nothing of the sort. I knew she was playing for time, because by the previous weekend she had not done much work on it and had come to my flat seeking advice. Great was the pleading from a few students for more time, but after consideration, I thought that tough love was the only thing to show and refused to accept any late essays, since the rest had passed theirs in. The students seemed to live in a world of relativity – everything can be modified and changed if you know the right strings to pull. So I thought that to insist – 'When I say this is the deadline, this *is* the deadline' would be better than to vacillate which would leave me open to future manipulation. 'They're going to hate me . . .' I mused.

When there was a knock at the door that evening, the situation became confused. A girl stood there holding an essay from a fellow class-mate, asking if it was too late to submit it? The story ran that the girl in question had gone home for a few days but had completed her essay ahead of time and given it to the friend to pass in. Her father needed her on the farm. From the low prices for produce in the market, I knew that the local farmers were not wealthy. Should I believe her? The bearer of the essay was not one of the most honest of students. She said that she had simply forgotten to bring the essay to class. I accepted the essay and asked her to pass on a message to the other girl to see me when she returned to town.

The following week, two of her class-mates (more trustworthy ones) approached me and asked quietly if the girl really did have to come to see me? They thought I might give her a grilling, which wasn't what I planned at all. They explained that she hadn't returned to College yet and asked me not to be hard on her because life for her family was very difficult. Her father was struggling on the land, her mother had died two years ago and she was the eldest child with two younger brothers. Her two uncles were putting her through College, since her father was unable to pay the expenses. Her class-mates were afraid that I'd unwittingly ask her about all these personal details which, even amongst her friends, she had difficulty talking about. I let the matter drop.

The essay from this struggling lass was one of the best researched and thoughtfully written from both classes – despite all the disadvantages of her circumstances . . . What a difference between her attitude and that of the first girl who had every advantage to study.

Chinese teachers of English are torn between the needs of their students on the one hand and the demands of their English departments on the other. Respected by their students for their advanced grasp of the foreign language, they are nonetheless bewildered by the vagaries of language usage. The

English language can be governed by structural regulations in grammar books, but in conversation it breaks free from such regulations. The correct usage of regional colloquialisms which defy logic most of the time, are another puzzle. They change rapidly over time as old phrases are replaced by new. Some colloquialisms practised by the students, like 'Long time no see' sounded permanently frozen in a time-warp. My heart went out to teachers faced with the problem of teaching the 'right form'. What is the 'right form' anyway? Can three or four versions of a phrase or sentence all be 'correct'? A teacher presented me with this test question:

'Place these words in the order of size: immense, vast, gigantic'. I couldn't choose between them, let alone the teacher.

'I am walking, I am sitting, I am boring,' a girl wrote.

'No you're not, you're a very interesting person!' I'd counter. Confusion clouded her face. After all, she had followed all the rules surrounding suffixes. Why is 'bored' correct and 'boring' wrong in this context? Why indeed?

Like a bower-bird, English has collected bits and pieces from other languages over the centuries, resulting certainly in a colourful language with a gigantic (or is it immense?) vocabulary, but there are disadvantages to this eclectic tendency. Further, many of the commonly-used verbs happen to be irregular. Each must be painstakingly and individually learnt. Chinese teachers tread an uncertain path through this field of 'grey areas', trying to capture the capricious 'correct form'. I admired their tenacity to keep going, year after year.

Presented with the arrival of babbling Westerners, some teachers became quiet and picked their words carefully when speaking to us. I longed to say 'Hey, lift up your heads. You're doing a great job. Anyone who can speak several Chinese languages and dialects, plus Romantic, alphabetic English – and teach it at that, is a marvel to behold!' Many overcame their reticence and beat a path to our door to ask questions generated from their course work.

I wrote home: 'A couple of classes of would-be teachers are sweating now because next month they will take the Band Four English examination. Great was the wailing last night from some of them. Their "listening" teacher is doing her best to train them, but every week she comes to us with questions from the curriculum and some of them are really curly.'

A male teacher asked me questions concerning an abstract poem which he wanted to write an essay on, to enter a literary competition. By about the fifth reading, the truth hit my naïve brain: it was about the sordid relationship between a pimp and a prostitute! How to delicately answer his questions without getting both of us horribly embarrassed? I wrote a carefully-worded note briefly saying what it was about, suggesting he find another poem. With deliberate nonchalance I slipped the note into his pigeon-hole in the bustling English Department. At least I hope I put it in the right pigeon-hole!

The poem was so obscure that I was not surprised he didn't comprehend its meaning fully. Why should such trash be introduced into China? I felt vaguely that I shared the blame for its import, if only because I was a Westerner.

It was a pleasure to see consternation turn to revelation on teachers' faces. I enjoyed delving into the mysteries of my collection of word usage books to fish out answers. I learnt that since God's will for my time in China was to concentrate on teaching English, anything to do with helping students and teachers was intellectually stimulating, a great joy and not a burden.

> 'For my yoke is easy and my burden is light.'
> (Matt. 11: 30)

I caught something of what Jesus meant when he said: 'My food is to do the will of him who sent me and to finish His work' (Jn. 4:34).

Being ill in China had its own special problems. I wrote home: 'I haven't felt in much of a letter-writing mood because I've had a bad cold. (wo gan mao le) with fevers and the works. I asked for a day off and that brought a large delegation of teachers from the Department around in the afternoon to commiserate. I alternated between coughing and speaking in a whisper because my voice had gone west. Everyone wore more layers of clothing than me. I was burning up with a temperature so received yet another well-meaning lecture: "You don't wear enough clothes!" '

We were amazed at the degree of their consternation over just a bout of 'flu. But after all, my predecessor was ill most of one term and was seriously ill twice, so they know that serious things can happen. They kindly brought us powdered milk and lots of apples.

I whispered to the Vice-Dean: 'Thank you for coming.'

'Oh, it is my duty, I mean it is my pleasure,' she replied, a little breathless. A sense of duty or a command from above had meant that she had cycled back out of hours to the campus to see me. With so much attention lavished on us, we decided that in future we would struggle to class no matter how we felt.

'Miss Belinda, please would you excuse us from class this afternoon? I must take my friend to the hospital to see the doctor.'

'I hope it isn't anything serious?'

'I have stomach pains,' the patient answered.

'I hope you're feeling better soon,' I said and turned to her companion; 'You're a kind mate for going with her.'

'Well, of course, it is my duty, she is my friend.' Such loyalty to the rules of friendship.

They have their endearing ways. One night I went to 'English Corner' feeling unwell and swaying a bit. I wondered what a stir would be created if I suddenly fainted into the pot plants. Afterwards two of my students walked part-way home with me and one had her arm round my shoulder. That was nice – someone to catch me!

My predecessor had written to me: 'Sometimes you might feel like some commodity that everyone wants to use without considering how you feel about it at all…'

Jeanette and I had a strange experience. We were told to report to Language Lab No. 1 to have our photos taken for the journal commemorating the anniversary of the College. Wearing our Sunday best we arrived expecting a five-minute round of shots.

Instead, we spent the next forty-five minutes in front of a grade one class who were sitting wearing headphones. I was ushered to the teacher's desk on the dais and seated in front of a computer screen and control panel for running the lab equipment. On one side was an overhead projector and on the other a TV screen and video recorder. They told me to put on headphones and then they pressed various commands and up sprang 'Top of the World' which I had to sing Karaoke style. I felt really silly but fortunately it's easy to sing and ironically is one of our songs from the tours. Then I had to give an impromptu English lesson, using a story invented on the spot. I wrote with one hand on the screen and waved with the other, trying to sound sensible at the same time. We all had a good laugh.

What has all this to do with photography, you may ask? That's what we were asking ourselves. All the time this valuable learning experience was going on, the photographer was methodically and slowly setting up his equipment, instructing his assistant and occasionally taking the odd shot. There were several breaks in the proceedings as the other AV staff fiddled with the technology which wasn't amenable to having its photo taken. During these times, I just chatted to the students who were too shy to say much, so I prattled on half to myself.

Meanwhile, Jeanette was sweating at the back of the room, wondering what intimidating delights were awaiting her. It turned out that they wanted her to look as though she was giving a lesson from my projected story. She carried on an intelligent discussion with poise and a deliberate sense of purpose. Her evocative gestures were highly effective too.

My photos were not a true depiction because I never used the language labs; I taught in ordinary classrooms. It was all so artificial – I instinctively reacted against it. I rushed out the next week and took photos of *my* classes in *my* classrooms. I think they really wanted to show off their equipment rather than us. My photo later appeared in the journal. To add to my embarrassment, the class in the lab became my grade ones and they well remembered every single detail of the episode.

We learnt to our cost that we had different perspectives on social outings from those around us. When invited out, we saw the occasion as just an enjoyable few hours spent in congenial company. The event ended when the concert or whatever was over. It appeared to me that those inviting us, and all the others who turned up on the day, saw it in wider terms: a most important side-line for the 'event' itself was the publicity it generated.

While I was still green in the ways of the culture, the chair-woman of the Students' Union politely invited us to spend some time rambling through the extensive gardens of the hotel where we celebrated National Day. We should have guessed something 'official' was afoot since Pauline herself asked us. Seizing an opportunity to explore beyond the confine of the campus, we looked forward to the coming Saturday. About eight second and fourth year girls also looked forward to Saturday, so much so they invited a lad from the college photography shop along as well. Thinking nothing of the presence of his over-active camera, we carried on in our own blithe and breezy fashion; jumping out from behind rocky outcrops, playing the fashion model from under trailing vines and, well, just being silly Australians. Click, click, click.

Our frolicking was a reaction to the timid and formal attitude of the classmates to the serious business of photo-taking. People stood perfectly still in small groups or with an individual in roughly the same posture for each shot. It is true that a slight smile was permitted. After the 149th roll of film had caught its last unique souvenir of the occasion, Jeanette and I were tired of the rigidity of it all. We set up our own creative poses, some with our somewhat hesitant subjects.

'No, no, no, don't do that, just stand there!' everyone else yelled.

'Yes, yes, yes' I thought but didn't say, 'I'm getting bored and you're far too young to be so staid.' Letting themselves go a little was an alien concept to them at first, but they thawed out somewhat. At lunch we jostled with the patrons of a large fast-food place. Just as we stood up to leave, a camera flashed from somewhere across the room. We groaned.

'We're going to get copies of the photos done. We'll get some for you too,' Sally said next day.

Within the week, a collection of 'Jeanette standing with girl A, with girl B, C, D.' 'Belinda with girl A, C, D', 'Jeanette and Belinda with the group of A, B, and E' and so on, appeared magically on my desk. So did a bank of photographs of Jeanette and Belinda acting the silly goats materialize on the stairwell where the 460 English Department students and teachers could see them. Silly and serious, there they were in full Technicolor.

Then all became clear. Was our little casual outing closer to an official function? I had a quiet word with the producer of the display who hadn't asked my permission beforehand. Had some copies gone on file? They would provide amusement for the security office. Still, we had had an enjoyable day despite the camera.

This incident was but a dress rehearsal for the College anniversary celebrations later in the year, when photographs of previous performances of the Australian team were pinned up for all the visiting 'old girls and boys' of the College to see. In a close-up, my partner and I were dancing to a rock 'n roll number in full costume. My 'hat' had changed a lot since that night. My students were delighted to point it out, to see my red face yet again.

During the first two months, one of the strangers whom I did let in beyond the gate was a Christian girl about my age, who decided that she wanted to be my friend. What a blessing from the Lord. She visited me twice a week before Jeanette arrived and would usually ring me first to see if there was anything I wanted her to buy on the way. I later met her fiancé and also her sister Holly. We learnt a lot about each others' countries and I appreciated her maturity and wide vision about issues. Unfortunately the students regularly compared us with the former Western teachers and we never seemed to live up to their expectations of the fun, teaching and singing which they had enjoyed in the past. Still, we can only be who we are, and cannot become super-heroes on the whim of people expecting a performance.

Nonetheless we had some enjoyable times with them. I wrote home about one memorable Saturday. 'This morning was special because we were in excellent company and had the park almost to ourselves. Some old men had brought their songbirds into an open area and chatted amongst themselves, while their birds did likewise. We think the birds are myna – a noisy variety. All the bauhinias are now out in glorious deep pink flowers bigger than one's hand.'

Extra-curricula studies revolved around art classes and learning Chinese. Once Jeanette suggested that she wanted to learn how to paint the traditional way, offers came thick and fast. She attended early morning classes with Art Department students and a lad from there gave her private coaching. He was so keen that she improve as much as possible, that he told her to practise for a few hours every day. Once when she suggested that they visit the local art shop, he replied, 'No I think you should stay here and paint!' We also both visited a neighbouring art teacher in his home for lessons. Certainly Jeanette's art works surpassed mine, but she met her match when we saw the remarkable standard of the students' work at their art exhibition. We kept telling ourselves: 'These are only students!'

A couple of fourth year girls volunteered to teach us *Putonghua* (Mandarin). If I used some Chinese in class, everyone laughed (with me, not at me). My language teacher and art teacher were the only ones who didn't laugh at my tentative attempts. Their suppressed giggles gave them away though. I had learnt

Chinese before I went away, but was a long way away from being able to carry on a conversation.

It never ceased to amaze me how much difference there was in attitude towards us between our warm-hearted students and staff, and people unconnected to us. A casual walk through the College or anywhere in the city would be constantly punctuated by people staring and young men invariably yelling out to us in English and Chinese. 'Hello' and 'How do you do?' probably exhausted their limited vocabulary. Often the phrase would be followed by laughter from their surrounding group of mates. In my first week I learnt to avoid walking in front of one of the boys' dormitories, because the residents would yell out from the balconies. Any bystander who hadn't realized I was in the street, would be quickly informed of my presence. In all my travels around China, I had never met this yelling phenomenon and the staring seemed worse here than elsewhere. I didn't detect any negative feeling in the remarks, and interpreted then as just cheekiness, irritating though it was, until . . .

'Miss Belinda, do you understand what people say to you in Chinese?'

More than the words she used, the pained look on her face conveyed that some of the comments in Chinese were deliberately barbed.

'Well, I've come all this way, spent all this money and that's the way they treat me!' was what I felt like saying, but I held my tongue. The extreme difference in reaction between 'my' students and the English Department generally and other people can be explained by the 'insider/outsider' mentality of the culture.

As Kevin B. Bucknall explains:

'. . . the Chinese view people as essentially either "insiders," who belong to the group or unit, or "outsiders," who are strangers. The latter can be treated with an indifference that can border on contempt. Trying to get assistance from another organization can be trying, as the people there feel no responsibility to assist, indeed quite often they feel the reverse.'[1]

The people 'outside' the English Department owed me nothing and stood to gain nothing from me, so were free to air prejudices against Westerners or make sport of me at whim. But 'my' delightful students had to be nice to me out of an ingrained practice of deference to teachers. They wanted to be friendly and I just might fail them if they weren't!

My students anyway, had by nature, warm and generous spirits. They wanted to make the most of the brief year they had talking with someone whose native tongue was English. Many a time my heart would skip a beat as I suddenly heard 'Hello Miss Belinda' and a familiar face came into focus out of the crowd. The string of questioning, giggling and fingering of my belongings for clues about what we'd been up to, made us feel like long lost friends or favourite aunts. Their uncoerced friendliness brought me to the

---

[1] Bucknall, K.B., *Kevin B. Bucknall's Cultural Guide to Doing Business in China* (Oxford: Butterworth Heinemann, 1994) p. 29

conclusion that they were the ones we should invest our lives in and not be overly distressed about the name-calling 'outsiders'. Easy to do in theory but not in practice.

Relationships between people in China are vitally important. Many students, worried about finding a 'good job' at the end of the College life, were infuriated that they had to battle the system of *guanxi* (*relationships based on mutual dependence*, with the active element, *feelings* and *emotion*, in short, *connections*).

> 'Of all the influences and elements that went into the forging of traditional Chinese attitudes and behaviour, none played a more critical role than lack of personal freedom ... Since people had to have permission for virtually everything they did outside of their ordinary routine, either from their parents, from village elders, from workplaces, or from government officials – and often from all of them – developing and maintaining co-operative relationships, called *guanxi* (or) connections, with key individuals in all of these categories, or knowing someone else who had the necessary relationship that they could call on for help, became a way of life ... The whole of China, socially, economically and politically, runs on personal connections, on *guanxi*.'[2]

It must be very hard to study diligently for years on end and at the same time worry that all one's efforts and good examination passes would be counted for

---

[2] Mente, *NTC's Dictionary*, p. 133

nothing, since one lacked useful connections to get any job.

Nepotism, a form of *guanxi*, whether as a blessing (for the favoured one) or a curse, has been an ingrained element of Chinese society for centuries. Before liberation the government recognized the problems which can easily ensue from nepotism.

'China's dynastic *guarner* or *mandarins* – government officials who administered the laws of the land on a regional and district level . . . were always outsiders who were assigned to different districts every three or four years, like military commanders of an occupying force. They were not assigned to their home districts, and were moved frequently, as a means of reducing the corruption that inevitably followed personal ties.'[3]

---

[3] Ibid., p. 134

12

'We'll remember your heart'
— Leaving —

The second semester was different in some ways from the first. The bubbliness of the students was beginning to evaporate. I suspected it had been partly the result of the sheer novelty of having a foreign teacher and, what is more, a female, in classes dominated by girls. By the second semester, the novelty had worn off. Now it was my turn to have the novel experience of being treated like part of the furniture. I had long ago become tired of my celebrity status and I longed to be accepted as just another teacher.

The atmosphere in the classrooms became more serious as the students faced the truth that this semester was the downhill run towards the final exams and an uncertain future in employment prospects for the graduates. Discussions about the unfairness of the system 'it's not what you know, but who you know' (*guanxi*), increased in frequency and intensity as the semester progressed.

By the end of first semester I had discerned a definite improvement in the Oral English skills of most of my students. The vast majority were diligent workers who stepped up the pace towards the end. There were also the ones who had jobs to go to after graduation, so they saw little point in trying hard and assumed they would pass the exams anyway.

'And leave you with a love that never dies.'

To stay or not to stay, that is the question.

With such insistence from the Department to sign a two-year contract at the beginning of our term, we knew it would be easy to have our contracts extended. Though our hearts ached to see our family and friends again, they ached also for the Chinese people who had found a permanent place in our affections. We felt keenly the uncertainty of the future that lay ahead of them. Perhaps by staying we could make a difference in their lives, and help them get that 'good job'. After two years learning from us, the enthusiastic ones would be able to chatter away like native speakers. Even our accent and colloquialisms might have penetrated their overly 'proper' English pronunciation by then. We prayed for God's abundant blessing in all its fullness to take root in their lives, and in the nation as a whole, for his 'shalom'.

'If I was staying, I would . . .' became a regular preface to analyses of our teaching methods during the latter half of second semester. What to change? What to try?

But we knew we were going home.

We had an inkling by the end of our stay of why people wanted to stay in China. This ancient country and people have a way of drawing one back, time and again. It was true that deep and special relationships had been formed, but, after a year how much did we really know about our friends? How much more could we discover about them and this fascinating culture if we stayed for another year? It felt as if the relationships had barely started. We had actually spent such little time with each student: two hours per class per week and that with almost forty students. It had been so inadequate.

The night before we left, a breathless Anita and Felicity raced up our stairs to tell us the news. Anita spoke with an air of importance. 'I have just come from a meeting of the Communist Party. I will probably be accepted as a Party member.'

They expected a shout of joy or some expression of excitement. Too stunned to be tactful, I asked foolishly: 'Why do you want to join the Party?'

A little taken aback, she thought for a bit then replied: 'Well, there are many advantages to being a Party member, for getting jobs and finding housing and things like that.' That was quite a distance from the zealous ideology of the past. Felicity wasn't going to join. I thought of the difference between the two girls. One came from a stable, loving family and the other from a family which had deep divisions in it. The difference in confidence, self-esteem and striving was evident. Did her decision to join reflect an unconscious need to find a father's protection in an unpredictable world I wondered? I longed for her to know the length and breadth of her heavenly Father's provision and care all her life.

I thought in the beginning I was going overseas to fulfil certain roles; primarily as a teacher of English, but also as a 'student' gaining a deeper education so that I could better serve and pray for China. The education I acquired would be an 'overlay' upon the foundation of my own identity, spiritual life, and my very being. I would return to Australia triumphantly full of faith, knowledge and experience. (All those goals were fulfilled within God's timing.) My pastor once preached that sometimes the Lord splits your heart into a million pieces in order to put it back together again the right way. What I found as soon as I arrived in China was that the Lord's plan was not to add an 'overlay' but to work on the very fabric and foundation of my make-up. The dross in my life needed to be dissolved away.

'I am the true vine, and my Father is the vinedresser. Every branch in me that does not bear fruit he takes away; and every branch that bears fruit he prunes, that it may bear more fruit.' (Jn. 15:1–2)

It isn't until you meet pressures that the cracks in the surface of your personality show through. I came to the staggering conclusion by the end of my stay that this transformation could have happened only if I had been taken completely out of my own environment for a length of time. Isolated from the familiar supports of home, I had to rely on the Lord entirely for sorting out every detail of my existence. Certainly, the Lord provided caring people around to help in practical ways, but their understanding of my felt needs was limited by language, culture and past experience. They had never lived in another country.

Needless to say there was a lot of kicking and screaming when the Lord began to change me: it was all the more painful because paradoxically, he used large doses of the 'dross' itself, to remove it. He dealt with the problem of loneliness, not by giving me companionship, but even deeper loneliness before Jeanette arrived. During that time I experienced what Karen Blixen expressed in *Out of Africa*: 'At times life on the farm was so lonely, and in the stillness of the evenings when the minutes dripped from the clock, life seemed to be dripping out of you with them, just for want of white people to talk to.'[1]

Now, back in Australia, any loneliness experienced is trivial compared to past experience. Pressures also show hidden strengths, abilities and flexibilities. I have more faith in God's provision and a 'lighter hold' on ministry projects – I hold them in an open hand instead of a tight fist.

'Lord give me faith' is a dangerous prayer for anyone to pray because the Lord takes away human assistance until we know that 'faith isn't faith until it's all we're hanging onto!' This was the caption above a photograph I once saw of a terror-struck kitten hanging perilously from the handle of a basket. This image helped me through many a crisis when I acknowledged I was in the same situation as the kitten. Beyond the point of panic, there is a tranquillity available when one realizes that the presenting problem is one that only God can solve. The tranquillity comes at a deeper level than surface emotions which may still be flustered. Over and over again, we would see the Lord solve everyday problems and dilemmas;

---

[1] Dinesan, I., (Karen Blixen), *Out of Africa and Shadows on the Grass* (Harmondsworth: Penguin, 1937) p. 26.

ever working to assure us that 'he was with us to the end of the age'.

This must be the experience of all Christian workers in a third world country. Surely, the day arrives sooner or later when everything inside you cries out: 'Lord, this is too much, I'm just not strong enough. I don't have the right personality. You made a mistake picking me, get someone who's tough.' I'd heard too many stories of crime and injustice, passed too many poor people on the street, too many frail elderly, disabled beggars, ragged children . . .

'That's why I picked you – because you are soft.' Early in my stay these words reassured me that the Lord knew exactly what he was doing. I drew enormous strength knowing that all the 'soft bits' in me were not only acceptable to Almighty God, but in fact what he wanted for the ministry.

I am indebted to the experience of being turned inside out by the Lord, though the process was painful. I can now better understand the disorientation people feel when they are transplanted into a new country or situation. I came just one tiny step closer to feeling the horror of being a war refugee, suddenly torn from home and hearth. As Gillian Bouras said: 'Now I know the whole agonizing process of migration intimately . . . This is how all migrants feel, surely. Far from believing with Henley, that we are the masters of our fates and captains of our souls, we feel, instead, like Lear's poor naked wretches biding the pelting of the pitiless storm.'[2]

---

[2] Bouras, *Foreign Wife*, p. 186.

Each day had rotated on its axis, illness and homesickness making the sluggish hours drag on. But now that the last day was rapidly approaching, we couldn't believe how quickly our time had gone. Towards the end of the semester, conversations inevitably came around to the obvious fact that Jeanette and I were going home and probably would not see any but a handful of them again. Everyone asked if we were going to come back for a visit, to which I would mumble a non-committal answer. My spirit and emotions told me this wasn't the last visit, but how or when we might return heaven knew.

One lad, Nigel, said in front of the rest of the group: 'We will miss you when you go.' I groaned, suddenly convicted of all the times when I had failed them and failed my own expectations of how I should teach and care for them.

'But I am so cranky sometimes. You've had a lot to put up with having me.'

'That doesn't matter,' he replied quickly. 'The students won't remember all that. They'll only remember your heart.'

13

The One-Child Policy

Before my time as a resident, I had not formulated my
own attitude towards the one-child policy, though
doubtless I was carrying around the silent baggage of
western attitudes. Like others, I was outraged at the
reports of enforced abortions in China. The crippling
fines and discriminations against the second child are
abhorrent to western understanding of human rights.
Such attitudes come from societies which have the
luxury of political freedom, material prosperity and
enough 'space' for each individual. Sadly not all
countries can offer these luxuries.

No one side of the argument brings an alleviation of
problems – just a new set of problems which later generations will have to tackle – one hopes without the
draconian tendencies of the early 1990s. While interference in one direction in the issue provokes a string
of unwanted results, inaction by the government and
people will foster other implications both now and
later. The Chinese government, when considering
demographic statistics and using only human logic,
made its decision for purely pragmatic reasons. They
believed they simply could not provide for China's 1.2

billion people in the coming decades. I cannot condone the policy but now 'after living in China' I can better understand how the government came to their decision to limit the population.

The journey by road to Guangzhou was a lesson for me in the extent of the problem. The highway linked up each village, town and city between the two places and covered a distance of approximately 560 kilometres. During the twelve long hours of travelling one way, I saw very little countryside. There was no point trying to work out where one city finished and another started. Villages merged into towns and cities engulfed towns and rice-fields alike. The peeling paint of tired, weathered structures cried out with the stress of municipalities trying to provide housing, education, employment as well as a reason to live, for each of its citizens. My imagination could not comprehend the size of the population lying beyond the narrow ribbon of what I could see through the car windows. The magnitude of the problems screamed at me in the run-down appearance of the roadside businesses and the weariness of the cyclists in the choking traffic, inching cautiously towards an uncertain destiny. I felt crowded by the concrete and glass and harried by the vehicles on every side of the car. The residents breathe the pollution and live in such conditions all their lives. Nevertheless, the life expectancy in China has risen from 40 years in 1949 to around 70 years today.

The one-child policy highlights substantial problems in food production for future generations. Only a small percentage of land out of a total of 9,561,000 sq. kilometres is suitable for growing crops. Mountains cover one third of the land, hills 9.9 per cent and plateaus 26.04 per cent (some of the latter are limited in use due to deforestation and erosion).

Tourists from all over the world flock to see the famous karst landscape along the Li River near Guilin in Guangxi Autonomous Region. From boats in every direction, they gaze at mountains rising like conical hats in the 'windows' framed by still other mountains. Though attracting tourist dollars, these mountains restrict available land for agriculture. A sizeable slice of Guangxi Autonomous Region is covered with similar terrain.

While on tour, we once visited a remote village in the mountains in Guangxi. Walking five kilometres along the rocky path, the spectacular scenery was constantly changing as mountains came into view, then disappeared behind other pinnacles. A song going through my head as I walked along seemed sadly fitting: 'The summer folk call it Paradise Mountain, but we call it Poverty Hill.'

The farmers were carefully tending every inch of land. Sweet-corn a metre high was growing up the sides of the mountains, even in single rows, until the incline defeated the farmers' efforts. We were told the average wage for a family here was \$A30/month. Guangxi is not the only province whose geography presents difficulties in coaxing the earth to yield sufficient bounty. People in other provinces contend with mountain ranges, deserts and changeable river courses, poor accessibility to remote parts, harsh climates in the north and west and often small or erratic rainfall in some areas. History has tragically taught that the land cannot cope with increased pressure to produce more and more to feed an ever-expanding population.

The government chose the pragmatic one-child policy after contemplating gloomy statistical projections – and disregarded human rights in the process. Perhaps they predicted a more sinister denial of rights, mass starvation, in a few decades' time. China suffered the worst famine in the history of the world in 1958–63 when 30 million people died. This was only one of several famines of unbelievable scale this century.

Wen-sheng talked about a famine in 1920: 'My father offered to sell me during the famine. We met a man with no son of his own and he offered to buy me for a bushel of millet. Dad asked me if I agreed. I said "Yes" but when my father started to leave me, I cried and wanted to go with him. In the end the bargain was called off. Dad gave back the millet and I went with him. We ate grass. We nearly died before we found a landlord who let us work his fields. My mother and sisters were already dead.'[1]

The population has exploded this century, despite the turbulence of wars and revolutions. In 1911 the population was estimated to be 374 million, in 1955 600 million and in the 1990 census 1,133,682,501. It is estimated that the population will be over 1.3 billion by the beginning of the twenty-first century. There is still a precarious margin between total food supply and the total number of consumers, although famine has largely been eliminated.[2] The leadership introduced the policy because they thought that

---

[1] Bloomfield, *China*, p. 35

[2] Murowchick, R.E., *Cradles of Civilization: China* (Norman: University of Oklahoma Press, USA, 1994) p. 35

over-population would seriously hamper reaching the economic goals of the Four Modernizations.

Although the policy denies the enjoyment of a large family, there is a sinister paradox which partly explains the recurring violent history China has suffered for thousands of years.

> 'A successful dynasty ensured peace within the country and this allowed the population to expand, putting pressure upon many aspects of the economy, but especially upon food supplies in years of poor weather. In addition, every sign of internal weakness was taken as an opportunity for those on the edges of China to demand more concessions or to raid more deeply into Chinese territory. Such external attacks only encouraged more popular anger with a government that could not provide adequate defence. Ultimately the combination of problems would bring such widespread discontent with the existing dynasty, that new aspirants hoping to wield a more effective dynastic power would arise, either inside or outside China or both.'[3]

If this summary of history is correct, it presages a continued cycle of violent political upheaval following an expansion in population, ironically due to peace, which in turn causes pressure on the land, unrest and finally rebellion again. Perhaps the one-child policy is an attempt to circumvent this historical certainty.

My friend asked a man in Beijing years ago what he thought of Mao Zedong. He sniffed and said that Mao

---

[3] Phillips, R. T., *China Since 1911* (London: MacMillan Press Ltd., 1996) p. 4

had caused the over-population of China. For years I naïvely puzzled how one man (no matter how friendly he was with countless women!), could *cause* such a huge increase. I later learned that Mao encouraged large families because he wanted to become the father-figure of a vast population. Today's cities groan under the problems caused by this short-sightedness. In Shanghai there are 2,000 inhabitants per square kilometre. The early communist leaders believed that massive amounts of labour were needed to transform the nation. People advocating birth control were accused of trying to 'kill off the Chinese people without shedding blood'.[4]

The 1953 census shot the estimate of 500 million people closer to 600 million. Even Mao was staggered by the facts. Serious birth control efforts started in 1956.

The one-child policy, introduced in 1979 encouraged couples to limit themselves to one child through a system of incentives and penalties. For the compliant, there was free medical treatment for the child to the age of eighteen, preferential admission to kindergarten, child-care facilities, free education, exemption from military service and transfer to rural areas to work. The mother would receive extended maternity leave and the family priority in obtaining housing, including larger quarters, a small cash subsidy and extra food rations.

The non-compliant would be immediately disadvantaged in competition for housing, kindergarten admission, etc. The child would be more likely to be

---

[4] Kaplan & Sobin, *Encyclopedia*, p. 28

sent to the countryside or selected for military service. For those with three or more children, sanctions were imposed. The fines, ranging from 5–15 per cent of parental income, were levied until the child reached fourteen or fifteen years of age. This money was to compensate the government for educating and other-wise caring for the 'excess' child. Cadres could be sacked or expelled from the Party if they themselves did not comply.

Billboards showing parents admiring their toddler (always a girl in view of the strong preference for male children) captioned 'Daddy, Mummy and me', and 'One Child is best' sprang up all over China. Many city couples decided they wanted only one child any-way, so the policy worked well there. When we talked to local people about the policy, they didn't give their own point of view but closed the subject by replying: 'Our government won't let us have more than one child.' I detected no strong feelings against the policy. But the majority of the population is rural and they have economic and traditional reasons to resist the policy. Male labour is more highly regarded than female, so if girls are born the parents want to keep trying until a boy arrives.

A student illustrated this preference for boys over girls. When she was born, she greatly disappointed her grandfather by not being a boy, but with time he came to love her deeply. When her sister was born, the same entrenched attitude reared its head again. One day, her grandfather locked her mother in the house, took the baby, put it in a tub and was going to let her drift down the river – to face whatever destiny. Fortunately her mother escaped and rescued the baby. Her sister has survived to adulthood though it seems only through the Lord's sovereignty in her life. She also told me that babies are abandoned by their parents on the steps of the hospital within walking distance of the college. The hospital can't or won't take care of them, so they are simply left to die. One wonders how many are abandoned because of gender or because the parents cannot afford to keep them and pay the fine.

When asked how they feel a skewed sex ratio will impact on their chances of having grandsons, people tend to reply that having grandsons depends on having sons first.[5]

There are concerns that when young men reach marriageable age they will have trouble finding wives. Country people either pay fines or bribe officials to ignore births. Since they own their own homes, housing incentives are meaningless. Many do not seek lengthy education so preference in school admission is not essential. People use many methods for getting around the regulations: by not registering marriages or female births, or, when the wife becomes pregnant, by moving to distant relatives until after the birth, or by joining the floating population. Under Deng Xiao Ping's economic incentive system, people were given more liberty from their work units which resulted in more freedom to move between states. A *Xinhua* reporter asked a peasant-turned-peddler what he would do about his lack of residence registration: 'You need residence registration in order to get grain and coal rations. We buy grain and coal at negotiated

[5] Dreyer, *China's Political System*, p. 246

prices. We have no use for residence registrations . . .
We have money and are far better off than you are.'
When he asked him about how he would educate his
large brood of unregistered or 'black' children, the
reporter was told: 'There is nothing that money cannot buy. We give some money under the table to the
person in charge of the school; the problem will be
solved in no time. They will go to one of the good
schools.'[6] Villages built by 'excessive birth guerrillas'
have sprung up on wastelands and the floating population is estimated to be between 70–100 million
people and growing.

I was told that the minority groups are exempt and
when I asked a student why, she replied: 'There aren't
many minority people.' (There are over fifty minority
groups in China today and *one* of them, the Zhuang,
has a population of 16 million!) I later read: 'By official government decree that they (Zhuang) can have
only two children; fines of over US$500 are levied
against families who exceed this quota.'[7]

The situation for minorities is complicated. Under
Deng Xiao Ping's reforms, minority groups were partially exempt from the family planning regulations.
The government policy varied according to the developmental level of individual groups and other
circumstances. The large groups considered relatively
advanced economically and culturally, living in urban
areas, could have two children or three, if the first
two were daughters. In practice, the groups which

---

[6] Ibid., p. 245
[7] Stevens & Wehrfritz, *Southwest China*, p. 71

were likely to be resistant to the issue received little more than lectures on the merits of family planning.[8]

If the 1.824 birth rate and .66 death rate are correct, then 13 million people are added to the population each year. Others believe the figure is 3–4 million higher – almost the entire population of Australia. Reducing the population growth rate to below 2 per cent in a short time is an amazing achievement. But this growth rate has serious implications for the government. A number of new jobs will need to be created each year, and at present chronic unemployment and underemployment inhibit the mechanization of industry and agriculture and hold down productivity. When basic needs must be met first, the rate of capital accumulation slows down. This delays the modernization of the economy and contributes to continuing shortages of housing, clothing, medicine and other necessities and also of consumer goods, educational opportunities and cultural advantages – living standards rise very slowly. Valuable farming land has to be seconded for housing and other purposes. Births are lowest amongst educated professionals and highest amongst the poor and marginally literate.

My students are the last generation of children born just before the regulations took effect, so many have brothers and sisters. To me they were polite, helpful, a pleasure to teach and always fun to be with. But many of those destined to become teachers fearfully foresee struggles trying to control naughty pupils in enormous classes. 'Little Emperors' is the name Chinese adults apply to these children. Since

---

[8] Dreyer, *China's Political System*, p. 295

they are not required to consider another sibling, potentially they may grow into very self-centred individuals. Military officers are worried about the recruits of the future. Also, with all the hopes of a family centred on the success of a single daughter or son, would the psychological burden become too great and affect their mental health? Parents are understandably concerned about the out-working of effects of childhood indulgence on society.

I noticed at college and elsewhere that in many family units the father has transferred to another city or province, leaving the mother to rear the child alone or with the assistance of a grandparent. Time will tell what effect this separation from the father figure will have on the child. There are probably economic advantages, but it means one household occupies two dwellings, and there is already a housing shortage in many localities. On a brighter note, children live close together, so they are never far from a playmate: the sounds of them playing in the alley below reassured me that they are not as lonely as a single western child in a suburb in the West can be. The future care of the elderly is a question left unanswered at this point of time. How could a married couple care for four infirm parents? Considering the nation as a whole, how could a smaller group of younger people support a huge population and still achieve high economic growth rates?

Since 1979, the Government has lost many of its economic controls over the population. Even threats against cadres are only partially effective because the position of cadre is not as desirable as it once was, and party membership not so eagerly sought after. Inflation has diluted the value of cash bonuses in cities. In a situation of acute housing shortages, but with almost everyone holding a one-child certificate, preference in housing means little. It is small wonder that the government is losing its ability to enforce compliance.

Epilogue

1997 Concert Tour

My return to the college less than a year after I had gone home, was a surprise for everyone and I hope it reinforced the notion that I was still committed to the students. Mr. Lu, George and Hannah met us at the airport and whisked three team members and myself off in the College vehicle. The others found their own way to the hotel. Bouncing through the streets, it was wonderful to see the place that had been so alien on that first night, but had quickly become so familiar to me. I pointed out landmarks to the team while talking non-stop to Hannah, so it all probably came out very garbled. Hannah was her same hospitable self. She gave me all the local news about students and teachers we knew and also mentioned that she had at last decided to apply for post-graduate study in Guangzhou. I was thrilled that she had taken this leap into the unknown. (A letter from her months later confirmed that she had accepted a teaching position at the College instead.)

Walking swiftly up the four flights of steps of the teaching building seemed strange; how many times had I trudged up them carrying heavy books and bags? As we walked in, the class erupted into excited applause. It was great to see my favourite class again and even better to hear them chattering on and on like native speakers. Their skills had improved exponentially in the intervening few months.

I prepared questions tailored to most of the students; Damien told me about his swimming accomplishments, Nigel about how hard the class had been studying (to the laughter of the rest of the class); Felicity and Anita about going shopping etc. I thought they would give hesitant one-sentence answers, but each held the floor confidently and told me all the latest news since my departure. They tossed around their penny worth of teasing comments to each other and asked me questions concerning life back home. In the class were women teachers we had associated with the most, including Lyla. They asked all sorts of questions and were as excited as the students.

Unfortunately I did not have a chance to talk to Felicity privately about the sudden death of her father. Anita had written to tell us the sad news.

I assumed I would meet friends after the concert that night. But we had to share the stage with a school who had so many items, each with a cast of thousands, plus the College items. The concert ended just at curfew time for the dormitories. Afterwards I only saw one of my students. I was heart-broken; to have spent a fortune going so far and seen my class for only an hour in the afternoon. I felt I should stay on stage during the Chinese items because of security reasons. I should have gone down to the audience. Sometimes my sense of duty needs to be over-ruled!

The typhoon season hit the city once again.

Felicity wrote after my return to Australia: 'I'm now telling you a piece of astonishing bad news. A strong typhoon came on September 9. Most of the trees, windows, doors, unsolid buildings are damaged. Half of the things on Anita's bookshelf had gone with the wind (including books, sheets, photos etc.) My house is quite good, just a piece of glass was broken. If you came back now . . . you wouldn't believe what you see. Luckily nobody in our college was killed in the typhoon. However, it's said that more than 80 people died and more than 800 people were injured by now in the city and the loss summed up to more than 650 million yuan . . . Now the people are rebuilding their homes, factories and so on. I'm sure the city will appear a new look.'

It had stood on the wharf alongside the others. A towering, imposing dock crane – capable of shifting shipping containers with ease and speed; now derelict. Its vertical and horizontal lines now lay in circular form. The giant hand of the typhoon had caught the top and twisted it down into a round ball of crumpled metal, with the ease of a child twisting a string of dandelions into a headband.

'This crane was Japanese. That one over there – the one still standing – is Chinese,' our tour guide said smugly.

I looked back at the crushed mass which was once a crane and wondered how they would clear it away.

Where do you start? The port authorities may have had the same thought: already it had lain untouched for seven months.

I brought Jeanette back a silk scarf . . .

1998 Concert tour

Have you ever opened your diary before the Lord and asked him to fill a particular day with appointments with people you want to see, but have no way of contacting otherwise? When I returned to the college during the 1998 tour, I had a prayer list of names of students and teachers and a yearning to meet them. But how? I knew that the College wouldn't necessarily set up meetings just for me; they would want other students as well to have 'practice time' talking with the Australians. The College now has over 5,000 students.

Our itinerary had been arranged to include my giving a two-hour lecture on the history and present state of education in Australia to teachers and senior students. At the same time at another location, the rest of the team would have an informal get-together with some (unspecified) students. As usually happens, details for the morning were changed late the night before. With the change of plans, I feared that I would be in one place talking to a roomful of mainly strangers while the others I wanted to meet, would be talking to our mob of strangers elsewhere. Over to you, Lord.

In the room for the get-together, amongst a crowd of younger ones, were a few of Jeanette's students – now blossomed into grade threes – and about half of my class, excitedly waiting for us. What a relief. Among the well-wishers was a girl who had received the rough end of my discipline one day in class – a slip I always regretted. Thank you Lord for another answer to prayer.

Gone were the middle school haircuts and self-conscious hilarity. My girls, now in fourth grade, had matured into poised and beautiful young women and the men had an air of confidence and ease. Their language skills had had another year to be polished into readiness for any career challenge. All of them I spoke to were keen to talk about their new teaching positions awaiting graduation day, or their bright prospects for such, awaiting confirmation. Most would start a fresh life in any one of the surrounding cities and one or two were taking up local jobs near the College.

I was thrilled to hear that all of them were streamed into the higher numbered and hence better-endowed, prestigious middle schools. That may have been because in a few months' time, the College would confer on them a Bachelor of Arts rather than a Diploma. They were also studying towards the dreaded Band Eight examination which would open further doors to career advancement. How far they have come in four years! At the end of the session, when we had talked ourselves out, I asked Felicity to come shopping with me in the afternoon. She flung her arms around my neck, thrilled to be asked.

'It's just like old times!' she enthused.

'You asked about my father's death in your letter and where we would live. You will be happy to know that we are still at the same college, but have moved into a larger home there.'

'Great, that's wonderful. How is your mother?'

'Oh, she is very busy every day. Remember my sister had a baby? My mother looks after her while my sister is working.'

The wheel of time – birth to death to new life: every problem, catastrophic at the moment, over time smoothed away, converted into some life-giving activity for another's sake. We are cared for by a Heavenly Father who sees ahead with solutions for every calamity.

Felicity sent Anita's apologies: she had been unwell in the morning. Certainly it seemed strange to see Felicity without Anita in tow. Before the performance at night, I had to slip out for something. I bumped into Anita who was on her way to her weekly class of tutoring a child in English.

'I am pleased to tell you that I will be teaching at number one middle school in the city when I graduate,' she announced proudly.

Felicity was confident of a job in a local school too, so the two friends would not be separated. Others asked me my opinion on whether college students should date or concentrate instead solely on their studies for the duration of their course? This is a thorny question. At the end of their college careers, most graduates find themselves separated to the four winds by employment needs with little opportunity for couples to be located permanently in one city. They are helped or hindered by the forces of *guanxi* in their search for work. The fortunate few find work in the same city. For a proportion of those failing in this endeavour, the State system will assign jobs in their home-towns or elsewhere. Elly groaned: 'If we don't take the job offered to us, we have to pay a lot of money to the government.'

'Why is that?'

'It's because the government has already paid out a lot of money to give us an education.'

There is no 'bad guy' you could pin the blame on. The cold reality was that the government also had a stake in this situation. Its agenda was the development of the nation and to do that teachers were required in all areas of the country, not just in the comfortable cities where graduates wanted to go. The underlying question in the young people's hearts was an emotional one: can I bear to say goodbye to the security and closeness of a relationship and college life, at such a pivotal time in my life when I am launching into an important phase of my career with all the attendant insecurities of my first year out, probably in another city – alone? With each individual in the relationship facing the same situation, forces greater than themselves propelling them in different directions, needs and desires become of secondary importance. Sally had a boyfriend in her new city, thus avoiding these problems.

I had prayed that I would have time to speak with Evelyn. While on the last tour we discovered that we were both Christians. I had spoken to her infrequently while a resident, while she bided her time for months interstate until the day she could join her husband permanently, following his transfer to the College. I was amazed to see her in the welcoming party, though surprised by Lyla's absence. At lunch-time next day, Evelyn re-appeared and we talked non-stop throughout the scrumptious meal. Her transfer had gone through so now she was happily living with her husband and teaching in the College.

My students were disappointed that they were not given tickets for the team's concert that night. Many others I knew, though I had not taught them, were in the audience, as well as many other staff members. We shared the concert programme with spectacular student performances of songs and dances. As I stepped between rows finding a seat to watch this part of the show, I saw a hand waving energetically and heard 'Belinda'. It was Lyla.

One name not on my ten-page prayer list was Holly since she was not part of the college. 'Hello Belinda!' A beaming Holly popped out of the crowd at the end of the concert.

'What are you doing here?' I gasped.

'We are filming the show for my television programme. It will appear on TV on Monday. Oh, I must tell you, Amanda is going to have a baby in July!'

They had tied the knot. The college gossip lines had also revealed another two pregnancies amongst the teachers.

There was no strangeness at all in relating to old friends. Everyone was so warm-hearted. Intimate conversations just started where we had left off two years ago. Sharing joys and pressing worries conveyed a sense of being part of the community. Why did I ever worry that I wouldn't fit into the campus community?

What a campus it is now. The pocket handkerchief of land that the college resides on is burgeoning with multi-storey teaching buildings, dormitories and other facilities. However, the site exuded an air of efficiency rather than cramped conditions. The library

and some of the departments were soon to be re-
located to the second campus, the students informed
me with pride.

The blackened kitchens and dining-rooms were
re-furbished and put to alternative purposes after the
new dining-room became fully operational. The con-
tentious two-hour lecture was held in one of them.
Fresh gardens were planted and old ones re-planted,
but why did they chop down the shady eucalyptus
trees and plant palms? Perhaps shade is more important to Australians than Chinese because we have less
cloud and harsh summers? I remembered the symbol-
ism of the heavy, ponderous cloud cover which
shrouds much of China, much of the year.

The Son is shining through the thick clouds. Thank
you Lord for the privilege of being part of your plans
in the Middle Kingdom. I started the journey thinking
I would be teaching some dancing as well as English.
That only eventuated into a brief few lessons with a
girl from the Art Department. That didn't matter at all
now. I had gained so much more experience than I
could have ever imagined possible in my short time in
the Middle Kingdom.

Appendix 1: Teaching Contract

The Contract with the College Issued by the State Bureau of Foreign Experts (Abridged form)

Party A – College Authorities
Party B – Foreign Teacher
The two parties, in a spirit of friendly co-operation, agree to sign this contract and pledge to fulfil conscientiously all the obligations stipulated in it.

Money

Party B's monthly salary will be 1,800 RMB (Yuan). Party A shall pay Party B's salary regularly by the month.

Laws

Party B shall observe the laws, decrees and relevant regulations enacted by the Chinese government and shall not interfere in China's internal affairs.

Party B shall observe party A's work system and regulations concerning administration of foreign experts and shall accept Party A's arrangement, direction, supervision and evaluation in regard to his/her work. Without Party A's consent, Party B shall not render service elsewhere hold concurrently any post unrelated to the work agreed on with Party A.

Party B shall complete the tasks agreed on schedule and guarantee the quality of work. Party B shall respect China's religious policy and shall not conduct activities incompatible with the status of an expert.

Party B shall respect the Chinese people's moral standards and customs.

Both parties should abide by the contract and should refrain from revising, cancelling or terminating the contract without mutual consent.

Party A has the right to cancel the contract with a written notice to Party B under the following conditions: Party B does not fulfil the contract or does not fulfil the contract obligations to the terms stipulated and has failed to amend after Party A has pointed it out. According to the doctor's diagnosis, Party B cannot resume normal work after a continued 30 day sick leave.

Party B has the right to cancel the contract with a written notice to Party A under the following conditions: Party A has not provided Party B with necessary working and living conditions as stipulated in the contract. party A has not paid Party B as scheduled.

Breach penalty

When either of the two parties fails to fulfil the contract or fails to fulfil the contract obligations according to the terms stipulated, that is, breaks the contract, it must pay a breach penalty of $US500–2,000 or equivalent in RMB (Yuan).

If Party B asks to cancel the contract due to events beyond control, it should produce certifications by the department concerned, obtain Party A's consent, and pay its own return expenses; if Party B cancels the contract without valid reason, it should pay its own return expenses and pay a breach penalty to Party A.

If Party A asks to cancel the contract due to events beyond its control, with the consent of Party B, it should pay Party B's return expenses; if Party A cancels without valid reason, it should pay Party B's return expenses and pay a breach penalty to Party B. This contract takes effect on the date signed by both parties and will automatically expire when the contract ends. If either of the two parties asks for a new contract, it should forward its request to another party 90 days prior to the expiration of the contract and sign the new contract with mutual consent. Party B shall bear all expenses incurred when staying on after the contract expires.

Arbitration

The two parties shall consult with each other and mediate any disputes which may arise about the contract. If all attempts fail, the two parties can appeal to the organisation of arbitration for foreign experts affairs in the state Bureau of Foreign Experts and ask for a final arbitration.

Duties of the person hired

- Taking teaching position *conversational English, English writing*, working five days __ hours a week.
- Making good preparations for classes, checking exercises, giving instructions, supervising examinations, grading examination papers and working out student's marks.
- Reporting feed-back information from teaching to the Dean and helping guide the language corner and other after-class activities.
- Carrying out the teaching programme in line with requirements of the college, using textbooks agreed upon by both sides, so that satisfactory results can be achieved.
- Assuring that the teaching programme is not interrupted or suspended, except of illness or other special reasons. No private travelling or vacation can be arranged in this period. Informing the Dean's office in case of illness.

Duties of the appointing side

- During the contract, the appointing side makes clear the teaching programme, provides necessary help to guarantee the fulfilment of the programme.

Boarding and lodging

- The College provides a suite of well-furnished rooms together with a gas stove, kitchen utensils, a refrigerator, a washing machine, telephone, water heater, etc.
- Gas, water and electricity are free. Telephone fee paid 40 RMB (Yuan) monthly by the college.

Medical care

- The person hired receives free medical care in the College's clinic. Medical care outside the college needs personal payment from the person hired.

Transportation

- The appointing side arranges a one day tour . . . once during the whole academic year. An overnight stay is not arranged. The appointing side will send a person to accompany the tour and the fee of lunch, drink and tickets during these twice touring is paid by the college.

Holidays and travelling

- Besides Chinese traditional holidays, the person hired can enjoy his (her) own important holidays like Christmas or National Day (three days).
- The College doesn't provide travelling fee, but will separately grant a certain allowance for one year's service or less. The allowance is about 2,200 RMB (100%)/year.

- The College pays the hired person a return plane
  ticket of the shortest way to his (her) country after
  finishing two years of work. Within one year of
  contract, the college pays the person hired the
  inner-China transportation fee . . . when he (she)
  enters or leaves China.

Appendix 2: Practical Tips

Suggestions about what to take:

Many of these items came from home, on the
assumption that they might not be readily available
in China. Few things were a waste of luggage space.
I have expanded the list to include things which also
would have been useful. They can all be shipped in
boxes before leaving. The quantities taken should be
more than enough for the length of stay. Excess
items can be given away to friends or donated to the
College clinic, etc. Some items such as coffee, block
chocolate may be available in China, but westerners
prefer richer flavours.
Consider: Customs regulations for taking food and
other items overseas.

Medical

comprehensive first-aid kit – including tweezers,
alcohol swabs, spare syringes, cream for stings/
itching (e.g. Aloe vera cream), cotton wool,
Band-Aid, bandages of several sizes, antiseptic, burn

dressings, glucose electrolyte oral powder for
rehydration following diarrhoea and gastro-enteritis
Tablets: antibiotics, malaria, coughs and colds, throat
lozenges, nausea, diarrhoea, stomach complaints, pain
relief, vitamins - C, iron, calcium, etc.

Personal

toiletries, hobbies, fly swat, sunscreen, dental floss,
insect repellant, tampons, prickly heat powder
(tropical areas)
Stout shoes for winter and summer. *Clothing*
if you are larger than the average Chinese, take
own clothes; don't expect to find your size in
shops there; women can try man-size socks and
T-shirts.

Products with abundant uses

Oil of Eucalyptus for:
Influenza: inhalant, chest and back rub, to sprinkle
on handkerchief.
Muscular aches and pains: massage.
Stains, grease marks on clothes: apply directly
before washing; for woolens and work clothes, add
oil to wash.
Sodium Bicarbonate for:
Cleaning: bathroom and fridge surfaces, battery
terminals.
Stain removal: on carpet, upholstery, coffee cups,
vases, etc.
Killing odours in fridges.
Add to water for relaxing bath.

Stationary

staples, glue stick, stapler, felt pens, Blu-Tack, sticky tape, thick chalk.

Food

baking powder, Sodium bicarbonate, bread improver, other baking aids, meat substitute products, packet sauces, custards, powdered drinks – cocoa, coffee, orange, etc.
wooden spoon, recipes with basic ingredients, dish mop (the dishwasher will have to be boiling)
Herbs and spices in many and various quantities, are really important for your tastebuds. Some, not all, spices and herbs are sold by Chinese herbalists for medicinal purposes. There is less variety in the markets.

Professional library for teaching English as a second language (ESL)

Dictionaries of own country's version of English, preferably with phonetic symbols, poetry collections.
ESL my collection included a general reference book on teaching ESL, 2 guides to English usage, 2 teaching writing guides, a folktales story book for whole language learning, 3 grammar texts, books with spelling and grammar exercises and games, a picture vocabulary for illustration purposes.
Hunt out second hand textbook shops, make friends with a local primary or secondary school librarian.

Gather your own collection of authentic English
literature – calendars, maps and pictures, etc. as per
the teaching chapter. Backing tracks of western
pop/folksongs for your concert debut.

Miscellaneous

general purpose batteries (Chinese ones have limited
life), definitely specialized batteries, e.g. for hearing
aid, watch, camera, etc.
pocket torch, computer *power surge protector*, all
auxiliary products, e.g. cartridges (Computer may
be more trouble than it's worth, though a lap-top is
more portable.) Carry all computer equipment as
hand luggage on the plane.

What not to take

No unnecessary valuables – eg. jewellery, ostentatious
clothing (shows off our higher standard of living
and hinders the making of relationships), perfume
or perfumed toiletries e.g. deodorant (attracts
mosquitoes), not truckloads of clothes (if you are
'Chinese size' you can buy them there or treat
yourself to a trip to the tailor, you won't be
disappointed).

Gift-Giving

So Auntie Amelia has just left you her fortune and
your feet have said: 'Go East young man!' Your

head is reeling with what to pack into your suitcase. Cost is another factor which dampens your enthusiasm for the adventure of living and working overseas: just how far will her fortune go? Plane tickets, en-route accommodation, visas, medical checks and innoculations have a habit of making enormous holes in your budget. That's where friends, family and colleagues can help. If they get caught up in your enthusiasm for teaching English for a year or working in an aid and development role, they will probably want to give a gift to help your dream materialize. You will know they are interested by the glint of vicarious enjoyment you see in their eyes when you talk about the adventure. Good intentions could translate into gifts which instead of being a blessing, become an embarrassing curse. You just don't know what to do with the pink fluffy slippers someone gave you, let alone the over-stuffed life-size koala. People dither about what is appropriate and appreciate a bit of guidance. Incurable shoppers prefer to buy you something rather than give money.

To educate the would-be givers, make a list of what you *need* – not what you *want*:
• Include everything, from major expenses – Hepatitis shots, shipping costs for your boxes – to minor ones – spare watch battery. (The cost of the list will probably astound you.)
• Make copies and circulate it around.

Here are a few things to include on your gift-list of what you may ask people to provide:

- New sturdy suitcase. Be honest. Will your old faithful one last another year of being badly mistreated by railway and airport staff? Is it waterproof and the locks impenetrable?
- Vitamins. Your diet will certainly change and will include wonderfully delectable and strange foods. But it may exclude meat and dairy products, so supplements are advisable, especially iron tablets for women.
- Toiletries. If you think you couldn't live without your favourite brands of shampoo or whatever, take them along. If you are going to a tropical zone, you don't need scented soap, hand-cream, etc. because the mosquitoes will love you. Do I have to say – leave the perfume bottle home?
- Clothes. Check out your destination's climate and availability of clothes' suppliers. Average size in Australia is very large size in Asia, even Australian size 10–12, so take all your essential clothes and especially footwear (socks/stockings too) for all seasons. Think of buying clothes there as a bonus; don't go expecting to buy essentials the day you arrive. You probably won't need as large a wardrobe as you have at home.

Setting up a support team

You will appreciate a variety of people to play a variety of roles. Seek out those with particular gifts in the following areas:

- Prayer. Need I say more? You will need faithful
  intercessors.
- Finances. Ask your finance person to receive your
  mail, pay bills and deal with related matters. Take
  as much money with you as you can
  (cash/travellers cheques of well-known currencies
  – American, British, Australian) thus avoiding
  having to go through a bank. For the same
  reason, suggest to donors they give you money
  before you go rather than after you have left.
- Parcel sending. This person will gather gifts from
  friends and supporters, advertise the next
  shipment at church and send boxes on a regular
  basis. Boxes should be bound, lined with plastic
  and almost impenetrable! Stick masking tape on
  each fold and corner of box and tape the rope as
  well. Ask a person who is attuned to the Holy
  Spirit, so that they may anticipate future
  needs/wants and think creatively.
- Newsletters. Efficient secretary to type up
  newsletters, copy and circulate to supporters by
  post/fax/email, keep up to date with changes of
  addresses, new additions, etc. Ask secretary to
  announce arrival of each newsletter at church,
  thus encouraging prayer support from the
  congregation (and more letters). Leave money for
  stamps and sundry expenses.

Bibliography

Allen, J., *Seeing Red: China's Uncompromising Take-over of Hong Kong* (Butterworth-Heinemann Asia 1997)

Andrews, J., *The Asian Challenge* (Hong Kong: Longman Group (Far East) Ltd 1991)

Bastin, J. & Benda, H. J., *A History of Modern Southeast Asia* (Sydney: Prentice-Hall of Aust. P/L Australia 1977)

Beeching, J., *The Chinese Opium Wars* (London: Hutchinson & Co. (Publishers) Ltd 1975)

Blixen, K., (under name Isak Dinesan) *Out of Africa and Shadows on the Grass* (Harmondsworth: Penguin Books Ltd 1937)

Bloomfield, R., *China: Tradition and Change* (Auckland: Longman Paul Ltd NZ 1993)

Bouras, G., *A Foreign Wife* (Melbourne: McPhee Gribble/ Penguin Books Australia 1988, 3rd Edition.)

Brooman, J., *China Since 1900* (Harlow: Longman Group UK Ltd 1993)

Bucknall, K. B., *Kevin B. Bucknall's Cultural Guide to Doing Business in China* (Oxford: Butterworth Heinemann 1994)

Chang, I., *The Rape of Nanjing* (New York: Basic Books USA 1997)

Childs, R., *Leading the Chinese Revolution: China 1921–1949* (Auckland: Macmillan Company of NZ Ltd 1987)

Chung, J., *Wild Swans* (London: Flamingo 1991)

Courtauld, C. & Holdsworth, M., *The Hong Kong Story* (Hong Kong: Oxford University Press 1997)

Crossman, E., *Mountain Rain* (Singapore: OMF 1987 4th Edition)

Diamond, J.A., 'Peeling the Chinese Onion' in *Nature* Vol. 391 No. 6666 (1998) 433–4

Dreyer, J. Teufel, *China's Political System* (London: Macmillan Press Ltd 1996 2nd Edition)

Eastman, L. E., *Thrones and Mandarins* (Cambridge: Harvard University Press USA 1967)

Ebrey, P. Buckley, *Chinese Civilization and Society* (New York: The Free Press-Macmillan Publishing Co. USA 1981)

Fairbank, J. K., Reischauer, E. O. & Craig A. M., *East Asia: Tradition and Transformation* (London: George Allen and Unwin Ltd 1975 2nd Edition)

Findlay, I., *Shanghai* (Hong Kong: The Guidebook Co. Ltd/London: Harrap Ltd. 1988)

Gernet, J., *A History of Chinese Civilization* (Cambridge: Cambridge University Press 1982)

Giese, D., *Astronauts, Lost Souls and Dragons* (St Lucia, Brisbane: University of Queensland Press Australia 1997)

Gray, J., *Rebellions and Revolutions: China 1800's to 1900's* (Oxford: Oxford University Press 1990.)

Hale, Dr T., *Don't let the Goats eat the Loquat Trees* (Grand Rapids: Zondervan Publishing House USA 1986)

Haw, S. G., *A Traveller's History of China* (New York: Interlink Books USA 1995)

Hawthorne, S. C., *Perspectives on the World Christian Movement Part I: Study Guide* (Christchurch: Centre for Mission Direction NZ 1994 2nd Edition)

Hibbert, C., *The Dragon Wakes – 1793–1911* (Harmondsworth: Penguin Books Ltd 1984)

Hinton, H. C., *An Introduction to Chinese Politics* (Melbourne: Wren Publishing P/L Australia 1973)

Johnston, B., *Boxing With Shadows* (Carlton South, Melbourne: Melbourne University Press Australia 1996)

Kaplan, F. M. & Sobin, J. M., *Encyclopedia of China Today* (Sydney: Book Wise (Australia) Ltd 1982 3rd Edition)

Keay, J., *Empire's End* (New York: Scribner USA 1997)

Lambert, T., *The Resurrection of the Chinese Church* (London: Hodder & Stoughton OMF 1991)

Lane, P., *China in the Twentieth Century* (London: BT Batsford Ltd. 1978)

Lyall, L., *Three of China's Mighty Men* (London: OMF Books 1973)

Lyall, L., *God Reigns in China* (Sevenoaks: Hodder & Stoughton 1985)

Lyall, L., *The Phoenix Rises* (Singapore: OMF 1992)

Mackerras, C., *Western Images of China* (Hong Kong: Oxford University Press 1989)

Mann, M., (Ed) *Library of Nations: China* (Amsterdam: Time-life Books Holland 1990 12th Edition)

Mente, B.L. De, *NTC'S Dictionary of China's Cultural Code Words* (Lincolnwood: NTC Publishing Group USA 1996)

Montgomery, J.W., *Giant in Chains* (Milton Keynes: Nelson Word Ltd 1994)

Murowchick, R. E., *Cradles of Civilization: China* (Norman: University of Oklahoma Press USA 1994)

Nelson, E.R. & Broadberry, R.E., *Genesis and the Mystery Confucius Couldn't Solve* (St. Louis: Concordia Publishing House USA 1994)

Patterson, G. N., *The China Paradox* (Heathmont, Melbourne: Word Publishing Australia 1990)

Phillips, R. T., *China Since 1911* (London: Macmillan Press Ltd 1996)

Rajendra, N. & V., & Lower, C., *A History of Asia* (Melbourne: Longman Cheshire P/L Australia 1984)

Ross, S., *China Since 1945* (Hove: Wayland (Publishers) Ltd 1988)

Spence, J.D., *God's Chinese Son* (New York: W.W. Norton & Co. Inc. 1996)

Stefoff, R., *Places and Peoples of the World: China* (New York: Chelsea House Publishing USA 1991)

Stevens, K. M. & Wehrfritz, G. E., *Southwest China off the Beaten Track* (London: Collins 1988)

Taylor, J.H., *Hudson Taylor* (Minneapolis: Bethany House Publishers USA - no date given)

Wang, L., *Blood Price* (Port Melbourne: William Heinemann Australia 1996)

Weiner, R., Murphy, M. & Li, A., *Living in China* (San Francisco: China Books & Periodicals Inc. USA 1991)

Williams, B., *Ancient China* (New York: Viking USA 1996)

Williams, S., *China Since 1949* (Basingstoke: Macmillan Education Ltd 1985)

Yueng, Y. M. & Chu, D. K. Y., 'Guangdong: Survey of a Province Undergoing Rapid Change' in *China Journal* (Hong Kong: Chinese University Press 1994)

Zhao Xilin (Eds), *Tourist Atlas of China*, English edition (Shanghai: China Cartographic Publishing House 1988)

Index

A Flame of Sacred Love
The Life of Benjamin Broomhall 1829–1911
Norman Cliff

Benjamin Broomhall, brother-in-law of Hudson Taylor, was one of the best known Christina laymen in Britain in the latter part of the nineteenth century.

As the General Secretary of the China Inland Mission he was a prominent figure in churches and at large conventions where he spoke on China and the cause of the missions. He was well known to Cabinet Ministers and members of Parliament for his uncompromising stand against the evils of slavery and the opium trade, and in his lifetime saw both evils largely eliminated.

Although he never set foot in China, Broomhill had a great influence on God's work in that land through hundreds of young people he selected and sent out, including five of his own children.

"Behind many a Christian visionary stand those whose complementary gifts of steady wisdom and practical management, under God, enable the vision to be realised, Here is the engrossing story of a husband and wife partnership playing exactly such a role. In no small measure, it was Benjamin and Amelia Broomhill who enables James Hudson Taylor's vision for the China Inland Mission to pass from dream to reality."
Rosemary Dowsett, OMF International, Conference and Training Ministry

Norman Cliff is the great grandson of Benjamin Broomhill. He has researched and written about the history of missions in China in the nineteenth and twentieth centuries, including events during the Sino-Japanese War from 1937–1945. As a minister he had pastorates in South Africa and Zimbabwe. He is now in retirement in Harold Wood, Essex.

ISBN 1–85078–328–4

**OM
publishing**

A Cracked Pot
... tales from the heart of life's journey
Lizzy Wilson

Lizzy Wilson, an Irish Midwife engaged in developmental work, takes us on a journey into the hearts and lives of people who are, for many different reasons, 'living separation' from those they love. With humour, warmth and great love of life and people, she shows the many ways in which a 'cracked pot', in the hands of its master creator, can make a difference in our hurting world with its kaleidoscope of needs.

These true short stories are based on Lizzy's experiences in may parts of the world, including war-torn Iraq, refugee Sudan, Australia, North Africa and Ireland.

This book will have you laughing out loud—and weeping with grief and frustration. It will make you call into question the modern Western emphasis on 'success' that has infiltrated even out thinking about Christian work, with the timely reminder that God asks rather for obedience and faithfulness.

"Here is someone who not only lives in the real world, but is more that able to communicate events, feelings and struggles of faith through vivid, memorable prose . . . I wish there were more books life this."
Adrian Plass

"If you haven't time for an unputdownable book, don't read this one. I was completely drawn in . . . sharing the joy and pain of women at the most vulnerable time of their lives. There's a searing reality, warmth and compassion born of Lizzy's own heart-break in this beautiful book which moved me to tears, yet made me rejoice. It's an experience I wouldn't have missed."
Michele Guinness

Lizzy Wilson is a midwife currently engaged in Primary Healthcare in North Africa. She has worked in many parts of the world including Iraq, Australia, Ireland and the Sudan.

ISBN 1–85078–305–5

OM
publishing

Becoming a Contagious Christian
How to Invest Your Life in Reaching Other People
Bill Hybels & Mark Mittelberg

Becoming a Contagious Christian is a proven action plan for impacting the spiritual lives of friends, family members, co-workers and others. The material flows out of the real-life experience of Bill Hybels, one of the foremost experts on reaching irreligious people with the Gospel, and of Mark Mittelberg, Willow Creek's evangelism trainer.

Powerful stories and teaching will help readers:

- Gain hope that their friends' lives can change.
- Be freed from the misconceptions of evangelism.
- Take steps to develop a 'contagious' character.
- Discover a natural approach to communicating their faith.
- Maximise opportunities to build relationships.
- Learn to articulate biblical truths in plain language.

Bill Hybels is senior pastor of Willow Creek Community Church in South Barrington, Illinois. Willow Creek is the best attended church in North America and is known for its outreach to unbelievers in the Chicago area. Bill is the author of numerous books, including *Tender Love, Laws of the Heart, Too Busy to Pray,* and *Fit to be Tied,* which he authored with his wife Lynne.

Mark Mittelberg is Evangelism trainer for Willow Creek Community Church and the Associate Director of Willow Creek Association. He is also the primary author of the *Contagious Christian Course,* a curriculum designed to help churches train their people in relation to evangelism.

ISBN 1–898938–60–1

alpha